Terraform Authoring and Operations Professional Study Guide

Amazon Web Services edition

Mattias Fjellström

This book is dedicated to all the professionals who are continuously striving to improve.

Contents

Part I: About This Book

In this part you will learn about this book and about the Terraform Authoring and Operations Professional certification.

- Chapter 1 - introduces the author and the book, and includes acknowledgements to people who helped make this a great book.
- Chapter 2 - takes you through what is expected of you before you head into the exam, and what you can expect the exam to be like.

Chapter 1: Preface

This is the first book I have ever written.

However, I have been writing a lot in my own blog **mattias.engineer** for the past few years. The things I have been writing about have often involved Terraform. My writing has evolved a lot since I started my blog, and writing a book has been very rewarding for me. Writing this book has been a fun project, and I expect it to continue to be a fun project as new editions of the certification are released. It is challenging to cover everything I would like to cover, and at the same time not make this book into a brick nobody will have time to read. I think I have done a pretty good job with this.

I chose to publish this book myself, via Leanpub. The reason for this is that I will never be able to consider this book to be completely finished. With Leanpub I can continually refine and edit my book and publish new versions when required. Another reason I like Leanpub is that I can write my book using plain text (Markdown) and keep the manuscript in source control (GitHub). Updating the book is as easy as opening up my code editor, making the necessary edits, and pushing the changes.

My own cloud journey started with AWS and Terraform back in 2017. Initially I was not even aware of the fact that I was using Terraform, because it was built into a custom Python wrapper referred to as *env.git*. Suffice to say I did not get the best experience of Terraform back then, but things have changed since then. I had a period where I ventured away from Terraform in favor of other similar tools, but during the past two years the pendulum has swung again and Terraform is now my first choice when it comes to Infrastructure as Code.

I am also a **HashiCorp Ambassador**, and have been since 2023. I was awarded this title for my writing on topics and tools related to HashiCorp, both in my own blog and on LinkedIn.

Concerning the **Terraform Authoring and Operations Professional** certification: I was one of a few who got the chance to do the exam during alpha testing. This took place in San Francisco during HashiConf in October 2023. I also took and passed the actual exam in September 2024 and it was hands down the best certification exam I have experienced. The reason for this is that it is lab based, so you get to actually use Terraform to solve problems.

1.1: Acknowledgements

I wrote this book during a short and intense period. Meanwhile, I was working full-time and trying to make the most of the Swedish summer and early autumn. Inevitably, this led to more than a few grammatical errors and missing punctuation. A few nonsensical sentences made their way into the manuscript. A few technical inaccuracies briefly lived among the pages of this book.

Luckily, there were people who volunteered to help me track down and correct these mistakes!

In alphabetical order, I wish to thank those who helped me make this a better book:

- Artem Hrechanychenko
- Bill Grant
- Carlos Ruiz
- Chris van Meer, a fellow HashiCorp Ambassador
- Gary Larizza, also a fellow HashiCorp Ambassador
- Mahendran Selvakumar
- Manu Chandrasekhar

As well as a few anonymous contributors who shall not be named but also not forgotten.

Thank you all!

Chapter 2: Introduction

You are reading this book because you want to prepare for the **Terraform Authoring and Operations Professional certification** - an excellent decision!

The professional certification for Terraform is similar in spirit to the professional certification for **HashiCorp Vault** or any of the Kubernetes certifications available from the Linux Foundation (i.e. CKAD, CKA, CKS). Common for all of these certifications is that they are **lab based**, taking place in a virtual environment. You will solve actual problems involving Terraform configurations and workflows. One aspect of the exam that this book can't possibly prepare you for is how the exam experience is really like.

The exam also includes **multiple-choice questions**. However, the main part of the exam is lab based.

How can this book help you prepare for the professional certification for Terraform? My goal is to cover the theoretical concepts you need to understand in order to solve problems you face during the exam. I will include plenty of examples throughout the book to solidify your understanding.

This short introductory chapter goes through what goes into the exam and the prerequisites you need to set up to get the most out of this book.

2.1: Terraform Associate Certification

To understand what the professional certification is, it helps to first talk a little bit about the associate certification.

The **Terraform Associate certification** is:

> [...] for Cloud Engineers specializing in operations, IT, or development who **know the basic concepts and skills associated with Terraform**. You understand what Terraform Enterprise features exist and can differentiate between Terraform Enterprise and Community Edition.

It is clear from the description that only a **conceptual** knowledge of concepts and skills associated with Terraform is required. You should have an understanding of the most common CLI commands, a good understanding of Terraform workflows, and the general structure of the HashiCorp Configuration Language (HCL). Finally, you should know the difference between the community and enterprise editions of Terraform.

The associate certification exam consists of multiple-choice questions, and you have one hour to complete the test.

If you work with Terraform on a regular basis, both writing configurations and running Terraform locally or in a CI/CD environment, then I believe you are prepared to take the associate-level exam today without any further preparation.

2.2: Terraform Professional Certification

The professional certification demands that you are comfortable to be put into unfamiliar Terraform environments and solve given problems hands-on.

The description of the professional certification sounds more menacing than the associate certification:

> This exam assesses both **advanced configuration authoring** and a **deep understanding of Terraform workflows**. Earning this credential reflects that the practitioner has **professional-level expertise in both domains**. [...] The professional-level exam is intended for practitioners who have **extensive experience with Terraform in a production environment**, and **understand the concepts covered in the associate exam**.

The exam itself is lab based, taking place in a live virtual environment. You will use Terraform hands-on to solve given problems. Read more about the virtual environment in The Lab Environment section later in this chapter.

It is strongly recommended that you pass the associate certification before you set out to tackle the professional certification. However, this is not mandatory.

There are a number of other prerequisites listed for the professional certification:

- Linux skills (e.g. list and edit files via command terminal)
- Experience using the **Terraform AWS Provider** in a production environment
- Experience using cloud credentials

- Familiarity with YAML, JSON, HCL, and CSV formats
- Understanding of the networking stack and networking protocols, including TCP/IP and UDP

This book covers what you need to know about Terraform (i.e. workflows, CLI, HCL, HCP Terraform). Along the way we will also touch upon some of the other prerequisites, most notably how to use the AWS provider and cloud credentials.

Remember, **there is no substitute for real-world experience**. If you have never used Linux before you jump into the Terraform professional certification exam, then you will most likely fail due to not knowing how the virtual environment works. This book will not teach you how to use Linux. To be fair, you do not need to be a master of Linux for the exam–but you should be comfortable using a Linux terminal; changing directories, setting environment variables, creating directories and files, piping output between commands, and so on.

The first version of this book, as with the first version of the professional certification, focuses on the Terraform provider for **Amazon Web Services** (AWS). If AWS is not your cup of tea, then you can sit tight and wait for the Microsoft Azure or Google Cloud Platform versions of the exam to be released.

Parts of the certification will involve performing Terraform operations with AWS resources, as well as using the AWS console. This means it is beneficial to have a background in using AWS when you prepare for this exam. If you don't have prior experience, you should also spend some time learning the basics of the AWS console to familiarize yourself with how to find things and how AWS works. Descriptions for the tasks you need to perform in the AWS console will be provided during the exam, but being familiar with the AWS console beforehand will definitely save you some time.

The exam is divided into **six exam objectives**. Each objective has a number of sub-objectives.

The exam objectives are as follows:

1. **Manage resource lifecycle**

    - Initialize a configuration using **`terraform init`** and its options
    - Generate an execution plan using **`terraform plan`** and its options
    - Apply configuration changes using **`terraform apply`** and its options
    - Destroy resources using **`terraform destroy`** and its options
    - Manage resource state, including importing resources and reconciling resource drift

2. **Develop and troubleshoot dynamic configuration**
    - Use language features to validate configuration
    - Query providers using data sources
    - Compute and interpolate data using HCL functions
    - Use meta-arguments in configuration
    - Configure input variables and outputs, including complex types
    - Analyze best practices for managing sensitive data, such as using Vault for secrets management
3. **Develop collaborative Terraform workflows**
    - Manage the Terraform binary, providers, and modules using version constraints
    - Configure remote state
    - Use the Terraform workflow in automation
    - Share data across configurations and workspaces
4. **Create, maintain, and use Terraform modules**
    - Create a module
    - Use a module in configuration
    - Refactor a module and use module versioning
    - Refactor an existing configuration into modules
5. **Configure and use Terraform providers**
    - Understand Terraform's plugin-based architecture
    - Configure providers, including aliasing, versioning, sourcing, and managing upgrades
    - Manage provider authentication
    - Troubleshoot provider errors
6. **Collaborate on infrastructure as code using HCP Terraform**
    - Analyze the HCP Terraform run workflow
    - Understand HCP Terraform workspaces and their configuration options, including access management
    - Manage provider credentials in HCP Terraform
    - Analyze policy as code and governance features

This book has one chapter covering each of the exam objectives.

Note that for the last exam objective (**Collaborate on infrastructure as code using HCP Terraform**) only multiple-choice questions are used. This means you will not be using the HCP Terraform portal during the exam.

You have a total of **four hours** to complete the exam.

One last thing, the registration fee for the exam is **295 USD**. This is a steep increase from the 70.50 USD for the associate level exam. Most of us are not comfortable with throwing away 295 USD, so before you sit down to take the exam make sure you feel in control of Terraform and all the contents of this book.

2.3: About the Terraform Binary Version

The current version of the certification exam uses **Terraform version 1.6**.

Terraform 1.6 introduced the **`terraform test`** command and the ability to write specific test files for your Terraform modules.

The exam does not cover things like:

- The **`removed`** block (available from version 1.7.0)
- Provider-defined functions (available from version 1.8.0)
- Cross-validation for variable validation blocks (available from version 1.9.0)

I will be using the latest available Terraform version as of this writing in my examples, but I will not be using any of the specific features exclusively available in Terraform 1.7 or later.

If you are unsure of whether a specific feature is available in Terraform 1.6 or not you should head on over to the Terraform GitHub repository[1] and go through the release notes.

2.4: Prerequisites For This Book

To follow along with the examples in this book, there are a few prerequisites to set up first:

- Sign-up for an **AWS account** unless you already have one. Go to AWS[2] and follow the instructions to set up your account. If you are able to sign in to the console you should be good to go. I recommend using your own private AWS account rather than one owned by your organization. This helps you avoid any permission restrictions that may be imposed by your organization.
- To simplify getting started with the AWS provider for Terraform, I recommend that you install and configure the AWS CLI. This will set up AWS CLI credentials that Terraform can automatically pick up and use. Instructions for how to install and configure the AWS CLI can be found in the AWS documentation[3].
- You should, of course, have **Terraform** installed. Brief instructions will be provided in the next chapter.

If you are new to AWS, I encourage you to carefully go through Chapter 3 that will guide you on how to get started with AWS. If you decide to skip that chapter, I assume you are familiar with the basics of AWS IAM authentication and how to authenticate the AWS provider for Terraform.

To follow along with the full journey presented in the next chapter, you will also need an HCP Terraform organization.

2.5: Resources and References

During the exam you will have access to the Terraform documentation, as well as limited access to the Terraform registry. You should spend some time to learn the layout and structure of these resources before the exam so that you can quickly find your way around during the exam. You do not want to spend precious time learning about how the Terraform documentation is structured during the exam, when you can do it before the exam.

A few important pages of the documentation to familiarize yourself with are:

- The Terraform documentation[4]. Pay extra attention to the following sections:
  - The Terraform CLI documentation[5]
  - The Terraform configuration language documentation[6]
- The AWS provider for Terraform documentation[7] in the Terraform registry.

You will not have access to the Terraform tutorials during the exam, so do not rely on them to find information. Don't worry about accidentally accessing a page you are not allowed to use during the exam, they will be blocked automatically.

> Note that you will not have access to Google, or any other search engine, during the exam. If that is your primary way of finding things in the documentation, then you might want to practice finding information directly from the documentation pages.

> Each lab scenario includes an info box with links to the relevant documentation for that particular scenario. You can click on the links to open them in new tabs. This means it is rare that you need to find something "from scratch" during the exam, you can use the provided links to get to the relevant documentation.

Remember that the documentation pages are also available for the multiple-choice questions, not just during the hands-on labs.

2.6: The Lab Environment

The exam takes place in a virtual Linux environment.

The lab scenarios and the multiple-choice questions are provided to you on a web page that you can access via the browser in the virtual environment.

You also have access to VS Code with the Terraform extension installed, and a terminal environment with the Terraform CLI installed. If you are not used to VS Code it could be a good idea to install it, together with the Terraform extension, and learn how it works.

The lab scenarios are **containerized**. The lab scenarios are independent from each other. If you completely mess up one scenario, the other scenarios are unaffected.

This also means that you have to set provider credentials for each lab scenario individually. So do not expect that you can set AWS credentials as environment variables in the first scenario and then forget about credentials for the rest of the exam.

Speaking of AWS credentials, these are provided to you in the info box of each scenario. They will also be visible in the *MOTD* (Message of the Day) when you open a terminal for each scenario. You will need the credentials to configure the AWS provider for Terraform, as well as signing in to the AWS console.

Since the lab scenarios are individually containerized you might accidentally mix the different environments up. If you are looking for something in the lab environment that should exist according to the instructions, but you can't find it, then chances are you have mixed up your lab environments. You can always open the correct terminal environments using the links in the info box.

Note that copying and pasting information will likely not work as you expect. It is recommended to perform copy and paste using your mouse:

- Select what you want to copy
- Right-click and select "copy"
- Right-click where you want to paste and select "paste"

> Clicking random keyboard shortcuts can accidentally open up different panels in the lab environment that you did not intend. If you end up in this situation and don't know how to get back to the exam, ask your proctor for guidance.

The instructions given in each lab are the **source of truth**. If you are in doubt about something related to a lab scenario, follow what the instructions tell you to do.

A multiple-choice question covers one specific concept, but a lab scenario spans multiple concepts. You are encouraged to try to solve as much as possible of each scenario, even if you can't solve the full scenario. You can still get points for partially solved problems.

> Remember that you have a total of **four hours** to complete the exam.
>
> Don't lose track of how much time you have left. There is a timer available on the exam web page during the exam.
>
> If you get stuck, try to solve other parts of the scenario if you can - or jump to a different scenario. Come back to where you got stuck later, sometimes it helps to just think about a different problem for a while.

It is a good idea to read through each lab scenario from start to finish before you start trying to solve it. Perhaps you can save some time if you know from the start what you will need to do later in the scenario.

During the exam you should use all the features available in the Terraform CLI to make sure you are writing good HCL code. This includes running **`terraform fmt`** and **`terraform validate`**. When you are about to apply a change make sure that the output from **`terraform plan`** is what you expect! Also don't forget to run **`terraform apply`** to actually apply the required changes.

2.7: Target Audience

The target audience for this book are Terraform practitioners with some experience of using Terraform in a production environment. Your primary target cloud provider is AWS. You should be familiar with how to write HCL, and how to use the Terraform CLI. You should know how to navigate the AWS console.

If this description does not fit you, the learning curve from following this book alone will be very steep. However, I do not expect you to be a Terraform guru or a certified

AWS professional. Perhaps you have been using Terraform for a long time, but you have still never experienced the need to refactor a Terraform configuration into separate modules while keeping your AWS production infrastructure running.

If you are a seasoned AWS and Terraform professional, with a black-belt in HCL and HCP Terraform, with multiple AWS certifications but you don't have the Terraform professional certification yet? Then you will not learn anything profoundly new from this book. You could still get some value out of it as a refresher before taking the exam.

2.8: Visual Elements of This Book

This book has a few specific elements to highlight different types of information. This section shows examples of these.

Best practices, or other types of good suggestions, appear like this.

Warnings or things to look out for appear like this.

Figure 2.1. A Terraform code snippet appears like this

```
# this is a comment!
variable "name_suffix" {
  type = string
}

resource "aws_vpc" "europe" {
  cidr_block = "10.100.10.0/24"

  tags = {
    Name = "vpc-${var.name_suffix}"
  }
}
```

Inline code looks like **`this`**.

Important concepts or names will be in **boldface** the first time they are introduced, or to highlight them in other parts of the text where it is appropriate. A few phrases are in *italics* to put some emphasis on them.

There will be a *few* diagrams expressing relationships between different parts of a Terraform configuration. The different Terraform blocks are displayed as in Figure 2.2.

Figure 2.2. Visual representation of Terraform objects

2.9: Looking Ahead

In the next chapter you will be taken on an end-to-end journey with Terraform. That chapter is intended to cover most of what working with Terraform is all about, without diving deep into any specific concept. The purpose is to set the stage, and make sure we are on the same page before we move on to cover the exam objectives. This book goes through the exam objectives in order, but that is not necessarily the best order for learning, thus it is a good idea to see the whole workflow at least once first.

Part III of this book is dedicated to the exam objectives. Each chapter in that part goes through one exam objective each. Each chapter contains theoretical concepts with plenty of examples as well as highlighting best practices where applicable.

This book covers a lot about Terraform, but it cannot possibly cover everything. To get the most out of this book, you should have used Terraform enough to be familiar with what a Terraform configuration looks like and be familiar with how the Terraform CLI works. Some of the contents of the book will be repetition for you, while other things will be new. After all, this book follows the exam objectives very closely so if a given feature is not part of an exam objective it might not be covered in this book, yet it could appear on the exam.

Happy learning!

You can find most of the code samples from this book in an accompanying GitHub repository at github.com/mattias-fjellstrom/terraform-professional-book-sample-code[8]. Links will be provided to specific code samples throughout the book where appropriate.

You can scan the QR code below to come to the GitHub repository with sample code:

Figure 2.3. QR code for the sample code repository

There is another GitHub repository for a changelog for the book available at github.com/mattias-fjellstrom/terraform-professional-book-changelog[9].

You can scan the QR code below to come to the GitHub repository with the changelog:

Figure 2.4. QR code for the changelog repository

Notes

1. https://github.com/hashicorp/terraform/releases
2. https://aws.amazon.com/resources/create-account/
3. https://aws.amazon.com/cli/
4. https://developer.hashicorp.com/terraform/docs
5. https://developer.hashicorp.com/terraform/cli
6. https://developer.hashicorp.com/terraform/language
7. https://registry.terraform.io/providers/hashicorp/aws/latest
8. https://github.com/mattias-fjellstrom/terraform-professional-book-sample-code
9. https://github.com/mattias-fjellstrom/terraform-professional-book-changelog

Part II: Getting Started

In this part we will take a deep plunge into Terraform and all that goes with it. We will also learn about the HashiCorp Configuration Language.

- Chapter 3 - goes through a day in the life of an engineer working on creating infrastructure with Terraform. This chapter is an overview that covers many of the exam objectives briefly.
- Chapter 4 - goes through the basics of the HashiCorp Configuration Language.

Chapter 3: Terraform 101

You are on a journey to achieve the **Terraform Authoring and Operations Professional Certification**. You have already been through the basics of Terraform more than a few times. Perhaps you have achieved the **Terraform Associate Certification**? Perhaps you are planning on taking both certifications in the coming weeks or months?

No matter what your situation is, there could be gaps in your understanding on authoring and operating Terraform. Perhaps there has been some time since you worked actively with Terraform.

To bring you up to speed, this chapter will go through a complete journey from installing Terraform locally all the way to configuring workspaces and deploy resources via HCP Terraform.

The full source code for this example is available in the GitHub repository at github.com/mattias-fjellstrom/terraform-professional-book-sample-code[1].

3.1: A Journey With Terraform

You want to write your first **Terraform configuration** and create cloud infrastructure on **Amazon Web Services** (AWS).

Terraform Configuration

I use the definition of **Terraform configuration** from the official documentation:

> A *Terraform configuration* is a complete document in the Terraform language that tells Terraform how to manage a given collection of infrastructure. A configuration can consist of multiple files and directories.

You have read most of the documentation on Terraform and AWS, you have watched more Terraform Tuesdays[2] than you can remember, and now you feel that you are ready to get your hands dirty with Terraform.

The first step you need to take is to install Terraform on your local system. You go to the Terraform documentation[3] to find the instructions relevant for your system.

In this imaginary scenario you are on a MacBook, so you make your life easy by using **Homebrew**:

Figure 3.1. Installing the Terraform CLI using Homebrew

```
$ brew tap hashicorp/tap
$ brew install hashicorp/tap/terraform
```

Once Terraform is installed you verify that it is available in your Terminal:

Figure 3.2. Verify that Terraform is installed by printing the version

```
$ terraform version
Terraform v1.9.4
on darwin_arm64
```

You want to create infrastructure on AWS, so you go to the AWS console[4] and sign in using your credentials. Once you are signed-in you arrive at the AWS console home (see Figure 3.3).

Terraform requires AWS credentials to be able to create infrastructure on AWS. You could let Terraform use your own AWS credentials, but it is a better idea to create dedicated credentials for Terraform.

You go to the **Identity and Access Management** (IAM) service by typing **IAM** into the search bar at the top and selecting the IAM service (see Figure 3.4).

You want to create a new **IAM user** for Terraform so you click on **Users** in the left-hand menu, then you click on **Create user** (see Figure 3.5).

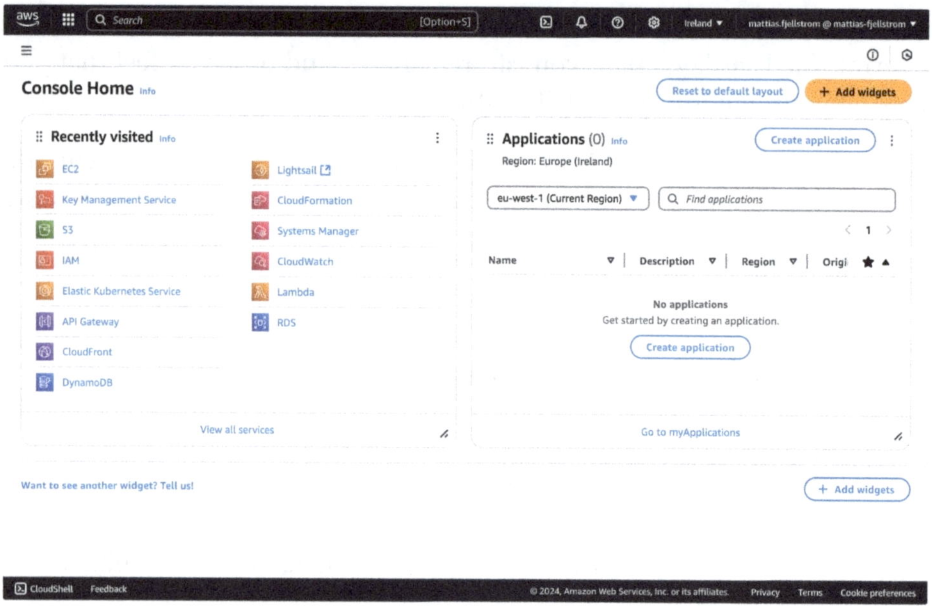

Figure 3.3. The AWS console home page that you arrive at after successfully authenticating and signing in to your AWS account.

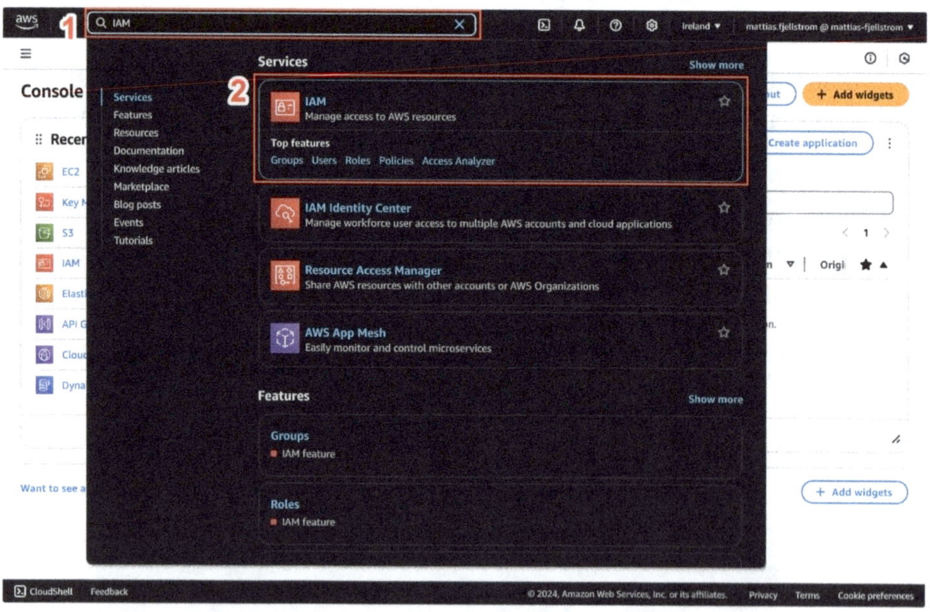

Figure 3.4. (1) Search for the IAM (Identity and Access Management) service in the search bar at the top of the AWS console and (2) click on the IAM service once it appears in the list.

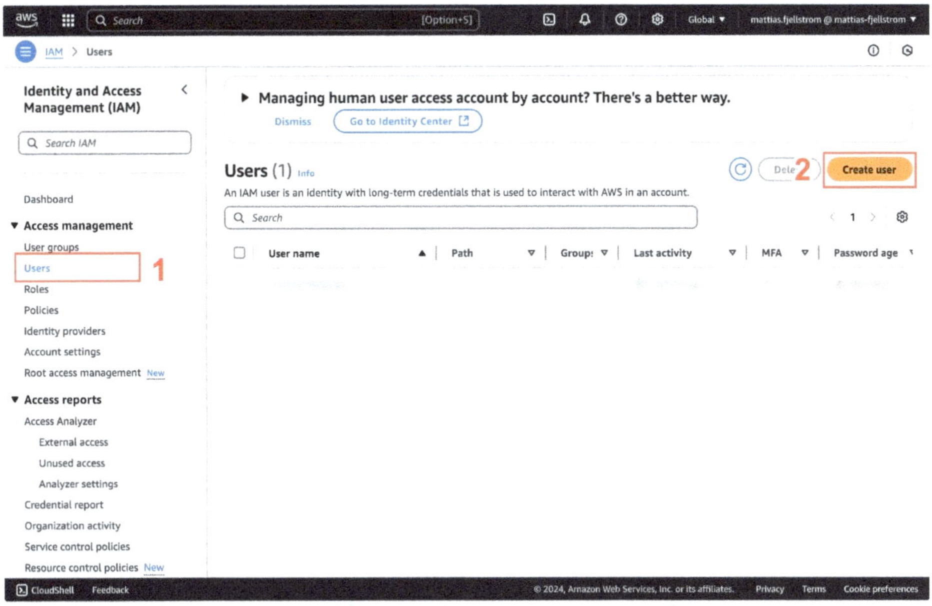

Figure 3.5. (1) On the IAM landing page, click on Users in the left-hand menu and (2) click on the Create user button to start the user creation process.

You enter **terraform** as the user name, then you click on **Next** (see Figure 3.6).

On the permissions page you select **Attach policies directly**. You search for **AdministratorAccess** in the search bar. You select the policy named **AdministratorAccess** and then click on **Next** (see Figure 3.7).

You understand that the **AdministratorAccess** permission is more than Terraform needs, but you are in an experimental mood so you let it slide for now.

You have arrived at the review page, and since everything looks good you click on **Create user** (see Figure 3.8).

Creating the user takes a few seconds. Once the green banner appears to inform you that the user has been created, you click on **View user** (see Figure 3.9).

On the user details page, you select the **Security credentials** tab and scroll down to the **Access keys** section and click on **Create access key** (see Figure 3.10).

You select **Application running outside AWS** in the list of use cases and then you click on **Next** (see Figure 3.11).

You write a short description for the access key and then you click on **Create access key** (see Figure 3.12).

You copy the values of both the **Access key** and the **Secret access key** and store them somewhere safe. Finally, you click on **Done** (see Figure 3.13).

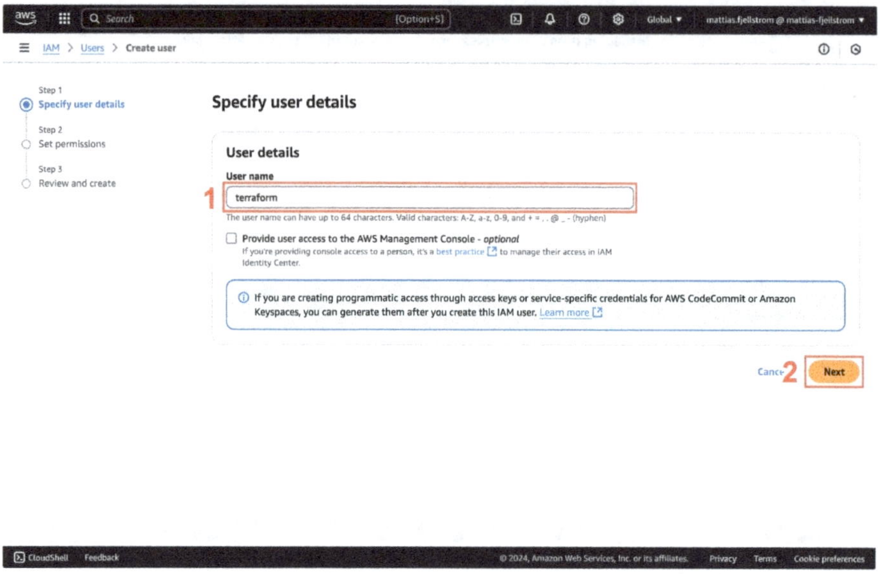

Figure 3.6. (1) Specify a user name for the new IAM user and (2) click on Next to proceed to the next step.

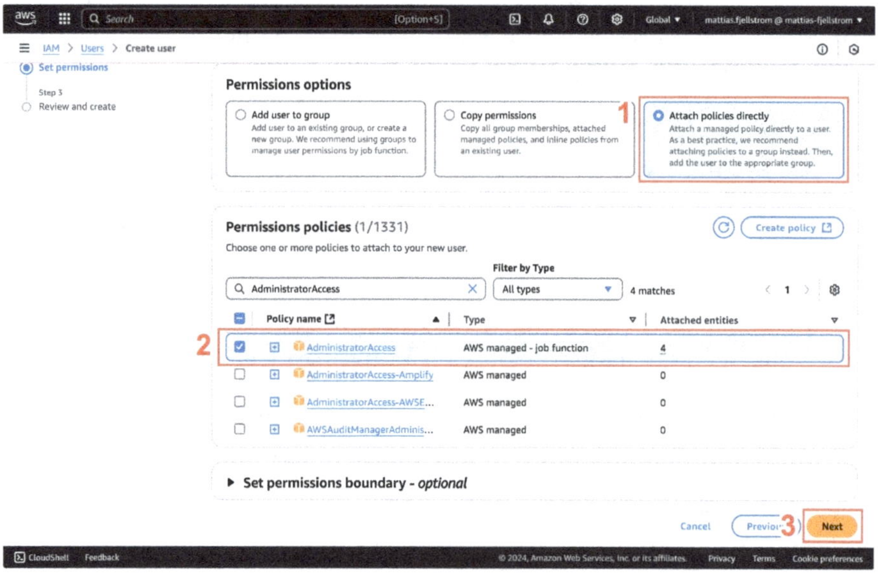

Figure 3.7. (1) Select Attach policies directly and (2) search for and select the AdministratorAccess policy once it appears in the list. Then (3) click on Next to proceed to the next step.

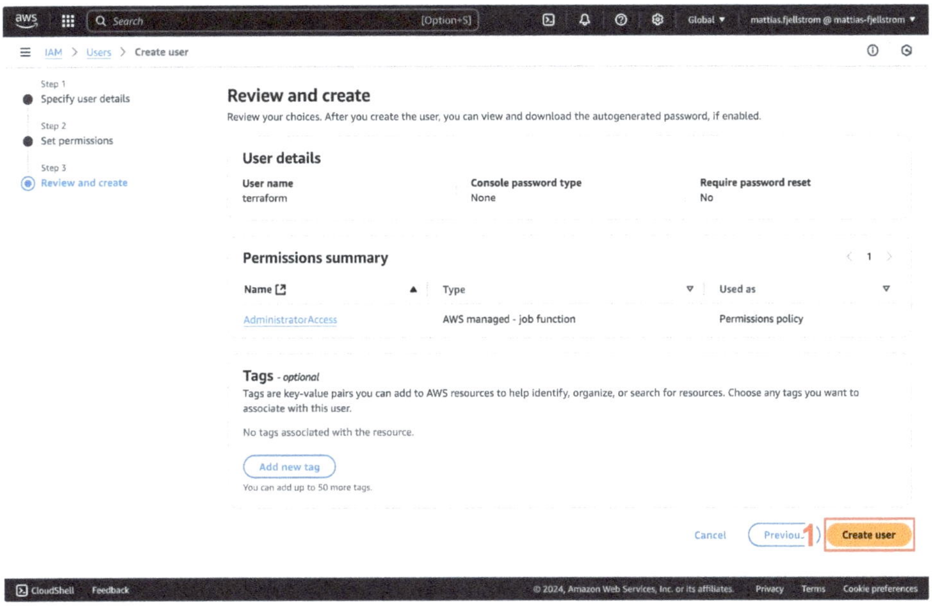

Figure 3.8. Review the details of the new IAM user for Terraform, and (1) if everything looks OK click on Create user to finish the user creation process.

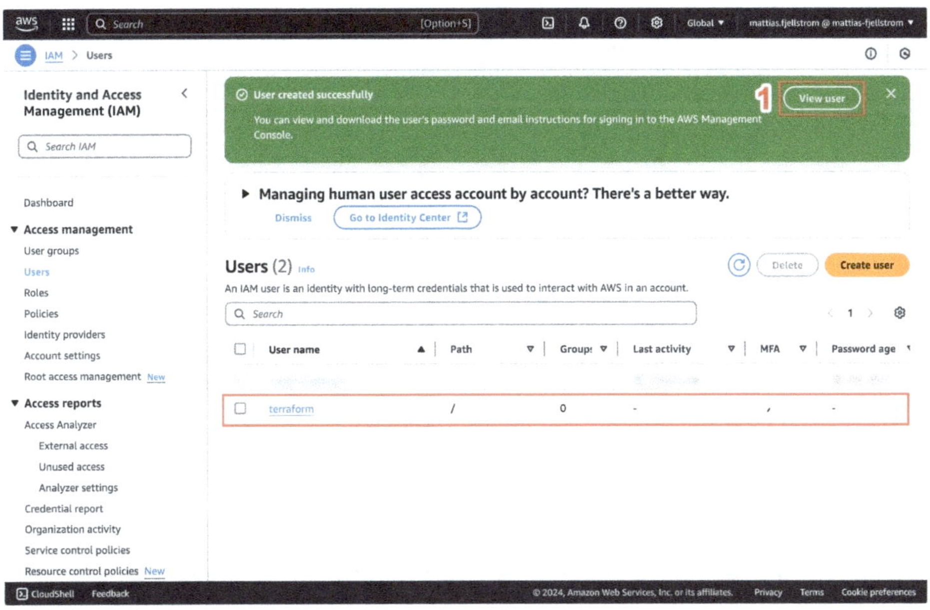

Figure 3.9. (1) Click the View user button on the green banner at the top of the screen, or alternatively click on the Terraform user in the list of IAM users at the bottom of the page.

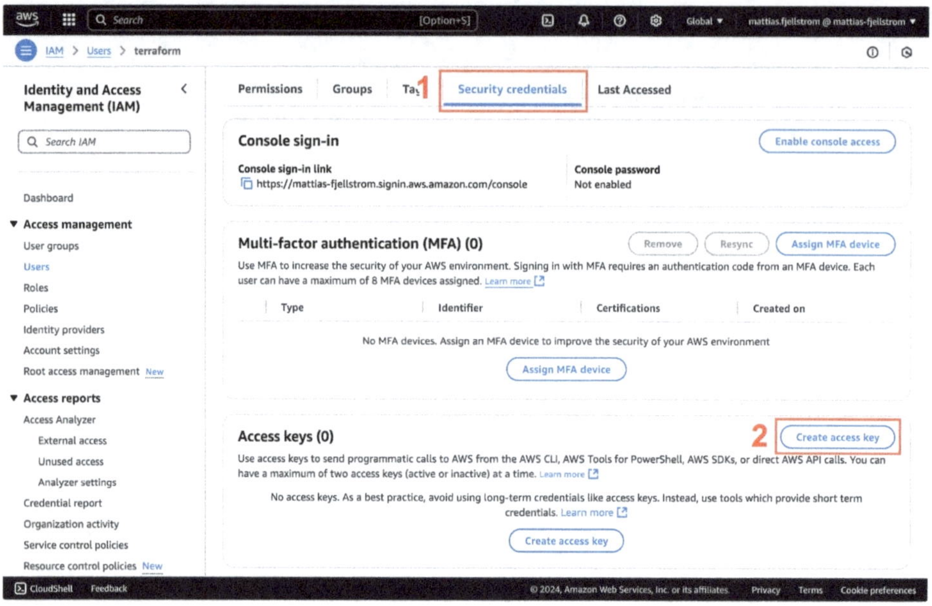

Figure 3.10. (1) Select the Security credentials tab on the user details page and (2) click the Create access key button to create a new set of access keys.

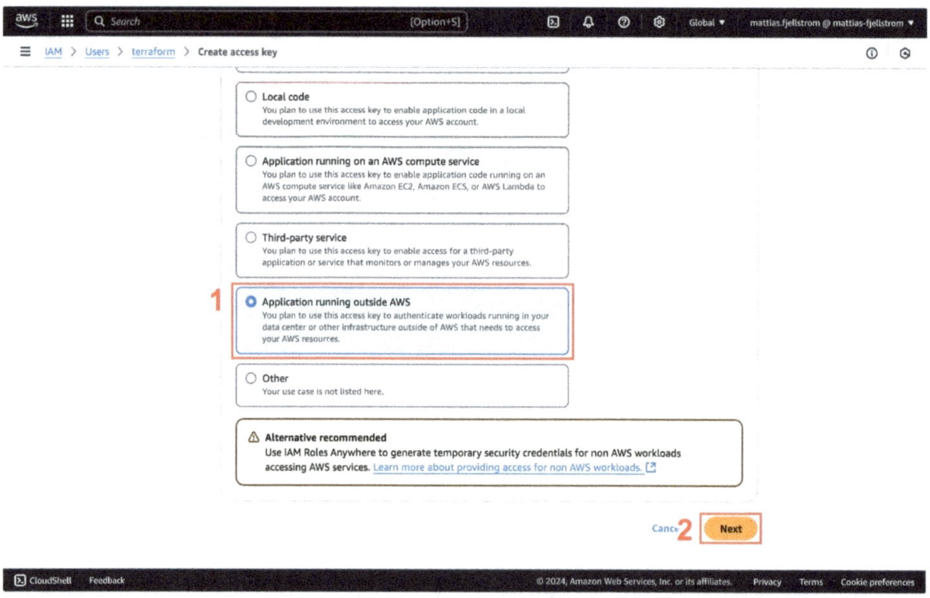

Figure 3.11. (1) In the list of use cases for the access keys select Application running outside AWS and (2) click on Next.

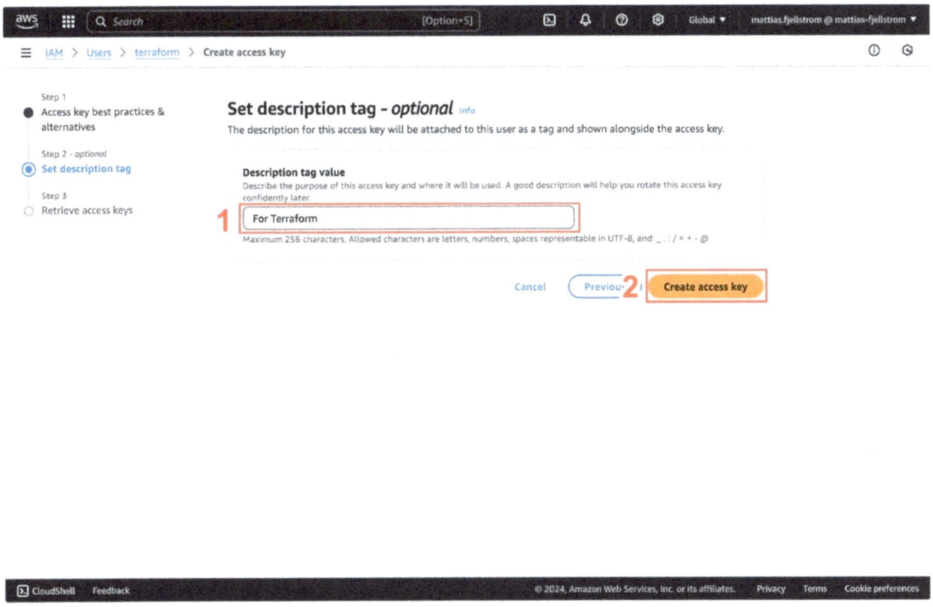

Figure 3.12. (1) Add a description for the access keys and (2) click on Create access key to finish creating the access key pair.

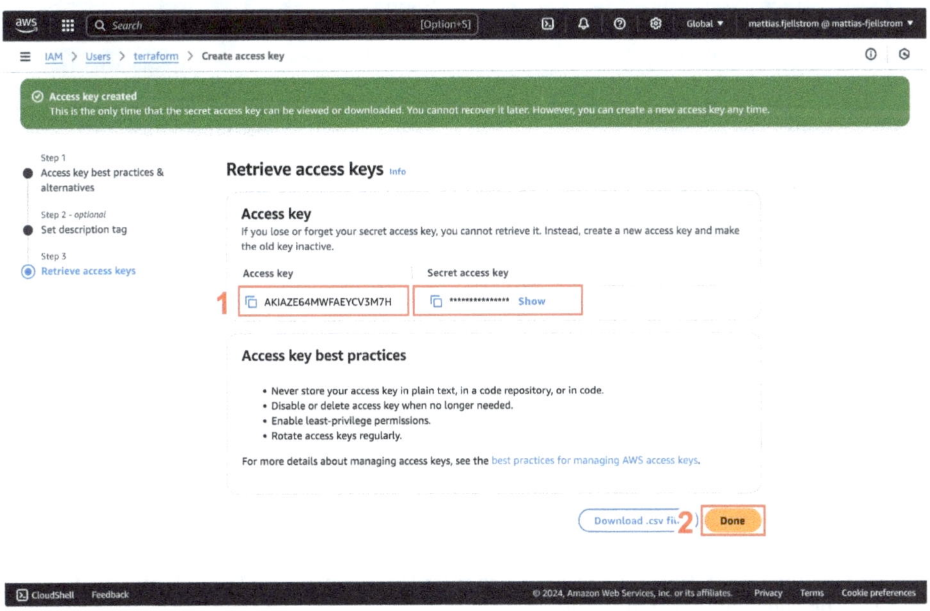

Figure 3.13. (1) Copy both the access key and secret access key and store them somewhere safe, then (2) click on Done.

You set up two **environment variables** with the AWS access key and secret access key in your terminal session:

Figure 3.14. Set two environment variables for the AWS access keys

```
$ export AWS_ACCESS_KEY_ID=<value you copied>
$ export AWS_SECRET_ACCESS_KEY=<value you copied>
```

Terraform is not able to create cloud infrastructure on AWS by itself. To do this, Terraform uses the **AWS provider for Terraform**. A provider is a bridge between Terraform and an external system, like AWS.

The AWS provider will automatically use the credentials that you set as environment variables in the terminal session when you run Terraform CLI commands.

You go to the Terraform registry[5] to read the documentation for the AWS provider. You click on **USE PROVIDER** in the upper right corner and copy the code snippet that is shown (see Figure 3.15).

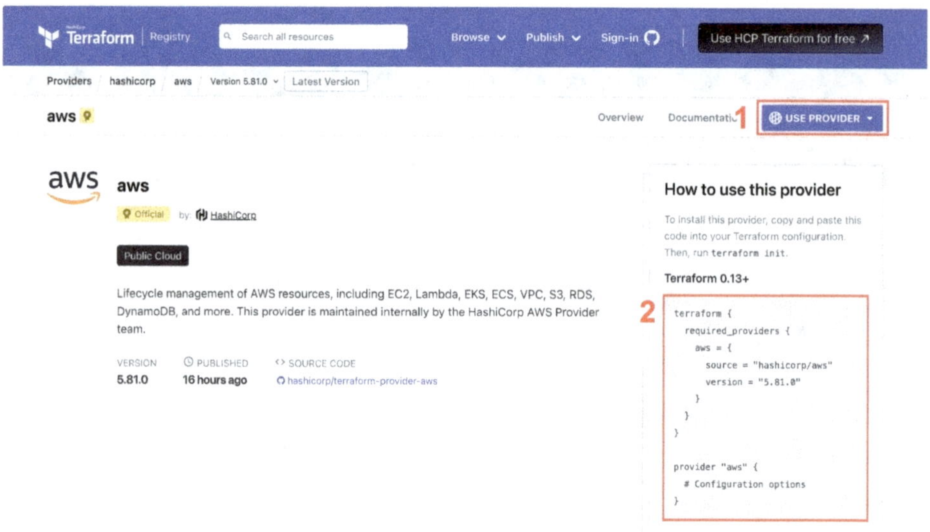

Figure 3.15. The documentation for the AWS provider for Terraform. (1) Click on USE PROVIDER, then (2) copy the code snippet that is shown.

You open your text editor to begin writing your Terraform configuration. You create a new file named **`terraform.tf`**, and you paste the code that you copied from the documentation:

Figure 3.16. terraform.tf

```
terraform {
  required_providers {
    aws = {
      source  = "hashicorp/aws"
      version = "5.81.0"
    }
  }
}

provider "aws" {
  # Configuration options
}
```

You use the **required_providers** block to tell Terraform which providers you intend to use. This block is nested inside of the **terraform** block. You can configure other settings for Terraform in the **terraform** block, but nothing that you need to worry about now.

You decide to move the **provider** block from **terraform.tf** to its own file named **providers.tf**:

Figure 3.17. providers.tf

```
provider "aws" {
  # Configuration options
}
```

It is a good organizational practice to split your Terraform configuration into logical pieces. Terraform will automatically stitch together all the files of the Terraform configuration into one piece.

You want to provision cloud infrastructure in Europe, and you know that the **AWS region** in Ireland is popular among AWS users. You want to configure the AWS provider for Terraform to use this region.

AWS Regions and Availability Zones

An **AWS region** represents a collection of data centers in a specific geographical location.

> A region is divided into **availability zones**. An availability zone is a smaller collection of one or more data centers. Availability zones within a region are far enough away from each other so as not to be affected by the same natural disasters or other infrastructure issues in the region.
>
> An AWS region has a *code name* that you specify in Terraform. A few common region code names are:
>
> - **`eu-central-1`** for Frankfurt
> - **`eu-west-1`** for Ireland
> - **`us-east-1`** for North Virginia
> - **`us-west-1`** for North California

You want to be able to easily use a different AWS region, so you turn the region name into a **variable**.

In your text editor, you create a new file named **`variables.tf`** and add a variable for the AWS region:

Figure 3.18. variables.tf

```
variable "aws_region" {
  type        = string
  description = "AWS region name"
  default     = "eu-west-1"
}
```

You give the variable a **default value** of **`eu-west-1`**, this is the code name for the AWS region in Ireland. If no other value is provided for this variable, the default value of **`eu-west-1`** will be used. You realize that providing sensible defaults for all your variables is a good practice.

To configure the AWS provider to use the selected region you edit the **`provider`** block in **`providers.tf`** to use the variable you just defined:

Figure 3.19. providers.tf

```
provider "aws" {
  region = var.aws_region
}
```

Variables are referenced in other parts of your Terraform configuration using the syntax **`var.<variable name>`**.

The infrastructure you want to create consists of a virtual network with a number of subnets. A **virtual network** is the digital equivalent of the computer network you have in your office or at home. In the AWS world a virtual network is called a **Virtual Private Cloud**, or VPC. A VPC can be split into smaller networks called **subnets**.

In Terraform, the **relationships** or **dependencies** between resources are important. Thus, you have created a diagram of how the resources of your infrastructure are related (see Figure 3.20). This is not an architectural diagram with fancy icons, but it will be useful as a guide when you write your HCL code.

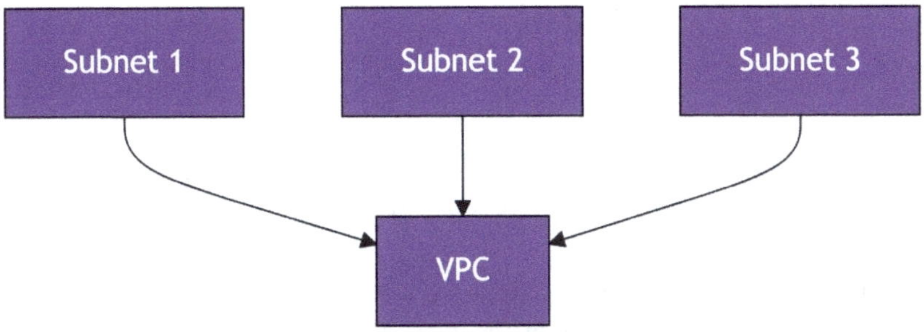

Figure 3.20. Relationships between your Virtual Private Cloud (VPC) and your subnets

You go to the AWS provider documentation[6] and learn about the VPC resource. You create a new file named **`main.tf`** and add a VPC resource to it:

Figure 3.21. main.tf

```
resource "aws_vpc" "this" {
  cidr_block = "10.0.0.0/16"

  tags = {
    Name = "vpc-${var.aws_region}"
  }
}
```

Resources are declared using a **`resource`** block. This block takes two **labels**, one for the **resource type** and one for the **resource name**.

The resource type of the VPC is **`aws_vpc`**. All resource types from the AWS provider has the prefix **`aws_`**. The resource name of the VPC is **`this`**. You can pick any resource name that makes sense to you.

Resource names

A **resource name** can contain letters, digits, underscores and dashes. It must start with a letter or an underscore.

There are a few recommended guidelines you should follow:

1. Primarily use lowercase letters and underscores. Start the name with a lowercase letter.
2. Avoid using dashes, even if they are allowed.
3. Avoid using the name of the provider or the resource type in the resource name (e.g. avoid `my_aws_vpc`)

No two resources of the same type can have the same resource name. If they did, it would be a conflict and Terraform would report an error.

The `aws_vpc` resource takes a number of **arguments** and nested blocks you can use to configure it according to your specification. Most of the arguments are optional. In this case you configure the following arguments:

- You set the `cidr_block` argument to the value of `10.0.0.0/16`. A CIDR block is a block of IP addresses that this virtual network consists of.
- You set the `tags` argument to a map with key-value pairs. You add one key called `Name` with the value `vpc-${var.aws_region}`. Tags are arbitrary key-value pairs you can add to most resources on AWS. The `Name` tag is special on AWS, it is used to display a friendly name of the resource in the AWS console. In the value of the tag you have used a method called **string interpolation** to build a string from two parts, `vpc-` and `var.aws_region`. Terraform will replace the reference to the variable by the value of the variable. If the value of the `aws_region` variable is `eu-west-1`, then the string interpolation will end up being `vpc-eu-west-1`.

You realize that you would like to use a variable for the `cidr_block` argument as well, to make this configuration more dynamic. In `variables.tf` you add a second variable:

Figure 3.22. variables.tf

```
# ... previous code is omitted ...
variable "vpc_cidr_block" {
  type        = string
  description = "CIDR block for the VPC network"
  default     = "10.0.0.0/16"
}
```

Next, you update the **aws_vpc** resource in **main.tf** to use the new variable:

Figure 3.23. main.tf

```
resource "aws_vpc" "this" {
  cidr_block = var.vpc_cidr_block

  tags = {
    Name = "vpc-${var.aws_region}"
  }
}
```

A virtual network must be split up into smaller networks called sub-networks, or **subnets**. Each subnet takes a smaller piece of the block of available IP addresses.

You go to the AWS provider documentation[7] to read about the subnet resource. Next, you add it to **main.tf** and configure it as required:

Figure 3.24. main.tf

```
# ... previous code is omitted ...
resource "aws_subnet" "first" {
  vpc_id     = aws_vpc.this.id
  cidr_block = "10.0.1.0/24"

  tags = {
    Name = "snet-${var.aws_region}"
  }
}
```

You realize that this is not good enough. You would like to use multiple subnets, and place one subnet in each availability zone of the AWS region.

How do you know how many availability zones are available in the AWS region you are using?

You can use a Terraform **data source** to query the provider for this information. A data source allows you to ask for information (or data) for existing infrastructure, or metadata related to resources or even the provider itself.

In the documentation[8] you find a data source for availability zones. You add the following block to **main.tf**:

Figure 3.25. main.tf

```
# ... previous code is omitted ...
data "aws_availability_zones" "all" {
  state = "available"
}
```

From the documentation you know that this data source has an attribute called **names**. This attribute contains the names of the availability zones within the region. In the AWS region named **eu-west-1** (i.e. Ireland) the availability zones have the names **eu-west-1a**, **eu-west-1b**, and **eu-west-1c**.

You update the **aws_subnet** resource in **main.tf** to place it in the first availability zone:

Figure 3.26. main.tf

```
# ... other code is omitted ...
resource "aws_subnet" "first" {
  vpc_id            = aws_vpc.this.id
  cidr_block        = "10.0.1.0/24"
  availability_zone = data.aws_availability_zones.all.names[0]

  tags = {
    Name = "snet-${data.aws_availability_zones.all.names[0]}"
  }
}
```

The **names** attribute is a list of strings. You select the first element in the list by adding the **[0]** selector. Remember that list indices start at 0, not at 1.

Another issue you have with your current Terraform configuration is that the **cidr_-block** is currently hardcoded for the subnet. You would like to make sure that the subnet CIDR block is part of the VPC CIDR block. Remember that you made the VPC CIDR block value into a variable, so it does not necessarily have the default value of **10.0.0.0/16**.

In the Terraform documentation[9] you find a **function** named **cidrsubnet** that can calculate CIDR blocks for you. You update the **aws_subnet** resource to use the **cidrsubnet** function:

Figure 3.27. main.tf

```
# ... other code is omitted ...
resource "aws_subnet" "first" {
  vpc_id            = aws_vpc.this.id
  cidr_block        = cidrsubnet(var.vpc_cidr_block, 8, 1)
  availability_zone = data.aws_availability_zones.all.names[0]

  tags = {
    Name = "snet-${data.aws_availability_zones.all.names[0]}"
  }
}
```

The value of **`cidrsubnet(var.vpc_cidr_block, 8, 1)`** will evaluate to **`10.0.1.0/24`** if the AWS VPC CIDR block has its default value of **`10.0.0.0/16`**. This is one example of a useful function that you should know about, there are a large number of functions available as can be seen in the documentation[10].

You want to create two additional subnets, so you copy and paste the **`aws_subnet`** resource two times and edit the relevant resource names and arguments so that they don't conflict with each other (remember that the combination of resource type and resource name must be unique):

Figure 3.28. main.tf

```
# ... other code is omitted ...
resource "aws_subnet" "first" {
  vpc_id            = aws_vpc.this.id
  cidr_block        = cidrsubnet(var.vpc_cidr_block, 8, 1)
  availability_zone = data.aws_availability_zones.all.names[0]

  tags = {
    Name = "snet-${data.aws_availability_zones.all.names[0]}"
  }
}

resource "aws_subnet" "second" {
  vpc_id            = aws_vpc.this.id
  cidr_block        = cidrsubnet(var.vpc_cidr_block, 8, 2)
  availability_zone = data.aws_availability_zones.all.names[1]

  tags = {
    Name = "snet-${data.aws_availability_zones.all.names[1]}"
  }
}

resource "aws_subnet" "third" {
```

```
  vpc_id            = aws_vpc.this.id
  cidr_block        = cidrsubnet(var.vpc_cidr_block, 8, 3)
  availability_zone = data.aws_availability_zones.all.names[2]

  tags = {
    Name = "snet-${data.aws_availability_zones.all.names[2]}"
  }
}
```

The subnet configurations are explicit and easy to understand. However, what if the AWS region has five availability zones and you need one subnet in each? Or what if the AWS region only has two availability zones? Then we would have an error in our Terraform configuration.

Either way, updating this Terraform configuration to match a given AWS region means there will be a lot of tedious and repetitive work.

You realize that you can use a loop **meta-argument** for your **aws_subnet** resource definition instead of copying and pasting resources.

There are two options for loops: the **count** and the **for_each** meta argument. In this particular scenario it is easier to use the **count** meta argument because we just want to create one subnet per availability zone.

You remove two of the **aws_subnet** resources you copied before, and edit the remaining **aws_subnet** resource to the following:

Figure 3.29. main.tf

```
# ... other code is omitted ...
resource "aws_subnet" "all" {
  count = length(data.aws_availability_zones.all.names)

  vpc_id            = aws_vpc.this.id
  cidr_block        = cidrsubnet(var.vpc_cidr_block, 8, count.index+1)
  availability_zone = data.aws_availability_zones.all.names[count.index]

  tags = {
    Name = "snet-${data.aws_availability_zones.all.names[count.index]}"
  }
}
```

The above resource definition will create one subnet for each availability zone in the list of availability zones for the selected region. Wonderful!

You are almost done, but you want your Terraform configuration to output the ID of the AWS VPC. You need the VPC ID for something that is not a part of this Terraform configuration. You can output values from Terraform using an **`output`** block.

You create a new file named **`outputs.tf`** and add the VPC ID as an output:

Figure 3.30. outputs.tf

```
output "aws_vpc_id" {
  description = "ID of the AWS VPC"
  value       = aws_vpc.this.id
}
```

You realize that you would also like to output all the subnet IDs. You add another output in **`outputs.tf`** for this, remembering that you created subnets using the **`count`** meta argument:

Figure 3.31. outputs.tf

```
# ... other code is omitted ...
output "aws_subnet_ids" {
  description = "IDs of all subnets in the VPC"
  value       = aws_subnet.all[*].id
}
```

You have used a splat expression `[*]` to reference all the subnets, and then selected the **`id`** attribute from each subnet.

You believe your Terraform configuration is done (for now) so you go to your terminal in the Terraform working directory and **initialize** Terraform using the **`terraform init`** command:

Figure 3.32. Initialize the Terraform configuration

```
$ terraform init
Initializing the backend...
Initializing provider plugins...
- Finding hashicorp/aws versions matching "5.81.0"...
- Installing hashicorp/aws v5.81.0...
- Installed hashicorp/aws v5.81.0 (signed by HashiCorp)
Terraform has created a lock file .terraform.lock.hcl to record the provider
selections it made above. Include this file in your version control repository
so that Terraform can guarantee to make the same selections by default when
you run "terraform init" in the future.

Terraform has been successfully initialized!
```

This command downloads the providers you have specified in **terraform.tf**, it downloads any external modules that you are referencing (none in this case), it connects to your **backend** where you will store the state file (you use the local working directory in this case).

Since the **terraform init** command did not encounter any errors, you move on to see what Terraform thinks will happen if it were to apply these changes. You do this using the **terraform plan** command, outputting the plan to a file named **actions.tfplan**:

Figure 3.33. Create a Terraform plan

```
$ terraform plan -out="actions.tfplan"
data.aws_availability_zones.all: Reading...
data.aws_availability_zones.all: Read complete after 1s [id=eu-west-1]

Terraform used the selected providers to generate the following execution plan.
Resource actions are indicated with the following symbols:
  + create

Terraform will perform the following actions:

  # aws_subnet.all[0] will be created
  + resource "aws_subnet" "all" {
      # details left out for brevity
    }

  # aws_subnet.all[1] will be created
  + resource "aws_subnet" "all" {
      # details left out for brevity
    }

  # aws_subnet.all[2] will be created
  + resource "aws_subnet" "all" {
      # details left out for brevity
    }

  # aws_vpc.this will be created
  + resource "aws_vpc" "this" {
      # details left out for brevity
    }

Plan: 4 to add, 0 to change, 0 to destroy.

Changes to Outputs:
  + aws_subnet_ids = [
      + (known after apply),
      + (known after apply),
      + (known after apply),
```

```
    ]
  + aws_vpc_id      = (known after apply)

Saved the plan to: actions.tfplan

To perform exactly these actions, run the following command to apply:
    terraform apply "actions.tfplan"
```

Since this is a new Terraform configuration there is no pre-existing infrastructure. Another way to put this is that there is no pre-existing **state**.

The output informs you that four resources will be created, and nothing will be changed or destroyed. This is good news for you and it was exactly what you expected. You move on to the apply phase, this is where Terraform orchestrates the provisioning of resources through the AWS provider.

You do this with the **`terraform apply`** command, passing it the plan file you created previously:

Figure 3.34. Apply the Terraform configuration

```
$ terraform apply "actions.tfplan"
aws_vpc.this: Creating...
aws_vpc.this: Creation complete after 2s [id=vpc-0a7fb0cec54e94498]
aws_subnet.all[1]: Creating...
aws_subnet.all[2]: Creating...
aws_subnet.all[0]: Creating...
aws_subnet.all[1]: Creation complete after 0s [id=subnet-0a8d2874de84569c5]
aws_subnet.all[0]: Creation complete after 0s [id=subnet-0cb036f1d8e17405c]
aws_subnet.all[2]: Creation complete after 0s [id=subnet-0027b4751205dd261]

Apply complete! Resources: 4 added, 0 changed, 0 destroyed.

Outputs:

aws_subnet_ids = [
  "subnet-0cb036f1d8e17405c",
  "subnet-0a8d2874de84569c5",
  "subnet-0027b4751205dd261",
]
aws_vpc_id = "vpc-0a7fb0cec54e94498"
```

The output tells you that the operation completed successfully and the correct number of resources have been created.

You now have your network infrastructure on AWS. To verify this, you go to the AWS console. This time you type **VPC** into the search box at the top and select the VPC service in the list (see Figure 3.35).

Next, you select **Your VPCs** in the menu on the left to see your VPC resources (see Figure 3.36).

You find the VPC named **`vpc-eu-west-1`** and select it to see its details (see Figure 3.37).

You click on the **Resource map** tab and see that this VPC contains three subnets, **`snet-eu-west-1a`**, **`snet-eu-west-1b`**, and **`snet-eu-west-1c`** (see Figure 3.38).

You are satisfied with what you have accomplished so far!

After some consideration you realize that you would like to collaborate on this Terraform configuration with your colleagues. You remember that your organization uses **HCP Terraform**, and you set out to migrate your current Terraform configuration to use HCP Terraform as a backend for state storage. This will allow your colleagues to work with the same configuration.

You go to HCP Terraform and sign in to your account using your HCP organization account. You arrive at the HCP Terraform landing page and you click on **Create a workspace** (see Figure 3.39).

A **workspace** in HCP Terraform is one instance of a Terraform configuration with its own state file.

Workspaces

There is a concept of a **workspace** in the Terraform CLI as well as in HCP Terraform, but it's not technically the same thing.

- For each CLI workspace a new state file is created for the same Terraform configuration.
- In HCP Terraform a workspace has a single state file. In Chapter 10 you will learn more about workspaces in HCP Terraform.

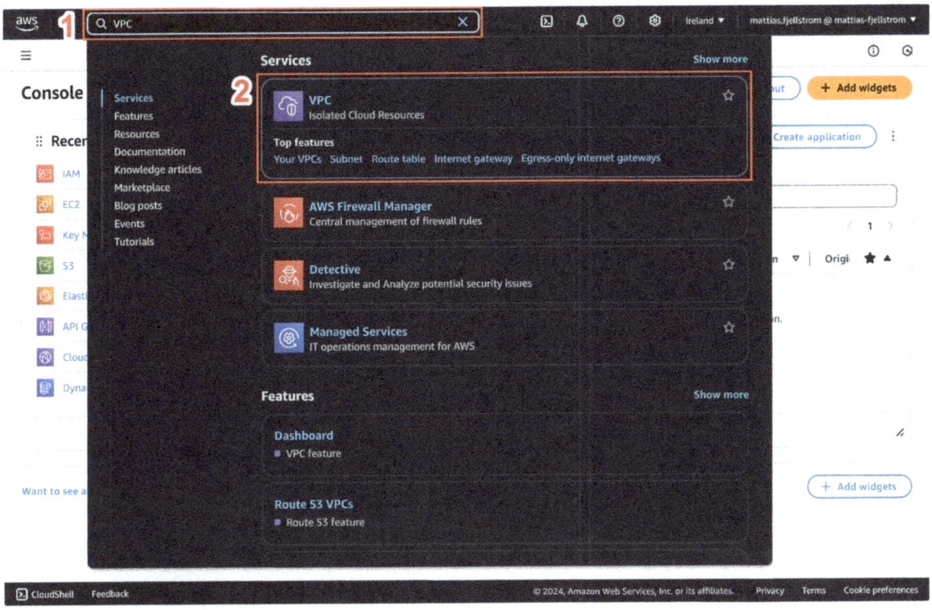

Figure 3.35. (1) Search for VPC in the search bar at the top of the AWS console, then (2) select the VPC service from the list once it appears.

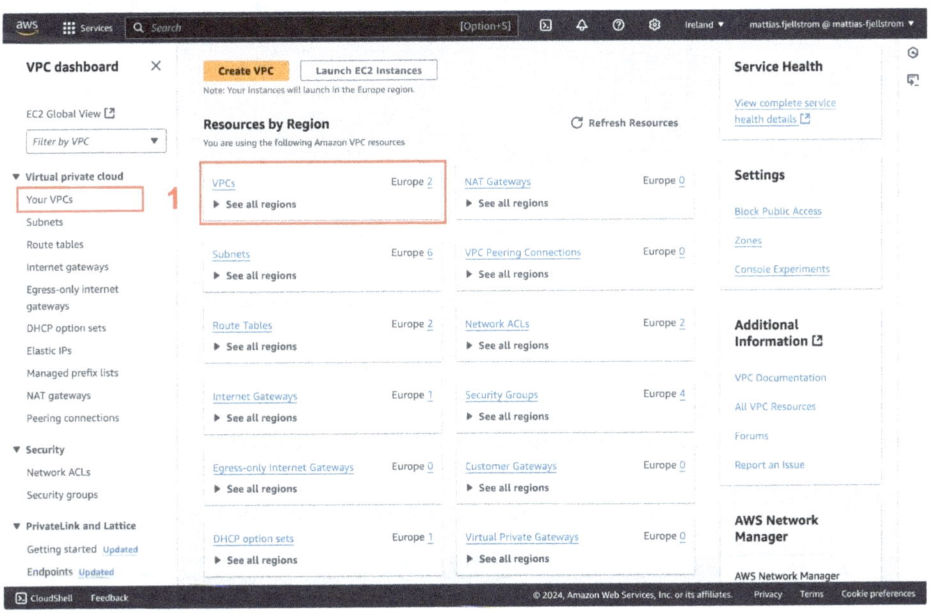

Figure 3.36. (1) Click on Your VPCs in the menu on the left, or click on the VPCs box in the middle of the page.

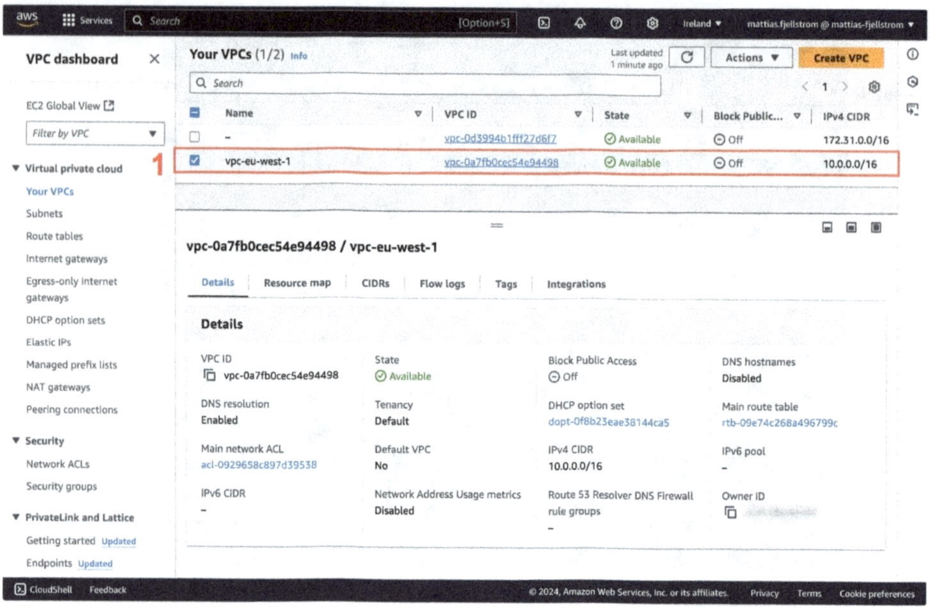

Figure 3.37. (1) Select the VPC named vpc-eu-west-1 from the list of VPCs.

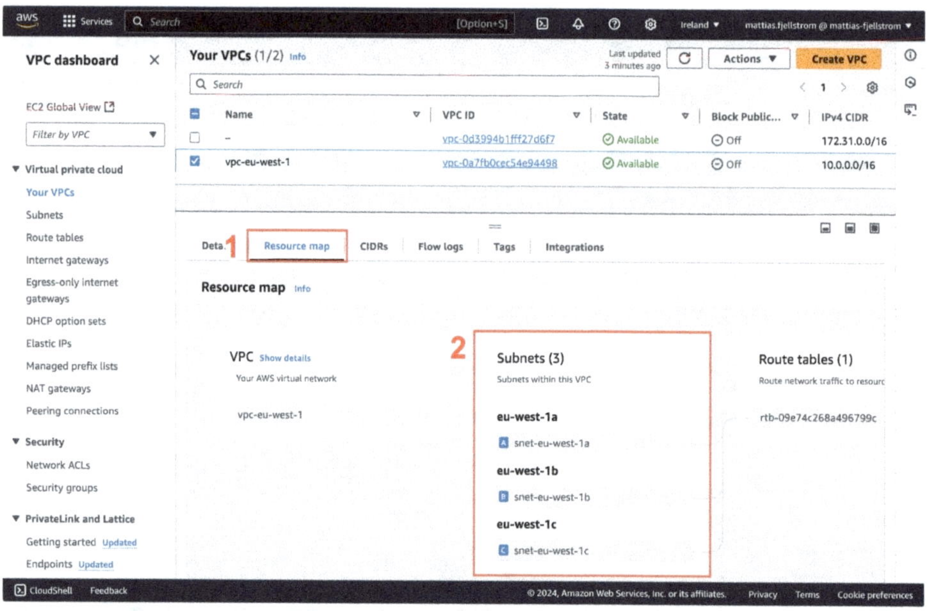

Figure 3.38. (1) Click on the Resource map tab and then (2) notice the list of subnets that are part of this VPC.

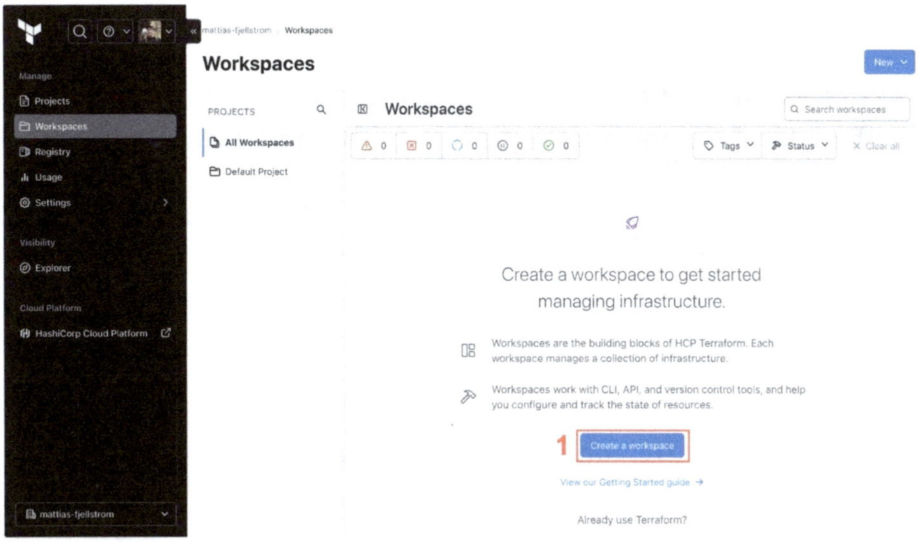

Figure 3.39. (1) On the HCP Terraform workspaces landing page, click on Create a workspace.

You specify that you want a **CLI-Driven Workflow** for the new workspace, this means HCP Terraform will be used for state storage and for running plans and apply[11] (see Figure 3.40).

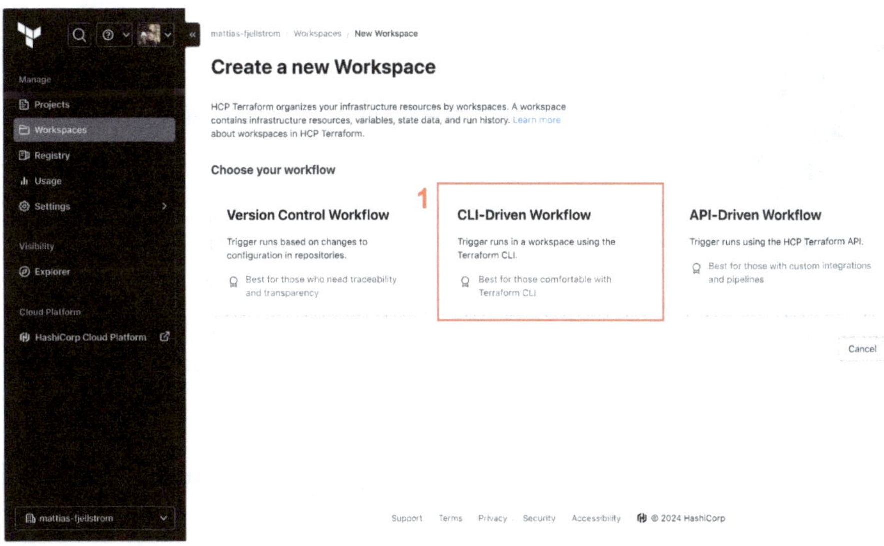

Figure 3.40. (1) Choose the CLI-Driven workflow for the new Terraform workspace.

There are three different types of workflows to choose from:

- The **version control workflow** requires that the Terraform configuration is placed in a Git repository and that you connect this repository to HCP Terraform.

- The **CLI-driven workflow** allows you to run Terraform from anywhere where you have the CLI (e.g. your laptop or a CI/CD pipeline), but you can utilize HCP Terraform for state storage and other features.
- The **API-driven workflow** is similar to the CLI-driven workflow but does not require the use of the CLI, you use the API directly instead. The API-driven workflow is the most advanced type of workflow but allows for some interesting use cases.

You configure your new workspace with a name of **aws-networking** on the next page, you place it in the **Default Project** and you give it a short description, then you click on **Create** (see Figure 3.41).

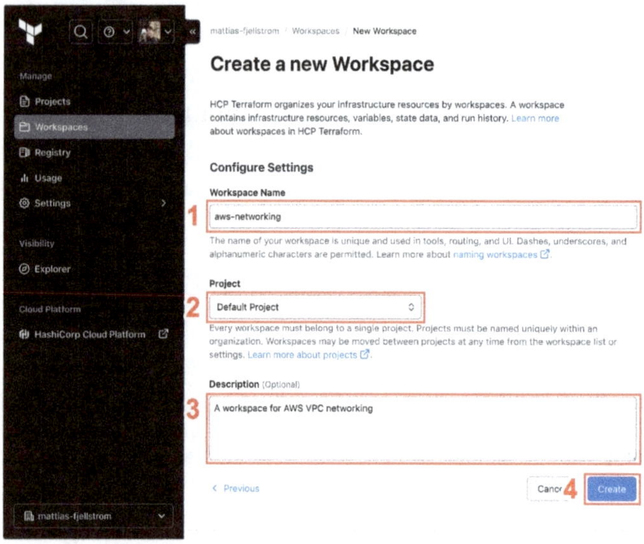

Figure 3.41. **(1) Enter aws-networking as the new workspace name, (2) let this workspace be part of the Default Project and (3) enter a description for the new workspace to indicate what it is. Finally, (4) click on Create to create the new workspace.**

Workspaces in HCP Terraform are part of a **project**, and projects are part of an **organization**.

Once the workspace is created, you copy the example code from the workspace overview page. You will need this code to configure your Terraform configuration to use the HCP Terraform workspace you created (see Figure 3.42).

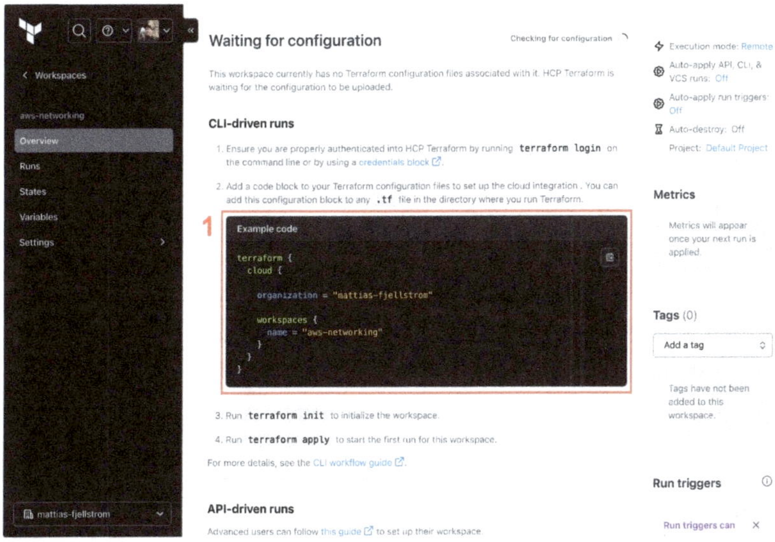

Figure 3.42. (1) On the new workspace overview page copy the example code for how to configure your Terraform configuration to use this HCP Terraform workspace.

Back in your code editor you edit the **terraform** block in **terraform.tf** using the example code you copied:

Figure 3.43. terraform.tf

```
terraform {
  required_providers {
    aws = {
      source  = "hashicorp/aws"
      version = "5.81.0"
    }
  }

  cloud {
    organization = "your-organization"
    workspaces {
      name = "aws-networking"
    }
  }
}
```

Currently, you have a state file in your local working directory. The **state file** is a record of the infrastructure that Terraform has created, with all their attributes. This is the single most important file you have in your Terraform working directory. The state file is named **terraform.tfstate** by default.

Now when you are migrating to use HCP Terraform as a backing system for your Terraform configuration you must migrate the state file from your local directory to the HCP Terraform workspace.

A state migration can take place between any state storage backends you are using, an example could be AWS S3 object storage. In Chapter 7 you will learn more about configuring remote state.

Normally, you would initiate a state migration between two different backends with the command **terraform init -migrate-state**, however, HCP Terraform is a bit of a special case. You just run a regular **terraform init** and follow the prompts:

Figure 3.44. Initiate a state migration to HCP Terraform

```
$ terraform init
Initializing HCP Terraform...
Do you wish to proceed?
  As part of migrating to HCP Terraform, Terraform can optionally copy
  your current workspace state to the configured HCP Terraform workspace.

  Answer "yes" to copy the latest state snapshot to the configured
  HCP Terraform workspace.

  Answer "no" to ignore the existing state and just activate the configured
  HCP Terraform workspace with its existing state, if any.

  Should Terraform migrate your existing state?

  Enter a value: yes

Initializing provider plugins...
- Reusing previous version of hashicorp/aws from the dependency lock file
- Using previously-installed hashicorp/aws v5.81.0

HCP Terraform has been successfully initialized!
```

To make sure the state file is migrated to HCP Terraform, you go to your HCP Terraform workspace and click on the **States** menu option on the left and then select the single state file available (see Figure 3.45).

You see the state file displayed as JSON, and you scroll through it to get an understanding of the format (see Figure 3.46).

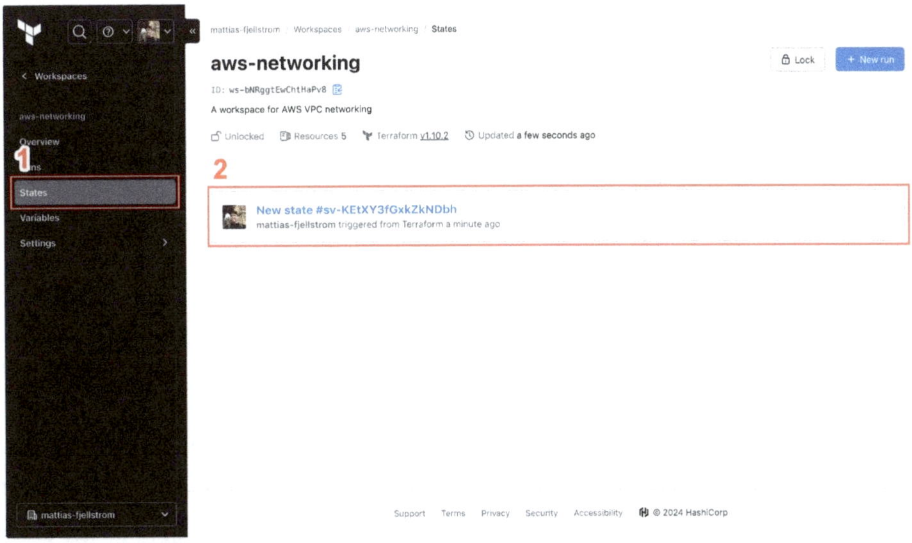

Figure 3.45. (1) From your workspace overview page select States in the menu on the left, then (2) click on the single state version in the list of state versions.

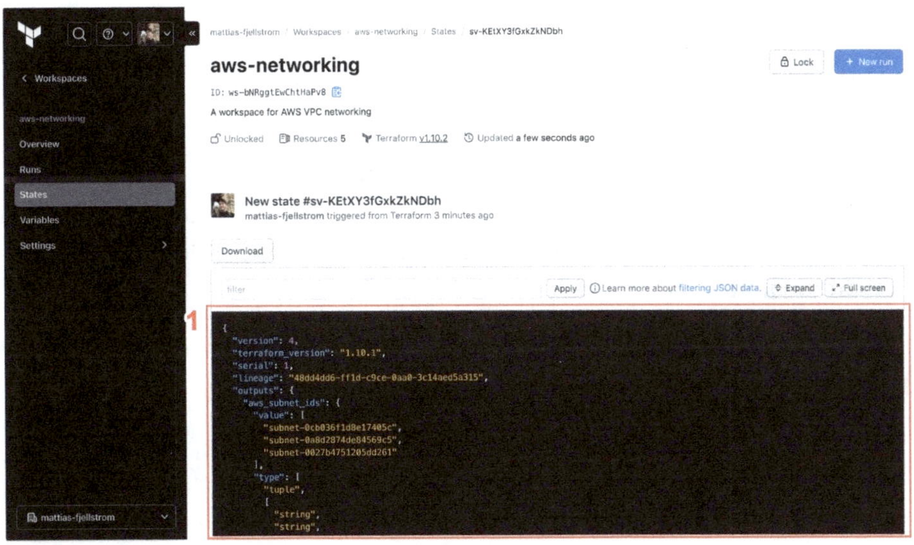

Figure 3.46. (1) Notice how the state file is available in plain JSON.

HCP Terraform keeps a record of all the state changes.

Now you would like to test your HCP Terraform workspace as the driver of your Terraform workflow by issuing **`terraform plan`** and **`terraform apply`** commands. However, you are certain that there are no changes to your infrastructure so you take a shortcut by issuing **`terraform apply -auto-approve`**:

Figure 3.47. Apply the Terraform configuration

```
$ terraform apply -auto-approve
Preparing the remote apply...
Waiting for the plan to start...

Terraform v1.9.4
on linux_amd64
Initializing plugins and modules...
```

When the run starts, you go to your HCP Terraform workspace and see that the run has been registered. You click on **See details** to get a better view (see Figure 3.48).

In the run overview you are met with a large red error message (see Figure 3.49).

You realize that HCP Terraform does not have access to the AWS credentials you configured for Terraform in your own terminal, this is why the apply operation failed!

To rectify the situation you go back to the workspaces overview page and select **Variables** in the left-hand menu (see Figure 3.50).

On the variables page, under **Workspace variables** click on **+ Add variable** (see Figure 3.51).

Specify that this should be an **environment variable**, give the variable the name **`AWS_ACCESS_KEY_ID`**, copy the value of the access key ID you saved from AWS earlier, mark the variable as **sensitive** and give the variable a description. Finally, click on **Add variable** (see Figure 3.52).

Repeat the process for an environment variable named **`AWS_SECRET_ACCESS_KEY`** with the value of the secret access key.

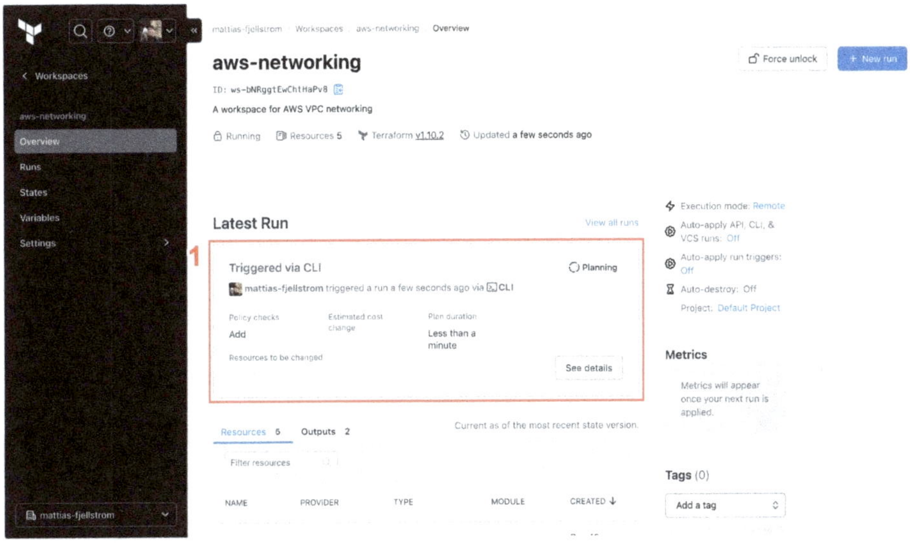

Figure 3.48. (1) From the overview of your workspace, click on the Latest run to see details about it.

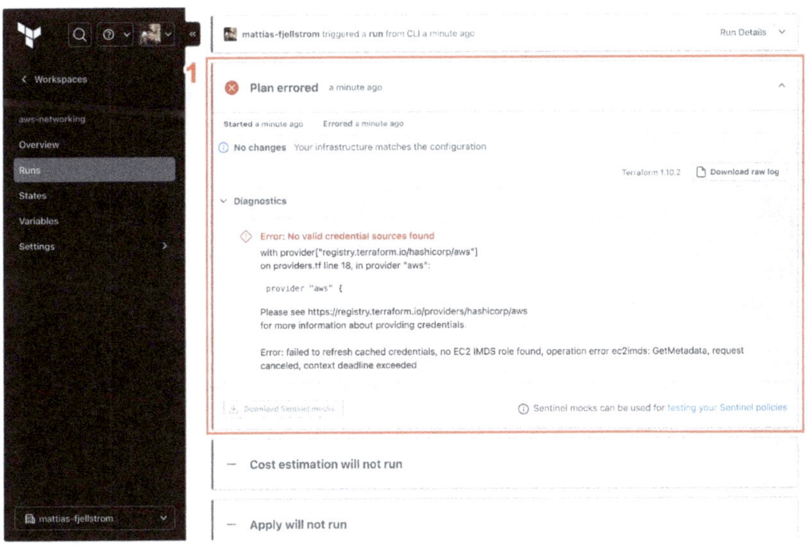

Figure 3.49. (1) Notice how the run has failed and that the error message says that no valid credential sources were found.

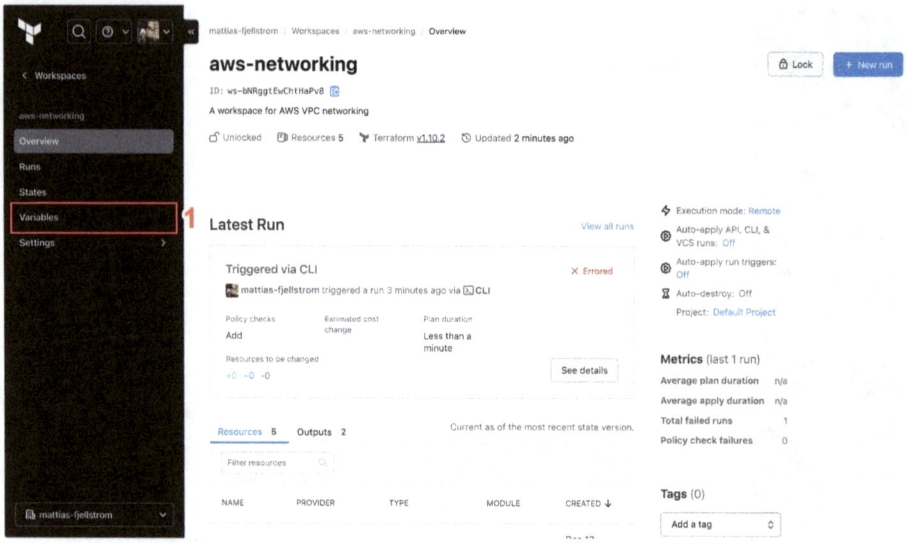

Figure 3.50. (1) From the workspace overview page, click on Variables in the menu on the left.

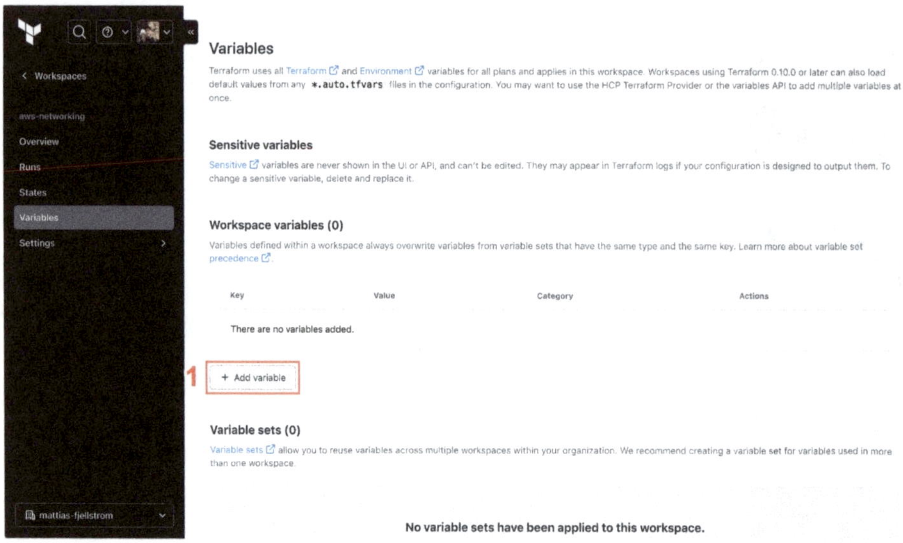

Figure 3.51. (1) Click on +Add variable to add a new variable to this workspace.

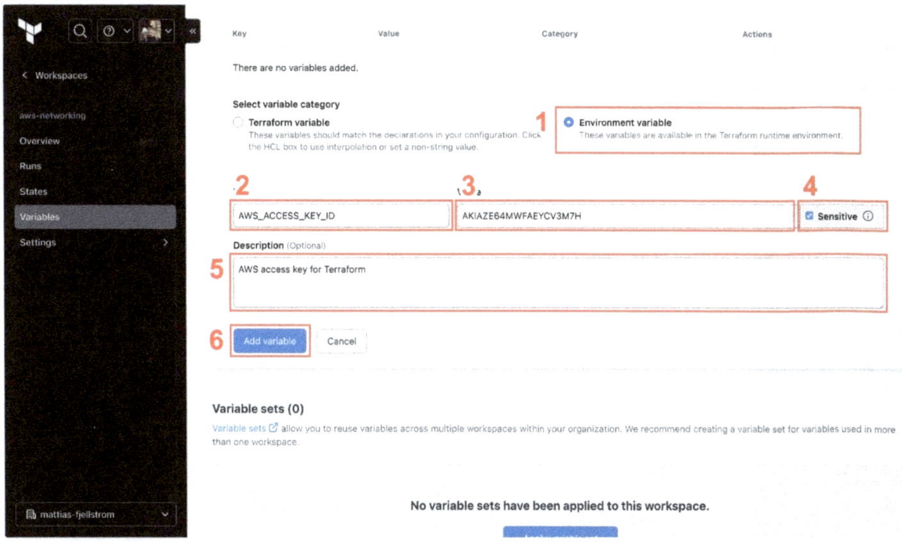

Figure 3.52. (1) Specify that this should be an environment variable, (2) provide the name AWS_-ACCESS_KEY_ID for the variable, (3) enter the value of the access key that you saved from AWS, (4) mark the variable as sensitive, (5) enter a description of the access key and (6) click on Add variable to add the variable to the workspace.

You initiate a new **`terraform apply`** from your terminal to see if HCP Terraform has everything it needs to work with your Terraform configuration:

Figure 3.53. Apply the Terraform configuration

```
$ terraform apply -auto-approve
Preparing the remote apply...
Waiting for the plan to start...

Terraform v1.9.4
on linux_amd64
Initializing plugins and modules...
data.aws_availability_zones.all: Refreshing...
aws_vpc.this: Refreshing state... [id=vpc-0a7fb0cec54e94498]
data.aws_availability_zones.all: Refresh complete after 0s [id=eu-west-1]
aws_subnet.all[1]: Refreshing state... [id=subnet-0a8d2874de84569c5]
aws_subnet.all[0]: Refreshing state... [id=subnet-0cb036f1d8e17405c]
aws_subnet.all[2]: Refreshing state... [id=subnet-0027b4751205dd261]

No changes. Your infrastructure matches the configuration.
```

In HCP Terraform you can also verify that the run has completed successfully (see Figure 3.54).

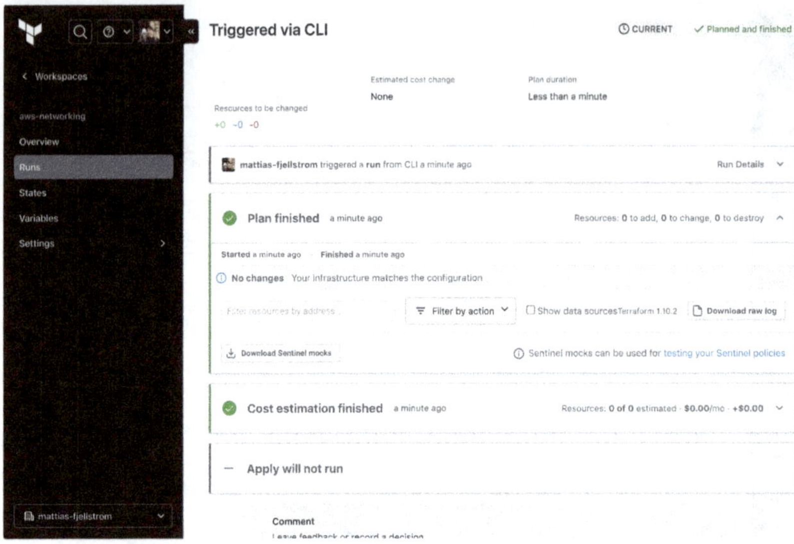

Figure 3.54. Verify that the new Workspace run has completed successfully.

The workday is over and it is time to go home. You are glad that you have accomplished a lot today!

Fast-forward a few months. You no longer need to use the Terraform configuration you created back in the day. It is time to end the lifecycle of this infrastructure.

You do this using the **`terraform destroy`** command:

Figure 3.55. Destroy the resources in your state

```
$ terraform destroy
Preparing the remote apply...
Waiting for the plan to start...
Initializing plugins and modules...
data.aws_availability_zones.all: Refreshing...
aws_vpc.this: Refreshing state... [id=vpc-0a7fb0cec54e94498]
data.aws_availability_zones.all: Refresh complete after 0s [id=eu-west-1]
aws_subnet.all[0]: Refreshing state... [id=subnet-0cb036f1d8e17405c]
aws_subnet.all[1]: Refreshing state... [id=subnet-0a8d2874de84569c5]
aws_subnet.all[2]: Refreshing state... [id=subnet-0027b4751205dd261]
# ... output hidden for brevity
Plan: 0 to add, 0 to change, 4 to destroy.

Do you really want to destroy all resources in workspace "aws-networking"?
  Terraform will destroy all your managed infrastructure, as shown above.
```

```
  There is no undo. Only 'yes' will be accepted to confirm.

  Enter a value: yes

aws_subnet.all[0]: Destroying... [id=subnet-0cb036f1d8e17405c]
aws_subnet.all[2]: Destroying... [id=subnet-0027b4751205dd261]
aws_subnet.all[1]: Destroying... [id=subnet-0a8d2874de84569c5]
aws_subnet.all[2]: Destruction complete after 1s
aws_subnet.all[0]: Destruction complete after 1s
aws_subnet.all[1]: Destruction complete after 1s
aws_vpc.this: Destroying... [id=vpc-0a7fb0cec54e94498]
aws_vpc.this: Destruction complete after 1s

Apply complete! Resources: 0 added, 0 changed, 4 destroyed.
```

`terraform destroy` is an alias for **`terraform apply -destroy`**, but you appreciate the clarity of the **`terraform destroy`** command.

Your journey with Terraform has come to an end, for now. In reality it is only the beginning.

We covered a lot about Terraform and a little bit about AWS and HCP Terraform in this section. Knowing what you have read here by heart is a good start on your professional certification journey.

The exam will test you on edge cases that move outside of this linear path that was presented in this chapter.

That is what the rest of this book is about!

3.2: Summary

This chapter explored a journey with Terraform. We started by installing Terraform on our local system, and we went through the design of a simple network architecture on AWS with Terraform.

We wrote the Terraform configuration, we provisioned our resources, then decided to migrate our state to HCP Terraform, and finally destroyed our infrastructure.

Refer back to this chapter to remind yourself of the big picture of working with Terraform.

Notes

1. https://github.com/mattias-fjellstrom/terraform-professional-book-sample-code/tree/main/aws/chapter03
2. Check out the **Terraform Tuesdays** series on YouTube by my fellow HashiCorp Ambassador, *Ned in the Cloud.* It covers bits and pieces of Terraform and the surrounding ecosystem.
3. https://developer.hashicorp.com/terraform/install
4. https://aws.amazon.com/console/
5. https://registry.terraform.io/providers/hashicorp/aws/latest
6. https://registry.terraform.io/providers/hashicorp/aws/latest/docs/resources/vpc
7. https://registry.terraform.io/providers/hashicorp/aws/latest/docs/resources/subnet
8. https://registry.terraform.io/providers/hashicorp/aws/latest/docs/data-sources/availability_zones
9. https://developer.hashicorp.com/terraform/language/functions/cidrsubnet
10. https://developer.hashicorp.com/terraform/language/functions
11. To better collaborate with others you should use a VCS-driven workflow (Version Control System). However, setting this up from scratch would make this chapter a lot longer and it would not contribute anything to the following story, so I decided to skip that in this example.

Chapter 4: Basics of the HashiCorp Configuration Language

In the previous chapter we saw many examples of the **HashiCorp Configuration Language** (HCL).

HCL is easy to learn and you might already know most of what you need to know about HCL, but in this chapter we will still cover the basics of HCL.

HCL consists of two primary constructs, **arguments** and **blocks**, and a a few related concepts, **values**, **expressions** and **functions**.

4.1: Arguments, Values and Expressions

An **argument** is the assignment of a **value** to a named entity:

```
name = "value"
```

Values can be one of three basic types: **`string`**, **`number`**, or **`bool`**. Values can also be of complex types, such as lists of strings or objects with many sub-arguments:

```
my_list = ["one", "two", "three"]
my_obj = {
  first  = "one"
  second = "two"
  third  = "three"
}
```

Values such as **`"one"`**, **`2`**, **`["three", "four", "five"]`** are called literal values.

Values can also be **expressions**. An expression is something that in the end evaluates to a literal value. Expressions can contain literal values, functions, and references. A few examples of expressions:

```
exp1 = min(1,2,3,6,3,0,9)
exp2 = var.do_it ? "I did it" : "I did not do it"
exp3 = [for name in var.names : lower(name)]
exp4 = aws_vpc.this.name
```

4.2: Blocks

A **block** is a piece of code with a **type** and zero or more **labels**. A block can contain arguments or other blocks (nested blocks).

Examples of blocks with zero up to two labels look like this:

```
# a block with zero labels
terraform {
  required_version = "1.6.0"
}

# a block with one label
provider "aws" {
  region = "eu-west-1"
}

# a block with two labels
resource "aws_security_group" "web" {
  name = "web"
  # other arguments ...
}
```

A block containing a nested block looks like this:

```
terraform {
  # a nested block
  required_providers {
    # an argument with a complex value (an object)
    aws = {
      source = "hashicorp/aws"
    }
  }
}
```

4.3: Functions

There are many **functions** in the HCL language for Terraform[1]. An example of what the use of a function looks like:

```
# name will evaluate to foo-bar-baz
name = join("-", ["foo", "bar", "baz"])
```

Functions will always be used in expressions for a value.

These are the main pieces of HCL to remember. By using the constructs described above you can write all of the Terraform code you can imagine. The difficulty of Terraform is not the HCL language, it is rather in complexities related to the resources we create using Terraform providers.

4.4: Terraform Specific Blocks

Below follows examples of the main root-level blocks available in Terraform, these are the blocks you will use in most Terraform configurations you write:

4.4.1: Resource block

The `resource` block represents infrastructure resources we want to create. It has two labels, one for the **resource type** and one for the **resource name** of the resource.

An example of a `resource` block:

```
resource "aws_security_group" "web" {
  # attributes
}
```

4.4.2: Data source block

The `data` block represents data sources, these are **existing** resources you want to read attributes from. It has two labels, one for the **data source type** and one for the **data source name**.

An example of a `data` block:

```
data "aws_security_group" "web" {
  # attributes
}
```

4.4.3: Variable block

The **`variable`** block represents **input** to our Terraform configuration. It has one label for the **name** of the variable.

An example of a **`variable`** block:

```
variable "aws_region" {
  type        = string
  description = "AWS region"
}
```

4.4.4: Output block

The **`output`** block represents **outputs** from our Terraform configuration. It has one label for the **name** of the output.

An example of an **`output`** block:

```
output "vpc_id" {
  value = aws_vpc.this.id
}
```

4.4.5: Terraform block

The **`terraform`** block allows us to configure the required Terraform binary version, the required provider versions, our state backend location, and possible HCP Terraform integration. This block has no labels.

An example of a **`terraform`** block:

```
terraform {
  required_version = "..."
  required_providers { ... }
  backend "s3" {
    # attributes
  }
}
```

4.4.6: Provider block

The **provider** block allows us to configure a given provider that we are using. It has one label representing the **name** of the provider.

An example of a **provider** block:

```
provider "aws" {
  region = "eu-west-1"
  # other attributes ...
}
```

4.4.7: Module block

The **module** block declares a **module**. A module is a reusable piece of Terraform configuration. It has one label representing the **module name**.

An example of a **module** block:

```
module "vpc" {
  source  = "terraform-aws-modules/vpc/aws"
  version = "5.13.0"
}
```

4.4.8: Locals block

The **locals** block can be used to create local values that can be referenced elsewhere in your Terraform configuration. This block has no labels.

An example of a **locals** block:

```
locals {
  local1 = "value1"
  local2 = "value2-combined-with-${local.local1}"
  local3 = 100
  local4 = true
  local5 = upper("abc")
  # other locals ...
}
```

You can use any number of **locals** blocks in your Terraform configuration. You could do this:

```
locals {
  local1 = "value1"
}

locals {
  local2 = "value2"
}
```

We will see all of the Terraform blocks presented here in use throughout the rest of the book.

Notes

1. Visit https://developer.hashicorp.com/terraform/language/functions to see a list of all the built-in functions.

Part III: Exam Objectives

This part covers each of the exam objectives that are part of the Terraform Authoring and Operations Professional exam.

- Chapter 5 - focuses on the Terraform CLI.
- Chapter 6 - focuses on features of the HCL language.
- Chapter 7 - focuses on how to collaborate on Terraform configurations using remote state, provider versioning, automation, and sharing data between different configurations.
- Chapter 8 - focuses on modules, how to use them, how to write one from scratch and how to refactor a Terraform configuration into modules.
- Chapter 9 - focuses on providers, and specifically on how to authenticate the AWS provider.
- Chapter 10 - focuses on benefits and features of HCP Terraform for collaborative Terraform development.

Chapter 5: Manage Resource Lifecycle

At the end of the day, Terraform is all about managing the lifecycle of resources. **Resources** are at the center of your Terraform configuration.

The first exam objective of the Terraform professional certification is **manage resource lifecycle** and it covers the following sub-objectives:

- Initialize a configuration using `terraform init` and its options
- Generate an execution plan using `terraform plan` and its options
- Apply configuration changes using `terraform apply` and its options
- Destroy resources using `terraform destroy` and its options
- Manage resource state, including importing resources and reconciling resource drift

In other words, this chapter concerns the use of the Terraform CLI.

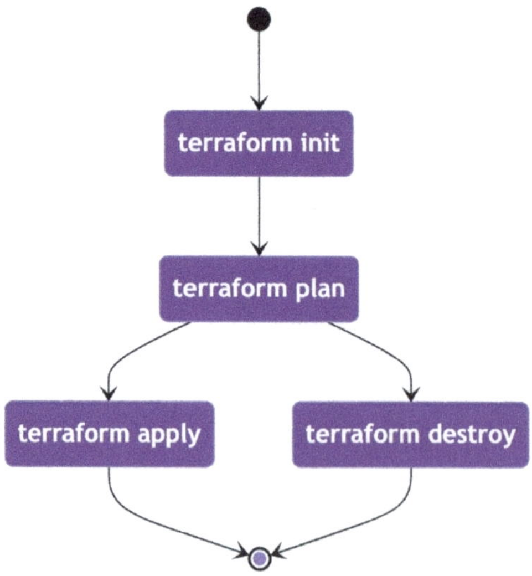

Figure 5.1. Using the Terraform CLI to manage the resource lifecycle

5.1: Initialize a Configuration Using terraform init and its Options

`terraform init` is the first command you run for all of your Terraform configurations. This is true for brand new configurations, as well as for existing configurations with an existing state.

The **`terraform init`** command initializes your configuration by downloading providers and modules, it connects to your state storage backend, and it creates the **`.terraform.lock.hcl`** file in your working directory unless it already exists. The lock file contains details of the providers that your configuration uses.

Create a **`main.tf`** file with the following content (sample code available at GitHub.com[1]):

Figure 5.2. A terraform block with one required provider.

```
terraform {
  required_version = ">= 1.6.0"

  required_providers {
    aws = {
      source  = "hashicorp/aws"
      version = "5.61.0"
    }
  }
}
```

Running **`terraform init`** for this simple Terraform configuration gives us the following result:

Figure 5.3. Initializing the Terraform configuration

```
$ terraform init
Initializing the backend...
Initializing provider plugins...
- Finding hashicorp/aws versions matching "5.61.0"...
- Installing hashicorp/aws v5.61.0...
- Installed hashicorp/aws v5.61.0 (signed by HashiCorp)
Terraform has created a lock file .terraform.lock.hcl to record the provider
selections it made above. Include this file in your version control repository
so that Terraform can guarantee to make the same selections by default when
you run "terraform init" in the future.

Terraform has been successfully initialized!
```

The output informs us of what Terraform is doing.

After running **terraform init** there is a new directory named **.terraform** in our working directory. The full contents of the working directory looks like this:

Figure 5.4. Working directory after running terraform init

```
$ tree -a .
.
├── .terraform
│   └── providers
│       └── registry.terraform.io
│           └── hashicorp
│               └── aws
│                   └── 5.61.0
│                       └── darwin_arm64
│                           ├── LICENSE.txt
│                           └── terraform-provider-aws_v5.61.0_x5
├── .terraform.lock.hcl
└── main.tf

8 directories, 4 files
```

The **providers** directory contains the provider binaries for the system architecture where you ran the **terraform init** command. In this case there is only the **aws** provider. If our configuration would have included external modules these would have been available under the **.terraform** directory as well.

Getting Help

Add the **-h** or **--help** flag to the **terraform init** command to get help:

```
$ terraform init -h
Usage: terraform [global options] init [options]

  Initialize a new or existing Terraform working directory by creating
  initial files, loading any remote state, downloading modules, etc.

Options:
  ...
```

This also works for all other Terraform CLI commands.

Three options for the **terraform init** command that are good to know about are:

- The **-upgrade** flag is used to upgrade the provider binaries, as well as installing new providers once they have been added to the Terraform configuration.
- The **-backend-config** flag is used to override settings related to the state backend configuration. This can be useful if you do not want to hard-code all the backend settings in your Terraform configuration.
- The **-migrate-state** flag is used to migrate your state file between different backends.

From the perspective of "resource lifecycle" we don't need to spend more time discussing the **terraform init** command. We run the command once to download the required provider binaries, download modules, and connect to our state storage, then we are good to go!

Note that the **terraform init** command can catch some of the most trivial mistakes you make in your Terraform configuration, for instance if you specify a provider version that does not exist. Errors from the **terraform init** command are usually very informative, so you should know what to do if you encounter them.

An example of what an error from Terraform init could look like:

Figure 5.5. Encountering an error during terraform init

```
$ terraform init
Initializing the backend...
Initializing provider plugins...
- Finding hashicorp/aws versions matching "6.61.61"...

│ Error: Failed to query available provider packages
│
│ Could not retrieve the list of available versions for provider hashicorp/aws:
│ no available releases match the given constraints 6.61.61
```

There was no AWS provider binary available with a version number of **6.61.61** and the error message from **terraform init** informs us of this.

5.2: Generate an Execution Plan Using terraform plan and its Options

The **terraform plan** command answers the question:

> *"What would happen if I apply the current Terraform configuration to my current state?"*

A Terraform **plan** is a record of changes that would be applied if the current configuration is used in a **terraform apply** command. There are a number of options for this command that are good to be familiar with as they can be useful during the exam.

If you run **terraform plan** the planned changes are output to the terminal. Planned changes can include:

- Creating new resources (this is considered the most safe of all the possible changes).
- Updating existing resources (with or without replacing the resources, be careful here!).
- Deleting resources.
- Refactoring your state in some way. This includes moving resources in the state and importing resources into your state.

To store the output from **terraform plan** in a file, add the **-out** flag:

Figure 5.6. Storing the Terraform plan output in a file named actions.tfplan

```
$ terraform plan -out="actions.tfplan"
...
```

You can name the plan file whatever you like. The **.tfplan** file ending is not an official convention but it clearly indicates what the file contains.

If you try to open the plan file you will notice that it is in binary format. To convert the file to JSON so that you can inspect it, run the **terraform show** command with the **-json** flag:

Figure 5.7. Output the contents of actions.tfplan as JSON

```
$ terraform show -json actions.tfplan
```

You can pipe the output of this command to a file for convenience:

Figure 5.8. Output the contents of actions.tfplan as JSON and store it in actions.json

```
$ terraform show -json actions.tfplan | jq > actions.json
```

Look through the plan file (**`actions.json`** in this case) to get a feel for the information that it contains. You will not need to be able to parse this file for the exam, it will suffice to look at the terminal output of the **`terraform plan`** command to determine what Terraform is planning on doing. The terminal output is formatted in a way that is easy for humans to read.

By default the **`terraform plan`** command makes a plan involving **all** the resources in the Terraform configuration. Sometimes it can be useful to plan changes for a single resource, or a few resources that have direct dependencies between them. You can do this using the **`-target`** flag together with the **resource address** of the resource you want to create a plan for.

Object Address

A resource has an **address** in your Terraform configuration, and in your Terraform state.

The address consists of the **resource type** followed by the **resource name**. To put it in a different way, it is the combination of the two labels in the **`resource`** block with a dot in between.

To illustrate what this looks like we have the following Terraform configuration containing a single **`aws_vpc`** resource:

```
resource "aws_vpc" "this" {
  # ... arguments
}
```

The resource address for the VPC resource is **`aws_vpc.this`**.

The resource address for a **data source** works in a similar way, but it starts with **`data.`**. Use the following data source:

```
data "aws_region" "current" {
  # ... arguments
}
```

> You can reference the data source using the address **data.aws_region.current**.
>
> The address of a **module** starts with **module.**. Now we have the following sample Terraform configuration:
>
> ```
> module "vpc" {
>   source  = "terraform-aws-modules/vpc/aws"
>   version = "5.13.0"
> }
> ```
>
> You can reference the module using the address **module.vpc**.
>
> Addressing a resource inside of a module builds upon what we learned above. An example of this is **module.vpc.aws_vpc.this**. If you have nested modules the address will be even longer, but you should now have a feeling for how all the addresses are constructed.

To illustrate how this works use the following Terraform configuration (sample code available at GitHub.com[2]):

Figure 5.9. A Terraform configuration with resources with a relationship.

```
resource "aws_security_group" "web" {
  name        = "web"
  description = "Security group for web servers"

  tags = {
    Name = "web"
  }
}

resource "aws_vpc_security_group_ingress_rule" "https" {
  security_group_id = aws_security_group.web.id
  cidr_ipv4         = "0.0.0.0/0"
  from_port         = 443
  to_port           = 443
  ip_protocol       = "Tcp"
}
```

This configuration creates a **security group** with a single **security group rule**. A security group is a basic firewall that allows or denies network traffic. The security group rule resource has an implicit dependency on the security group resource through the reference in the **security_group_id** argument.

We can run a **terraform plan** command specifically targeting the rule resource:

Figure 5.10. Create a plan for the security group rule resource

```
$ terraform plan -target=aws_vpc_security_group_ingress_rule.https

Terraform used the selected providers to generate the following execution plan.
Resource actions are indicated with the following symbols:
  + create

Terraform will perform the following actions:

# aws_security_group.web will be created
  + resource "aws_security_group" "web" {
    # arguments ...
  }

# aws_vpc_security_group_ingress_rule.https will be created
  + resource "aws_vpc_security_group_ingress_rule" "https" {
    # arguments ...
  }

Plan: 2 to add, 0 to change, 0 to destroy.

Warning: Resource targeting is in effect
```

Note that the use of the **-target** flag is only for exceptional situations, e.g. recovering from errors or mistakes. It is not something you should use in your default workflows.

The output indicates that two resources will be created, even though we targeted a single resource. This is because there was a dependency between the rule and the security group.

If we instead target the **aws_security_group** resource we get a different result:

Figure 5.11. Create a plan for the security group resource

```
$ terraform plan -target=aws_security_group.web

Terraform used the selected providers to generate the following execution plan.
Resource actions are indicated with the following symbols:
  + create

Terraform will perform the following actions:

  # aws_security_group.web will be created
  + resource "aws_security_group" "web" {
      # arguments ...
    }
```

```
Plan: 1 to add, 0 to change, 0 to destroy.

Warning: Resource targeting is in effect
```

In this case only the security group resource will be created.

If your Terraform configuration has one or more variables you need a way to provide values for these variables when you run **terraform plan**. There are a few ways of how you can do this. To illustrate how this works, imagine you have a Terraform configuration with a single variable like this:

Figure 5.12. A Terraform configuration with a single variable

```
variable "aws_region" {
  type = string
}
```

To provide a value for the **aws_region** variable we have the following options:

- We could add a default value argument in the **variable** block, i.e. **default = "eu-west-1"**.
- We can supply the value as part of the **terraform plan** command; this is done by adding the flag **-var="aws_region=eu-west-1"**. If you have multiple variables you add one **-var** flag for each of them.
- We can create a **variables file** (see the box below) where we specify the values for all variables.
- We can set an environment variable named **TF_VAR_aws_region** to the value we want (e.g. **export TF_VAR_aws_region=eu-west-1**).

Variable Files

A **variable file** is a file using the **.tfvars** or **.tfvars.json** file ending. It is a simple file containing key-value pairs assigning values for all variables for a given Terraform configuration.

As an example, imagine your Terraform configuration has the following variables:

```
variable "aws_region" {
  type = string
}
```

```
variable "user" {
  type = object({
    name = string
    age  = number
  })
}
```

We can create a file named **terraform.tfvars** with the following content:

```
aws_region = "eu-west-1"
user = {
  name = "Jane"
  age  = 35
}
```

We can provide this variable file to Terraform using the **-var-file** flag:

```
$ terraform plan -var-file=terraform.tfvars
```

The naming of the variable file is important. If you give it the name **terraform.tfvars** or **terraform.tfvars.json** Terraform will automatically use it, so there is no need to explicitly provide it in your CLI commands.

The same goes for any file named ***.auto.tfvars** or ***.auto.tfvars.json**. Terraform will automatically use all the variable files following this convention, and any file you explicitly provide using the **-var-file** flag. All the variables will be merged.

The **terraform plan** command is perhaps the most useful command in the Terraform CLI, and you should use it always! During the exam the **terraform plan** command will be your most used command. Use it to make sure that the changes you are about to make are what you expect.

Now we move on to the main command for creating infrastructure: **terraform apply**.

5.3: Apply Configuration Changes Using terraform apply and its Options

Once you have a plan file you can tell Terraform to perform the actions that this plan contains with the command:

Figure 5.13. Apply a plan file

```
$ terraform apply "actions.tfplan"
```

If you do not have a plan file you can still issue the **terraform apply** command and Terraform will run a plan operation for you and then ask you to confirm that you want to apply the changes (requiring you to reply **yes**).

There are situations where you want to just apply the changes without confirming them, this is done by adding the **-auto-approve** flag:

Figure 5.14. Automatically approve an apply operation

```
$ terraform apply -auto-approve
```

Be careful with the **-auto-approve** flag in your daily work, but perhaps you will use it during the certification exam just to shave off a few seconds of time!

As with the **terraform plan** command, the **terraform apply** command requires values for any variables that your Terraform configuration contains. You can use the same set of flags for variables as for the **terraform plan** command.

Something to be aware of for the certification exam and real-life is what happens if the plan file you are using is **stale**. A stale plan file means that something has changed in the infrastructure since the plan file was created. The plan is no longer accurate. This could be if someone manually edited something outside of Terraform.

To see what this looks like first apply the following sample Terraform configuration (sample code available at GitHub.com[3]):

Figure 5.15. A sample Terraform configuration to illustrate a stale plan file.

```
terraform {
  required_version = ">= 1.6.0"

  required_providers {
    aws = {
      source  = "hashicorp/aws"
      version = "5.61.0"
    }
  }
}

variable "aws_region" {
  type     = string
```

```
  default = "eu-west-1"
}

provider "aws" {
  region = var.aws_region
}

resource "aws_security_group" "web" {
  name        = "web"
  description = "Security group for web servers"

  tags = {
    Name = "web"
  }
}

resource "aws_vpc_security_group_ingress_rule" "https" {
  security_group_id = aws_security_group.web.id
  cidr_ipv4         = "0.0.0.0/0"
  from_port         = 443
  to_port           = 443
  ip_protocol       = "Tcp"
}
```

Save this Terraform configuration to **main.tf**, then apply it:

Figure 5.16. Apply the Terraform configuration

```
$ terraform apply -auto-approve
...
```

Edit the inbound rule in the Terraform configuration to the following (sample code available at GitHub.com[4]):

Figure 5.17. Update the security group rule resource.

```
# ... other code is omitted ...
resource "aws_vpc_security_group_ingress_rule" "https" {
  security_group_id = aws_security_group.web.id
  cidr_ipv4         = "0.0.0.0/0"

  # open all ports between 1 and 1024
  from_port         = 1
  to_port           = 1024
  ip_protocol       = "Tcp"
}
```

This change is not something we would actually want to do for our security group, but this is for illustrative purposes only. Now generate a plan file for these changes:

Figure 5.18. Create a new plan output file

```
$ terraform plan -out="actions.tfplan"
```

The output will tell us that the ingress rule will be updated in-place, meaning that Terraform expects that this ingress rule exists. Before we apply these changes, go to the AWS console and remove the ingress rule from the security group that this Terraform configuration created.

Now apply the plan:

Figure 5.19. Apply the changes in the Terraform plan file

```
$ terraform apply "actions.tfplan"
aws_vpc_security_group_ingress_rule.https: Modifying... [id=sgr-02b21a2051274e077]
|
| Error: updating VPC Security Group Rule (sgr-02b21a2051274e077)
|
|   with aws_vpc_security_group_ingress_rule.https,
|   on main.tf line 29, in resource "aws_vpc_security_group_ingress_rule" "https":
|   29: resource "aws_vpc_security_group_ingress_rule" "https" {
|
| operation error EC2: ModifySecurityGroupRules, https response error
| StatusCode: 400, RequestID: 7451ee72-9e9b-46a1-ade4-216e2f07d7b8, api
| error InvalidSecurityGroupRuleId.NotFound: The security group rule ID
| 'sgr-02b21a2051274e077' does not exist
```

The error message clearly indicates what is wrong in this case. However, that might not always be the case. Be aware that if you would be given a plan file you have not generated yourself these types of errors could occur. Try to minimize the time between creating a plan file and applying the changes.

5.4: Destroy Resources Using terraform destroy and its Options

To remove the infrastructure Terraform has created we use the **`terraform destroy`** command. This command is really just an alias for **`terraform apply -destroy`**. This is clear from the help output for this command:

Figure 5.20. Help for the terraform destroy command

```
$ terraform destroy -h
Usage: terraform [global options] destroy [options]

  Destroy Terraform-managed infrastructure.

  This command is a convenience alias for:
      terraform apply -destroy

  This command also accepts many of the plan-customization options accepted by
  the terraform plan command. For more information on those options, run:
      terraform plan -help
```

You could also generate a **destroy plan** using the following command:

Figure 5.21. Create a destroy plan

```
$ terraform plan -destroy -out="actions.tfplan"
```

Then you can pass the destroy plan to `terraform apply`:

Figure 5.22. Apply the plan as usual

```
$ terraform apply "actions.tfplan"
```

A destroy plan is just another plan, so you pass it to the **`terraform apply`** command without specifying anything about what types of actions you want Terraform to take.

Since **`terraform destroy`** is an alias for **`terraform apply -destroy`**, all the other flags to the **`terraform apply`** command are also available for the **`terraform destroy`** command (including **`-auto-approve`**).

When you run a **`terraform destroy`** operation it is extra important to double check the plan output to see exactly what infrastructure is being deleted. If you use this command during the exam it is very important that you are sure it is the right thing to do.

5.5: Manage Resource State, Including Importing Resources and Reconciling Resource Drift

You can refactor your Terraform configuration and state using two different methods:

1. An imperative method with the Terraform CLI.
2. A declarative method with refactoring blocks in HCL.

Both methods will be covered in this section. You should be aware that the declarative method is the preferred and recommended method.

Manipulating Terraform State with the CLI

To manipulate your Terraform state using the Terraform CLI there is a family of commands available for this:

```
$ terraform state -h
Subcommands:
    list                List resources in the state
    mv                  Move an item in the state
    pull                Pull current state and output to stdout
    push                Update remote state from a local state file
    replace-provider    Replace provider in the state
    rm                  Remove instances from the state
    show                Show a resource in the state
```

Be very careful when you use these commands since they could directly edit your state file (e.g. the **`terraform state rm`** command). There are two safe commands in this family that you can use for troubleshooting and verification:

- **`terraform state list`** lists all the resources in your state with their corresponding resource address.
- **`terraform state show <addr>`** shows a specific resource in your state with the address specified in **`<addr>`**.

Apart from those two commands I do not recommend that you use the **`terraform state`** commands unless you see no other way of doing it. If that is the case, first make sure you are certain that there is no other way of doing it. Then make sure one more time. And if you really have to, make a backup of your state file before you do anything!

Sometimes you want to import resources into your state. This is common if resources have been created using some other method, and now you want to manage the resources using Terraform.

To **import** resources into your state you can use the **terraform import** CLI command. This command looks like this:

Figure 5.23. The import command used to import resources into your Terraform state

```
$ terraform import ADDR ID
```

You need to know two things to use this command:

- The address (written as **ADDR** in the command above) of the **resource** block to which you import the resource. This means you need to define the resource as usual using a **resource** block in your Terraform configuration.
- The **ID** of the resource you want to import. The format of the ID varies depending on what resource provider you are using and what resource type you are importing.

As an example of how to import a resource into your Terraform state let's start with the following Terraform configuration that we have seen before, save it to a file named **main.tf** (sample code available at GitHub.com[5]):

Figure 5.24. main.tf

```
terraform {
  required_version = ">= 1.6.0"

  required_providers {
    aws = {
      source  = "hashicorp/aws"
      version = "5.61.0"
    }
  }
}

variable "aws_region" {
  type    = string
  default = "eu-west-1"
}

provider "aws" {
  region = var.aws_region
}

resource "aws_security_group" "web" {
  name        = "web"
  description = "Security group for web servers"
```

```
  tags = {
    Name = "web"
  }
}

resource "aws_vpc_security_group_ingress_rule" "https" {
  security_group_id = aws_security_group.web.id
  cidr_ipv4         = "0.0.0.0/0"
  from_port         = 443
  to_port           = 443
  ip_protocol       = "Tcp"
}
```

Apply the configuration using **terraform apply** to recreate the infrastructure we destroyed earlier.

Now add the following block to **main.tf** (sample code available at GitHub.com[6]):

Figure 5.25. main.tf

```
# ... other code is omitted ...
resource "aws_vpc_security_group_ingress_rule" "ssh" {
  security_group_id = aws_security_group.web.id
  cidr_ipv4         = "0.0.0.0/0"
  from_port         = 22
  to_port           = 22
  ip_protocol       = "Tcp"
}
```

The address of this resource is **aws_vpc_security_group_ingress_rule.ssh**.

Next we go to the AWS console and search for EC2 in the top search bar (see Figure 5.26).

A security group is a network resource, and you can find it by going to the VPC service page in AWS. However, for legacy reasons it is also listed under the EC2 service.

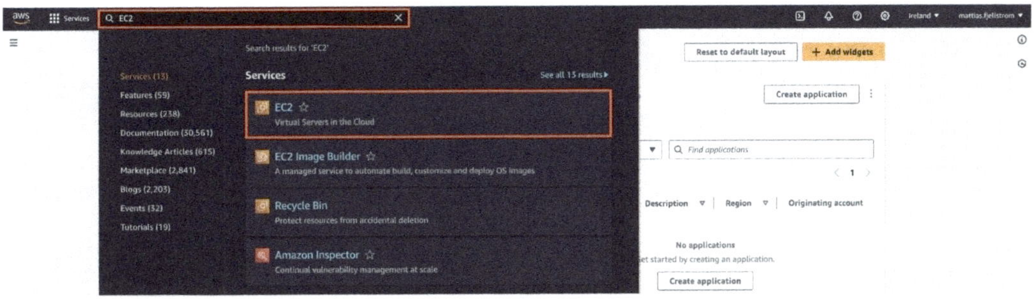

Figure 5.26. Search for and open the EC2 service

In the left-hand menu click on **Security Groups**, select the security group named **web**, select the **Inbound rules** tab, and finally click on **Edit inbound rules** (see Figure 5.27).

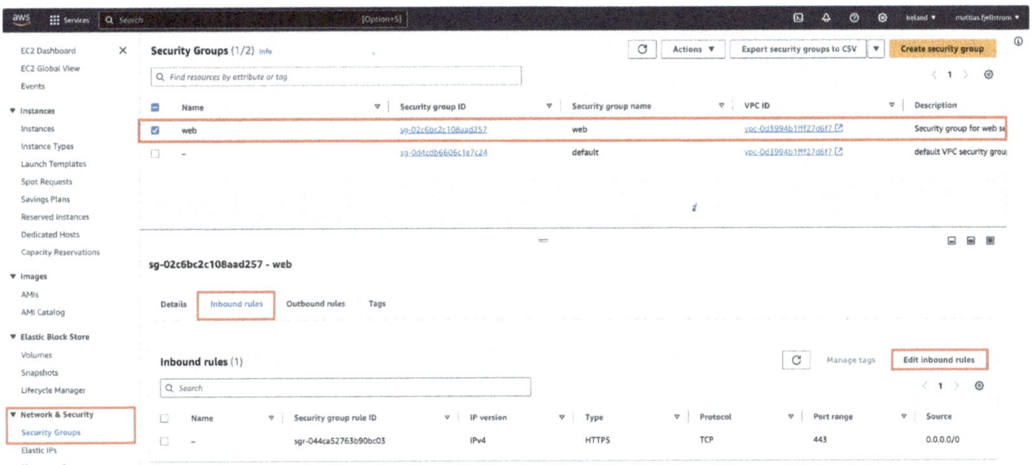

Figure 5.27. Overview of the web security group ingress rules

Click on **Add rule** and configure the rule with a type of **SSH** and a source of **Anywhere-IPv4**, then click on **Save rules** (see Figure 5.28).

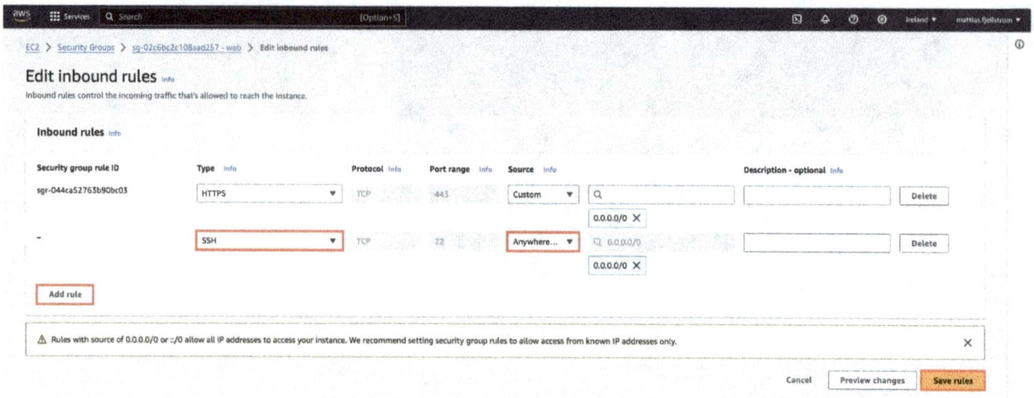

Figure 5.28. Configuring a new ingress rule for the security group

Back in the overview of the web security group, make a note of the security group rule ID of the SSH rule you just created (see Figure 5.29).

Figure 5.29. Copy the resource ID of the new security group rule

This is the ID of the resource we want to import[7]. In this case the security group rule ID is **sgr-014622bf796ad7f44**.

Now we have all the pieces needed to run the import command:

Figure 5.30. Importing a resource using the Terraform CLI

```
$ terraform import aws_vpc_security_group_ingress_rule.ssh sgr-014622bf796ad7f44
aws_vpc_security_group_ingress_rule.ssh: Importing from ID "sgr-01..."
aws_vpc_security_group_ingress_rule.ssh: Import prepared!
  Prepared aws_vpc_security_group_ingress_rule for import
aws_vpc_security_group_ingress_rule.ssh: Refreshing state... [id=sgr-01...]

Import successful!
```

The import was successful!

There is a declarative way to import resources, and this is the preferred way of doing it.

A declarative approach allows us to run **`terraform plan`** to preview what changes will be made. When we used the **`terraform import`** command above we just issued the command and hoped for the best. The state file was updated in-place for us.

To use the declarative approach for importing a resource we add the definition of the resource we want to import but instead of running the **`terraform import`** command we add an **`import`** block to our Terraform configuration:

Figure 5.31. Using an import block to import a resource

```
import {
  to = aws_vpc_security_group_ingress_rule.ssh
  id = "sgr-014622bf796ad7f44"
}

resource "aws_vpc_security_group_ingress_rule" "ssh" {
  security_group_id = aws_security_group.web.id
  cidr_ipv4         = "0.0.0.0/0"
  from_port         = 22
  to_port           = 22
  ip_protocol       = "Tcp"
}
```

The **`import`** block takes the same information as the **`terraform import`** command did, i.e. a destination resource address and the ID of the resource we want to import.

Next we run **`terraform plan`** to review what will happen, and if everything looks OK we run **`terraform apply`**.

If you do not want to add the **`resource`** block for the resource you are importing you could have Terraform do it for you. Just be aware that Terraform will read all the attributes of the resource and include all of them in your configuration, without regards for what attributes are important or even required.

Create a new Terraform configuration in an empty directory. Create a new file named **main.tf** and add the following blank Terraform configuration (except for the **terraform** and **provider** blocks):

Figure 5.32. An empty Terraform configuration except for the terraform and provider blocks

```
terraform {
  required_providers {
    aws = {
      source  = "hashicorp/aws"
      version = "5.61.0"
    }
  }
}

provider "aws" {
  region = "eu-west-1"
}
```

In my AWS environment I have a security group with ID **sg-0f5e1fb310a0e7880** that I would like to import into my state. Note that you will have to create a new security group in your AWS environment, or use an existing one. Once you have a security group to import, copy its resource ID (the ID should follow the format **sg-***).

Add an import block to **main.tf** specifying the resource ID and the desired resource address:

Figure 5.33. An import block in HCL

```
import {
  id = "sg-0f5e1fb310a0e7880"
  to = aws_security_group.web
}
```

Note that we do not add the corresponding **aws_security_group** resource, Terraform will do this for us.

Now run **terraform plan** but add the **-generate-config-out** flag with the value of a new configuration file named **network.tf**:

Figure 5.34. Create a plan for the coming resource import

```
$ terraform plan -generate-config-out=network.tf
aws_security_group.web: Preparing import... [id=sg-0f5e1fb310a0e7880]
aws_security_group.web: Refreshing state... [id=sg-0f5e1fb310a0e7880]

Terraform will perform the following actions:

  # aws_security_group.web will be imported
  # (config will be generated)
    resource "aws_security_group" "web" {
      # ... attributes
    }

Plan: 1 to import, 0 to add, 0 to change, 0 to destroy.
```

Open the new file **network.tf** to see the imported resource. As you can tell there is much more configuration than you would have specified yourself. You can remove any default values from the configuration.

Now let's move on to talk about **resource drift**.

There is a flag we can add to the **terraform plan** and **terraform apply** commands for working with drift: **-refresh-only**.

There is an additional CLI command to reconcile resource drift by updating your state file in-place to match the actual resources. This is the **terraform refresh** command. Note that this command will only make sure that your state file matches the reality, it will not update your Terraform configuration to also match the reality, so this you need to make sure to do yourself.

It is recommended to **not** use the **terraform refresh** command since it updates the state file in-place.

> ### Drift
>
> Resource drift is when your Terraform state no longer matches the actual infrastructure. This is commonly associated with manual updates to infrastructure taking place outside of your Terraform workflows.

> It does not have to be manual changes that caused the drift, it could be any two processes competing with each other (e.g. another Terraform configuration, or maybe a custom script someone is running on their laptop as a cron job).
>
> It is a good idea to try to avoid resource drift as much as possible, but sometimes it happens and this is when it is good to know how to reconcile your Terraform state again.

Let's walk through an example of reconciling resource drift.

We continue with our current Terraform configuration which should now look like this (sample code available at GitHub.com[8]):

Figure 5.35. An example Terraform configuration for exploring resource drift.

```
terraform {
  required_version = ">= 1.6.0"

  required_providers {
    aws = {
      source  = "hashicorp/aws"
      version = "5.61.0"
    }
  }
}

variable "aws_region" {
  type    = string
  default = "eu-west-1"
}

provider "aws" {
  region = var.aws_region
}

resource "aws_security_group" "web" {
  name        = "web"
  description = "Security group for web servers"

  tags = {
    Name = "web"
  }
}

resource "aws_vpc_security_group_ingress_rule" "https" {
  security_group_id = aws_security_group.web.id
```

```
  cidr_ipv4         = "0.0.0.0/0"
  from_port         = 443
  to_port           = 443
  ip_protocol       = "Tcp"
}

resource "aws_vpc_security_group_ingress_rule" "ssh" {
  security_group_id = aws_security_group.web.id
  cidr_ipv4         = "0.0.0.0/0"
  from_port         = 22
  to_port           = 22
  ip_protocol       = "Tcp"
}
```

A drift can be many things, for instance the deletion of a resource. In the AWS console, still at the overview page of the web security group ingress rules click on **Edit inbound rules**. Next, click on **Delete** on the SSH rule we added previously, then click **Save rules** (see Figure 5.36).

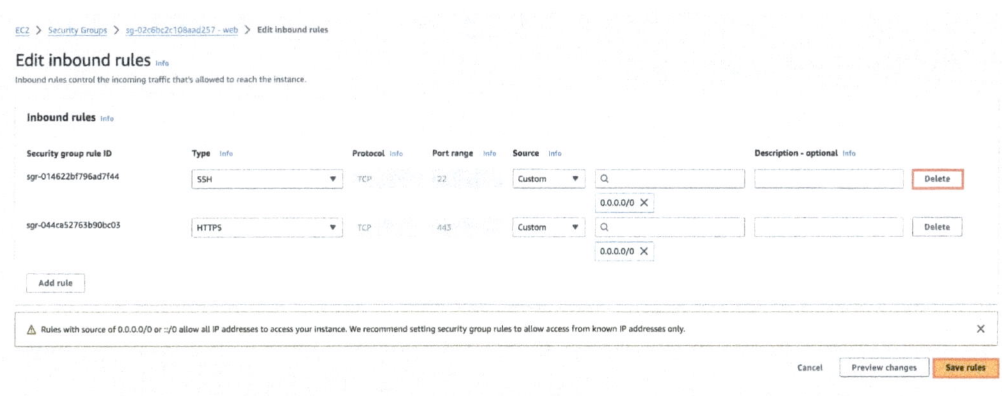

Figure 5.36. Manually introduce resource drift by deleting a security group rule

In your terminal, run **`terraform plan`** but add the **`-refresh-only`** flag (the output is truncated):

Figure 5.37. Run a refresh-only plan operation

```
$ terraform plan -refresh-only
aws_security_group.web: Refreshing state... [id=sg-017ce4f1cd5967a24]
aws_vpc_security_group_ingress_rule.https: Refreshing state... [id=<truncated>]
aws_vpc_security_group_ingress_rule.ssh: Refreshing state... [id=<truncated>]

Note: Objects have changed outside of Terraform

│ Warning: AWS resource not found during refresh
│
│   with aws_vpc_security_group_ingress_rule.ssh,
│   on main.tf line 37, in resource "aws_vpc_security_group_ingress_rule" "ssh":
│   37: resource "aws_vpc_security_group_ingress_rule" "ssh" {
│
│ Automatically removing from Terraform State instead of returning the error,
│ which may trigger resource recreation.
│ Original error: couldn't find resource
```

Terraform informs us that the SSH rule was not found in AWS, and that it will be removed from the state if we apply the changes.

Now we can do one of two things:

1. Accept that the SSH rule is gone. Perhaps we did not want it. If so, then we run the **`terraform apply`** command and delete the SSH security group rule from the Terraform configuration.
2. Recreate the SSH rule.

If we go with option 2, first run the **`terraform apply -refresh-only`** command:

Figure 5.38. Run an apply operation with the refresh-only flag

```
$ terraform apply -refresh-only -auto-approve
...
Apply complete! Resources: 0 added, 0 changed, 0 destroyed.
```

Next run a normal **`terraform apply`**:

Figure 5.39. Run a normal apply operation

```
$ terraform apply -auto-approve
...
Apply complete! Resources: 1 added, 0 changed, 0 destroyed.
```

Terraform has now recreated the security group rule that was missing.

Resource drift can be much messier than this. For instance, if you have multiple resources that depend on each other. You will likely encounter some variation of this in the exam, where the state does not match the reality. So it is important to feel comfortable with these commands.

On the other hand, a drift can be as simple as one or two attributes have changed values on a given resource. This is where the **`terraform plan`** command will be valuable, it will tell you that there are planned changes and you can determine if they make sense or if something is amiss.

Backup Your State File

During the exam, it is a good idea to back up the state file before you modify it. Especially if you use imperative approaches for editing the state file.

You can make a simple backup with the following command:

```
$ cp terraform.tfstate backup.tfstate
```

For production use of Terraform, you should keep the state file and its backup in separate locations (e.g. in different AWS S3 buckets in different AWS regions).

5.6: Summary

This chapter has covered the **manage resource lifecycle** exam objective in detail.

Managing the lifecycle of your resources involves understanding what happens during the standard Terraform workflow: **`terraform init`**, **`terraform plan`**, **`terraform apply`**, and **`terraform destroy`**. These are the most common commands you will run with the Terraform CLI.

I did not mention the **`terraform fmt`** or **`terraform validate`** commands. These are also useful to know about, and I encourage you to learn about them. However, since they are not strictly part of the exam objective I've left them out of this book. For the exam you could keep **`terraform validate`** in mind since it can capture a few trivial mistakes that you might make.

Sometimes you go beyond what the standard workflow entails and work with existing infrastructure. We saw how to use the **`terraform import`** command to import existing infrastructure into our Terraform configuration and also how to do it in a more controlled way using an **`import`** block.

Finally, we reconciled resource drift using the **`terraform plan`** and **`terraform apply`** commands by adding the **`-refresh-only`** flag.

The next chapter covers the **develop and troubleshoot dynamic configuration** exam objective.

Notes

1. https://github.com/mattias-fjellstrom/terraform-professional-book-sample-code/tree/main/aws/chapter05/figure5.02

2. https://github.com/mattias-fjellstrom/terraform-professional-book-sample-code/tree/main/aws/chapter05/figure5.09

3. https://github.com/mattias-fjellstrom/terraform-professional-book-sample-code/tree/main/aws/chapter05/figure5.15

4. https://github.com/mattias-fjellstrom/terraform-professional-book-sample-code/tree/main/aws/chapter05/figure5.17

5. https://github.com/mattias-fjellstrom/terraform-professional-book-sample-code/tree/main/aws/chapter05/figure5.24

6. https://github.com/mattias-fjellstrom/terraform-professional-book-sample-code/tree/main/aws/chapter05/figure5.25

7. You can find the format of resource IDs by looking at the contents of the state file for a similar resource, make a note of the ID and find it in the AWS console. Or, you could go to the documentation for the resource type you are importing and read the import documentation at the bottom.

8. https://github.com/mattias-fjellstrom/terraform-professional-book-sample-code/tree/main/aws/chapter05/figure5.35

Chapter 6: Develop and Troubleshoot Dynamic Configuration

The **HashiCorp Configuration Language** (HCL) contains many features you can use to create dynamic, robust, and maintainable Terraform configurations and modules.

The **develop and troubleshoot dynamic configuration** exam objective covers the following sub-objectives:

- Use language features to validate configuration
- Query providers using data sources
- Compute and interpolate data using HCL functions
- Use meta-arguments in configuration
- Configure input variables and outputs, including complex types
- Analyze best practices for managing sensitive data, such as using Vault for secrets management

To successfully follow along this chapter you should already have some experience using HCL. It is enough to once or twice have written a Terraform configuration using the most common blocks (**`resource`**, **`data`**, **`variable`**, **`output`**, and so on).

This chapter focuses on specific issues and concepts related to writing Terraform configurations, it does not walk through the process from scratch.

6.1: Use Language Features to Validate Configuration

If you write a Terraform configuration that only you will consume, then it is easy to fall into the trap of taking shortcuts. Perhaps you hardcode values in your configuration that would be better configured as variables. Perhaps you add many variables to your configuration but skip out on adding useful descriptions and

validations. Perhaps you use implicit assumptions that hold true most of the time, but perhaps not all of the time. Taking shortcuts generally means you are making your Terraform configuration less user-friendly.

You can **validate** values passed to your **variable** blocks. You do this using the **validation** block nested inside of a **variable** block (sample code available at GitHub.com[1]):

Figure 6.1. An example of a validation block for a variable

```
variable "name_suffix" {
  type = string

  validation {
    condition     = can(regex("^[a-z]+$", var.name_suffix))
    error_message = "Should only contain lowercase letters"
  }
}
```

A **validation** block has no labels. It takes two arguments:

1. **condition**
2. **error_message**.

The **condition** argument is a boolean expression that must evaluate to **true** for the validation to pass. If the **condition** argument evaluates to **false**, Terraform will halt the execution and report the error message specified in the **error_message** argument.

The **condition** in the **validation** block above checks if the value passed to the **name_suffix** variable contains lowercase letters, and nothing else. This is an example of the use of **functions** (i.e. **can** and **regex**). More on functions later in this chapter.

If we run **terraform plan** for this configuration while passing in an invalid value for the variable we get the following result:

Figure 6.2. Run a plan operation with an invalid variable value

```
$ terraform plan -var="name_suffix=ABC"

Planning failed. Terraform encountered an error while generating this plan.

│ Error: Invalid value for variable
│
│   on main.tf line 1:
│    1: variable "name_suffix" {
│      ├────────────────
│      │ var.name_suffix is "ABC"
│
│ Should only contain lowercase letters
│
│ This was checked by the validation rule at main.tf:4,3-13.
```

The plan fails! We can tell from the output that the failing validation was in the **name_suffix** variable. The error message from the **validation** block is also displayed.

A best practice when designing Terraform configurations and modules is to add validation for your variables to not allow garbage values for your variables that will generate errors further along in the execution.

You can include any number of **validation** blocks for a variable (sample code available at GitHub.com[2]):

Figure 6.3. A variable with multiple validation blocks

```
variable "name_suffix" {
  type = string

  validation {
    condition     = can(regex("^[a-z]+$", var.name_suffix))
    error_message = "Should only contain lowercase letters"
  }

  validation {
    condition     = length(var.name_suffix) == 10
    error_message = "Must be exactly 10 characters long"
  }
}
```

A **validation** block can only refer to the variable you are adding the **validation** block to. In the examples above you can only reference the **name_suffix** variable, but no other variable or object. However, you can use most of the available functions to build your validations.

There are more options for including validation in HCL. The general term for these types of validations is **custom conditions**.

Each custom condition has the same arguments as the **validation** blocks above: **condition** and **error_message**.

There are two options for introducing custom conditions for resources.

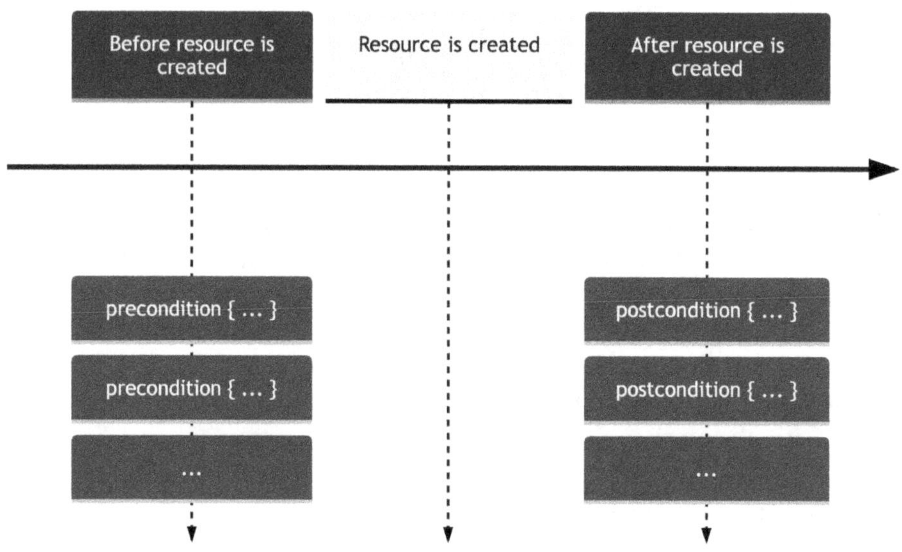

Figure 6.4. Resource lifecycle validation points

- Before a resource is created in a **precondition** block.
  The **precondition** block is evaluated before the resource is created. The **condition** argument must evaluate to **true**, otherwise the resource will not be created. This block is used to make sure one or more important conditions are satisfied before creating a resource.
- After a resource has been created in a **postcondition** block.
  The **postcondition** block is evaluated immediately after a resource has been

created. If the **condition** evaluates to **false** Terraform will halt and report an error. This block is used to check attributes on the resource that is only known after it has been created to make sure some condition is fulfilled.

You can use both types of custom conditions for the same resource. An example of what this looks like (sample code available at GitHub.com[3]):

Figure 6.5. A resource with a lifecycle block and custom conditions

```
resource "aws_instance" "web" {
  instance_type = "t3.micro"
  ami           = data.aws_ami.ubuntu.id

  lifecycle {
    precondition {
      condition     = data.aws_ami.ubuntu.architecture == "x86_64"
      error_message = "The selected AMI must use x86_64 architecture."
    }

    postcondition {
      condition     = self.public_dns != ""
      error_message = "VPC does not have public DNS hostnames enabled"
    }
  }
}
```

In the **postcondition** block you can reference the resource itself to check its attributes using the **self** reference object.

Both types of custom conditions for resources are added inside of the **lifecycle** block.

A different example of using a **precondition** block for a resource is to validate values from multiple input variables (sample code available at GitHub.com[4]):

Figure 6.6. Using resource lifecycle custom conditions to validate multiple variables

```
variable "check1" {
  type = bool
}

variable "check2" {
  type = bool
}

resource "aws_security_group" "web" {
  # other arguments omitted
```

```
  lifecycle {
    precondition {
      condition     = alltrue([var.check1, var.check2])
      error_message = "All checks must be true"
    }
  }
}
```

If we try to run a plan for this configuration where one of the input variables is **false** we encounter the following error:

Figure 6.7. Resource lifecycle validation error during a plan operation

```
$ terraform plan -var="check1=true" -var="check2=false"

Planning failed. Terraform encountered an error while generating this plan.

│ Error: Resource precondition failed
│
│   on main.tf line 14, in resource "aws_security_group" "web":
│   14:       condition     = alltrue([var.check1, var.check2])
│     ├────────────────
│     │ var.check1 is true
│     │ var.check2 is false
│
│ All checks must be true
```

You can configure custom conditions for **outputs** too. Custom conditions for outputs are used to make sure a condition is fulfilled, because if it is not then the output value might be inaccurate or useless.

Custom conditions for outputs are specified in a nested **precondition** block. However, in my experience they are of limited use in real-life as well as during the exam. Hence I will not cover them here.

The last custom condition you should be aware of for the exam is the **check** block. This block is used to validate parts of your configuration outside of the lifecycle of any specific resource.

An example of a **check** block (sample code available at GitHub.com[5]):

Figure 6.8. A check block used for a website health-check

```
check "liveness" {
  data "http" "mattias_engineer" {
    url = "https://mattias.engineer"
  }

  assert {
    condition     = data.http.mattias_engineer.status_code == 200
    error_message = "My blog is not responding!"
  }
}
```

In this **check** block, a scoped (nested) **http** data source is used to send an HTTP request to **https://mattias.engineer**. The **assert** block validates that the response status code is equal to 200. The contents of the **assert** block should look familiar by now, it is the **condition** and **error_message** arguments as in the other custom conditions.

To see what happens if the condition of the check fails, update the example shown above to expect a status code of 201 (or anything other than 200) and run **terraform plan**:

Figure 6.9. A failing check block assertion

```
$ terraform plan
data.http.mattias_engineer: Reading...
data.http.mattias_engineer: Read complete after 1s [id=https://mattias.engineer]

Terraform used the selected providers to generate the following execution plan.
Resource actions are indicated with the following symbols:
 <= read (data resources)

Terraform will perform the following actions:

  # data.http.mattias_engineer will be read during apply
  # (config will be reloaded to verify a check block)
 <= data "http" "mattias_engineer" {
      # ... attributes
    }

Plan: 0 to add, 0 to change, 0 to destroy.

│ Warning: Check block assertion failed
│
│   on main.tf line 7, in check "liveness":
│    7:     condition     = data.http.mattias_engineer.status_code == 201
```

```
│      ├──────────────────────
│      │ data.http.mattias_engineer.status_code is 200
│
│ My blog is not responding!
```

As you can tell from the output, there is a warning stating that the status code was not what was expected. However, *there was no error.*

The **`check`** block is special in the sense that if the **`condition`** evaluates to **`false`** it will only produce a warning, but it will not stop Terraform from continuing. This allows you to include checks that do not interfere with the rest of the Terraform execution.

In HCP Terraform you can set up continuous checks where HCP Terraform periodically (daily) runs the checks included in your Terraform configuration.

Closely related to validating parts of your Terraform configuration using custom conditions is the topic of testing. The Terraform test framework was part of the 1.6 release. However, it is unclear whether this will ever be a part of the exam at all. However, testing should be a part of your real life workflow for your modules.

6.2: Query Providers Using Data Sources

In its most basic form, a **data source** represents **existing infrastructure**. Think of this as infrastructure that has been created through some other means than the Terraform configuration you are currently working on:

- A resource that is created directly in the AWS console.
- A resource that is part of an AWS CloudFormation stack.
- A resource that is part of a different Terraform configuration.

A data source can also represent something closer to what the name suggests: plain **data**. A few examples of this:

- Data for the current AWS region that the provider is configured for

  ```
  data "aws_region" "current" {
    # ... arguments
  }
  ```

- Data about the current AWS account and user/role running Terraform:

```
data "aws_caller_identity" "current" {
  # ... arguments
}
```

- The ID of an Amazon Machine Image (AMI) that fulfills a set of filter criteria:

```
data "aws_ami" "ubuntu" {
  most_recent = true

  filter {
    name   = "name"
    values = ["ubuntu/images/hvm-ssd/ubuntu-jammy-22.04-amd64-server-*"]
  }

  owners = [
    "099720109477",
  ]
}
```

When you define a data source in your Terraform configuration, Terraform will read the data that the data source represents and make it available to you to use as required.

The AWS provider has a one-to-one mapping between a **resource type** and a corresponding **data source**. There is a resource type named **aws_security_group**, and a corresponding data source named **aws_security_group**, and so on.

This means that you can always share resources between Terraform configurations by creating the resource in one configuration, and reading it with a data source in a different configuration. Just remember that you are creating an invisible dependency between the two Terraform configurations.

There are other ways to share attributes of resources between Terraform configurations, we will see more of this in Chapter 7.

In HCL, a data source is configured using the **data** block:

Figure 6.10. A generic data block

```
data "type" "name" {
  # arguments
}
```

The **data** block has two labels:

- The first label is the **data source type**.

- The second label is the **data source name** used to reference this data source.

As with **resource** blocks, the combination of the data source type and the data source name must be unique within your Terraform configuration.

To reference a data source in an expression, you use the syntax **data.<type>.<name>**. Note how this is different from expressions for a **resource** block: **<type>.<name>**.

A concrete example of a useful data source is the **aws_subnet** data source:

Figure 6.11. An AWS subnet data source

```
data "aws_subnet" "this" {
  filter {
    name   = "tag:Name"
    values = ["subnet-eu-west-1a"]
  }
}
```

The **aws_subnet** data source has a large number of optional arguments and blocks. You can use any of them to pinpoint the exact subnet you are searching for. In the example above a single **filter** block was used to find a subnet that has a **Name** tag set to the value of **subnet-eu-west-1a**.

You can reference attributes for this subnet in any expression, for instance in an **output** block:

Figure 6.12. Referencing attributes of a data source

```
output "subnet_id" {
  value = data.aws_subnet.this.id
}
```

What happens if the data source you have configured does not correspond to an existing resource in AWS? This is a common error you will encounter, both in real life and perhaps during the exam.

Using the **aws_subnet** data source shown above in a **terraform plan** command gave me the following result:

Figure 6.13. Error when a data source has no corresponding existing resource in AWS

```
$ terraform plan
data.aws_subnet.this: Reading...

Planning failed. Terraform encountered an error while generating this plan.

│ Error: no matching EC2 Subnet found
│
│   with data.aws_subnet.this,
│   on main.tf line 13, in data "aws_subnet" "this":
│   13: data "aws_subnet" "this" {
```

The error message is clear: *no matching EC2 subnet found.* In this situation you need to look through how you have configured the data source and make sure that the arguments are what you expect. Also, make sure you have configured the AWS provider with the correct region.

Let's go through a different example of a data source. Imagine we have a Virtual Private Cloud (VPC) in our AWS account. The VPC has been set up using the following Terraform configuration (sample code available at GitHub.com[6]):

Figure 6.14. A Terraform configuration for a simple AWS VPC

```
resource "aws_vpc" "this" {
  cidr_block = "10.0.0.0/16"

  tags = {
    Name = "my-network"
  }
}
```

To create a subnet for this VPC in a different Terraform configuration we can first use a data source to get a reference for the VPC. Technically we can hard-code the reference to the resource by copying its resource ID and pasting it into our configuration, but this is not a good solution. If the VPC is replaced by a new VPC you would have to find the new resource ID of the VPC and update your configuration.

In the documentation[7] we find the AWS VPC data source:

Figure 6.15. A generic AWS VPC data source

```
data "aws_vpc" "this" {
  # arguments
}
```

There are a number of arguments we can use to find the correct VPC. This is very similar to the **aws_subnet** data source we saw above. In this case it could make sense to find the VPC by the **Name** tag that we have added to it.

To do this we configure the data source like this:

Figure 6.16. A configured AWS VPC data source

```
data "aws_vpc" "this" {
  tags = {
    Name = "my-network"
  }
}
```

Now we can keep building our Terraform configuration using the data source to ask for additional information about this VPC.

As mentioned above, we want to create a subnet in this VPC. We do this with the **aws_subnet** resource[8] (sample code available at GitHub.com[9]):

Figure 6.17. Creating a subnet in the VPC, referencing the VPC data source

```
data "aws_vpc" "this" {
  tags = {
    Name = "my-network"
  }
}

resource "aws_subnet" "main" {
  vpc_id     = data.aws_vpc.this.id
  cidr_block = cidrsubnet(data.aws_vpc.this.cidr_block, 4, 1)

  tags = {
    Name = "Main"
  }
}
```

Note that I have referenced the data source in both the **vpc_id** and **cidr_block** arguments.

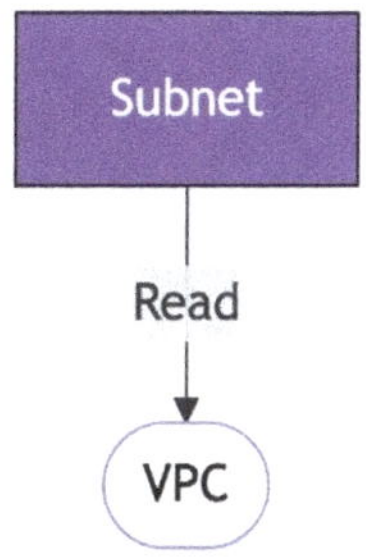

Figure 6.18. Referencing a VPC data source when creating a subnet resource

I want to bring up one last data source that is very important when working with EC2 instances (virtual machines) on AWS: the **aws_ami** data source.

An EC2 instance is based on a machine image, or Amazon Machine Image (AMI). This could be your favorite Linux distribution, or perhaps the latest version of Windows Server.

An AMI has a unique ID. AMIs are regional resources, meaning they are created within the context of an AWS region. An AMI for the latest version of Ubuntu with a specific hardware architecture has a unique AMI ID in Ireland (**eu-west-1**), and it has a different AMI ID in Stockholm (**eu-north-1**). Each new version of an image has a different AMI ID.

To obtain a given AMI ID, you can use the **aws_ami** data source. You can use any number of **filter** blocks and some arguments in order to narrow down the specific AMI ID you want to find. There are many filters available and there is no room to cover them all here, you can find them in the AWS CLI documentation[10].

An example of this data source for an Ubuntu Server 24.04 image satisfying a number of filters:

Figure 6.19. An AWS AMI data source for an Ubuntu 24.04 image

```
data "aws_ami" "ubuntu" {
  owners      = ["099720109477"]
  most_recent = true

  filter {
    name   = "name"
    values = ["ubuntu-pro-server/images/*24.04*"]
  }

  filter {
    name   = "virtualization-type"
```

```
    values = ["hvm"]
  }

  filter {
    name   = "root-device-type"
    values = ["ebs"]
  }

  filter {
    name   = "architecture"
    values = ["x86_64"]
  }
}
```

The example above shows the most common filter names you will encounter for the **aws_ami** data source. The **owners** argument is a list of AWS account numbers. In this example it contains the account number for Canonical (the maintainers of Ubuntu).

You are not expected to know account numbers like this during the exam, but you might have to configure an **aws_ami** data source to find a specific AMI ID.

6.3: Compute and Interpolate Data Using HCL Functions

The HCL language has a large number of **functions** to perform various tasks. These are similar to functions in other programming languages.

For the exam it will be beneficial to go through the **full** list of available functions and at least read the headline of what the function does.

You will have access to the documentation during the exam so you do not need to memorize how each function works, but if you don't know a certain function even exists it will be tedious and time-consuming to go through them all during the exam just to see if a certain function could help you solve a problem.

To see a list of all the available built-in functions go to the documentation[11].

In this section I would like to go through just a few functions that I think are important to know for the exam.

Before I do that, there is a powerful command you can use to experiment with functions in Terraform: **terraform console**. This command starts an interpreter (or REPL) where you can test Terraform functions (among other things):

Figure 6.20. Using the Terraform console to experiment with functions

```
$ terraform console
> split(" ", "the lazy fox jumps over the dog")
tolist([
  "the",
  "lazy",
  "fox",
  "jumps",
  "over",
  "the",
  "dog",
])
>
```

6.3.1: String Functions

In my own experience, string functions are among the most used functions. So it is a good idea to have a grasp of what types of string functions exist. I will mention a few in this section.

To check if a string starts with a specific substring, use the **`startswith()`** function:

Figure 6.21. Using the startswith() function

```
> startswith("abcdefgh", "abc")
true
> startswith("abcdefgh", "abd")
false
```

Likewise, to check if a string ends with a specific substring, use the **`endswith()`** function:

Figure 6.22. Using the endswith() function

```
> endswith("abcdefgh", "fgh")
true
> endswith("abcdefgh", "fgi")
false
```

You can join together multiple strings with an optional separator (set the separator to an empty string to effectively remove it) using the **`join()`** function:

Figure 6.23. Using the join() function

```
> join("-", ["this", "is", "my", "joined", "string"])
"this-is-my-joined-string"
```

To find a specific pattern of text in a string you can use the **`regex()`** function:

Figure 6.24. Using the regex() function

```
> regex("(\\d\\d\\d\\d)-(\\d\\d)-(\\d\\d)", "2024-09-14")
[
  "2024",
  "09",
  "14",
]
```

With the **`regex()`** function you can capture substrings from the input. In the example above I captured three things from the input date string: the year, the month, and the day.

The **`trimprefix()`** function can be used to remove leading characters from a string:

Figure 6.25. Using the trimprefix() function

```
> trimprefix("https://mattias.engineer/blog", "https://")
"mattias.engineer/blog"
```

There are many more string functions that can greatly simplify your life when working with Terraform, I highly recommend that you look through all the available string functions (while you go through all the other functions, too).

6.3.2: IP Network Functions

There are four functions available for helping you work with IP addresses. These functions assume you know the basics of expressing IP-addresses using CIDR notation.

The **`cidrhost(prefix, hostnumber)`** function takes a CIDR **`prefix`** argument and a **`hostnumber`** argument, and returns an IP address representing that host number in the CIDR range:

Figure 6.26. Using the cidrhost() function

```
> cidrhost("10.0.0.0/16", 1)
"10.0.0.1"
> cidrhost("10.0.0.0/16", 100)
"10.0.0.100"
```

With this function you could create a number of AWS EC2 instances, each with a private IP from a given range:

Figure 6.27. Using the cidrhost() function when creating AWS EC2 instances

```
resource "aws_subnet" "web" {
  vpc_id     = aws_vpc.default.id
  cidr_block = "10.0.10.0/24"
}

resource "aws_instance" "web" {
  count      = 10
  private_ip = cidrhost(aws_subnet.web.cidr_block, count.index)

  # other arguments ...
}
```

See the section on loops with count and for_each later in this chapter for details on the **count** meta-argument.

The **cidrsubnet(prefix, newbits, netnum)** function can help you split a large CIDR block into smaller blocks. This is useful for creating a VPC with a number of subnets. Instead of having to manually calculate the desired CIDR ranges for subnets you can instead do it automatically.

This function takes a CIDR block in the **prefix** argument, the size of the new CIDR block in **newbits**, and finally the network number of that size in **netnum**:

Figure 6.28. Using the cidrsubnet() function

```
> cidrsubnet("10.0.0.0/16", 8, 1)
"10.0.1.0/24"
> cidrsubnet("10.0.0.0/16", 8, 100)
"10.0.100.0/24"
```

An example of how to use this function in a Terraform configuration (sample code available at GitHub.com[12]):

Figure 6.29. Using the cidrsubnet() function to create a VPC with many subnets

```
resource "aws_vpc" "this" {
  cidr_block = "10.0.0.0/16"
}

resource "aws_subnet" "all" {
  count = 10

  vpc_id     = aws_vpc.this.id
  cidr_block = cidrsubnet(aws_vpc.this.cidr_block, 8, count.index)
}
```

This Terraform configuration creates a VPC with ten subnets.

6.3.3: Filesystem Functions

HCL has a number of functions that interact with the local filesystem. During the exam you might need to open a file to read its content, and then do some further processing with it.

The **`file(path)`** function reads the contents of a file located at **`path`**.

How do you specify the **`path`**?

- Assuming you are working in the **root** module and the file you want to read is located together with your Terraform configuration, then you can simply read the file using **`file("myfile.txt")`**.
- Continuing on the previous example, if the file is located in a sub-directory named **`files`** then you read it as **`file("files/myfile.txt")`**.
- It gets tricker if you are reading a file inside of a **module** (see Chapter 8). If the file is located in the module directory, then you should use the syntax **`file("${path.module}/myfile.txt")`**. The **`path.module`** built-in value is the path to the current module. This also works for the root module, so to be safe you can always read files using **`file("${path.module}/directory/filename")`**.

There is another function called **`fileset(path, pattern)`** that can list all the files at a **`path`** named according to a **`pattern`**.

Imagine you have a directory named **`files`** full of **`.csv`** files, and you must read all the files into Terraform. You can get the list of files using **`fileset("${path.module}/files", "*.csv")`**.

An example of using both the **`file()`** and **`fileset()`** functions in a concrete example is this (sample code available at GitHub.com[13]):

Figure 6.30. Read and process a number of CSV files as local values in Terraform

```
locals {
  # read all csv filenames
  files = fileset("${path.module}/files", "*.csv")

  # count the number of rows in each file
  rows = [for file in local.files : length(
    split("\n", file("${path.module}/files/${file}"))
  )]

  # sum all the row numbers
  sum = sum(local.rows)
}
```

Here I am using **local values** in the **`locals`** block, more on the use of local values later in this chapter.

The example performs the following steps:

- List all the CSV files located in the **`files`** directory using the **`fileset`** function.
- Loop through all CSV files, opening the file with the **`file`** function.
- Splitting the contents of each file on line breaks (**`\n`**) using the **`split()`** function.
- Counting the number of rows in each file using the **`length()`** function.
- Finally, summing all the numbers of rows using the **`sum`** function.

JSON

JSON stands for **JavaScript Object Notation** and is widely used in many contexts.

A small data sample describing a list of users in JSON format looks like this:

```
{
  "users": [
    {
      "name": "Jane Doe",
      "email": "jane.doe@example.com"
    },
    {
      "name": "John Doe",
      "email": "john.doe@example.com"
    }
```

```
  ]
}
```

There are two functions in the Terraform language to help you work with JSON data:

- **`jsonencode()`** to encode a string to JSON.
- **`jsondecode()`** to decode a string from JSON.

YAML

YAML is easier to type and read than JSON due to less use of special characters (`{}`, and `[]`). Indentation is *very* important when working with YAML.

YAML is widely used in Kubernetes manifests, AWS CloudFormation templates, and more.

A small data sample describing a list of users in YAML format looks like this:

```yaml
users:
  - name: Jane Doe
    email: jane.doe@example.com
  - name: John Doe
    email: john.doe@example.com
```

There are two functions in the Terraform language to help you work with YAML data:

- **`yamlencode()`** to encode a string to YAML.
- **`yamldecode()`** to decode a string from YAML.

CSV

CSV stands for **Comma-Separated Values**.

CSV is concise due to the fact that we don't have to repeat field names (such as **name** and **email**).

A small data sample describing a list of users in CSV format looks like this:

```
name,email
Jane Doe,jane.doe@example.com
John Doe,john.doe@example.com
```

For CSV files there is only one function in the Terraform language, the **csvdecode()** for decoding a string to CSV format.

An example of using the **csvdecode()** for the data shown above:

```
> csvdecode(file("test.csv"))
tolist([
  {
    "email" = "jane.doe@example.com"
    "name" = "Jane Doe"
  },
  {
    "email" = "john.doe@example.com"
    "name" = "John Doe"
  },
])
```

The last filesystem function I want to cover is **templatefile()**. This function takes a **template** and a map of keys and values to include into the template file. This is easiest explained using an example.

Imagine we have the following template file named **config.hcl.tpl**, where the special syntax is the Go templating language:

Figure 6.31. config.hcl.tpl

```
name = "${name}"

tags {
  %{ for k, v in tags ~}
  ${k} = "${v}"
  %{ endfor ~}
}
```

This template has two required keys: **name** and **tags**. The **name** key should be a string, and the **tags** key should be a map of key-value pairs.

Then we have the following Terraform configuration where we use the **local provider** that can create files in our local filesystem (sample code available at GitHub.com[14]):

Figure 6.32. A local file resource created using the templatefile() function

```
resource "local_file" "config" {
  filename = "config.hcl"

  content = templatefile("config.hcl.tpl", {
    name = "mattias"
    tags = {
      age   = "getting older"
      hobby = "terraform"
    }
  })
}
```

I create a file named **config.hcl**. The content of the file is generated using the **templatefile()** function. This function takes the name of the template (**config.hcl.tpl**, located in the same directory as the Terraform configuration) and the map of key-value pairs with values for **name** and **tags**.

Applying this Terraform configuration results in a new file being created with the following content:

Figure 6.33. A configuration file in HCL generated using the templatefile() function

```
name = "mattias"

tags {
  age = "getting older"
  hobby = "terraform"
}
```

The **templatefile()** function is very useful in automation scenarios where you need to build a specific configuration file containing values from the rest of the infrastructure that you create.

6.4: Use Meta-Arguments in Configuration

Meta-arguments are special arguments that are available for all resources no matter what type. These meta-arguments are built into Terraform itself. Meta-arguments allow you to build some dynamic behavior into your resources.

In this section, we will go through a few common meta-arguments that are important to master for the certification exam.

6.4.1: Loops With count and for_each

Imagine you want to create 100 resources of the same type with almost identical configuration. Is there an easier way to do it than to explicitly create 100 **`resource`** blocks? It turns out there is.

There are two types of *loop* constructs in Terraform, these are controlled using the two meta-arguments **`count`** and **`for_each`**. Loops in HCL are declarative, similar to what you find in functional programming languages.

Creating multiple resources of the same type is more common for some resource types than others. For a given Terraform configuration:

- You will likely only create a **single VPC**, but you might create **multiple subnets** in the VPC.
- You will likely only create **one or a few security groups**, but each group will contain **many security group rules**.
- You will likely only create a **single S3 bucket**, but you might create **multiple blobs** in the bucket.

The above examples are generalizations. Sometimes it will be of interest to create a large number of VPCs, and perhaps only a single subnet in each VPC.

The **`count`** meta-argument creates a number of copies of a resource based on the value of the **`count`** argument.

An example of using a fixed value for the **`count`** meta-argument (sample code available at GitHub.com[15]):

Figure 6.34. Using a fixed value for the count meta-argument

```
resource "aws_vpc" "this" {
  cidr_block = "10.0.0.0/16"
}

resource "aws_subnet" "all" {
  count      = 3
  vpc_id     = aws_vpc.this.id
  cidr_block = cidrsubnet(aws_vpc.this.cidr_block, 8, count.index)
}
```

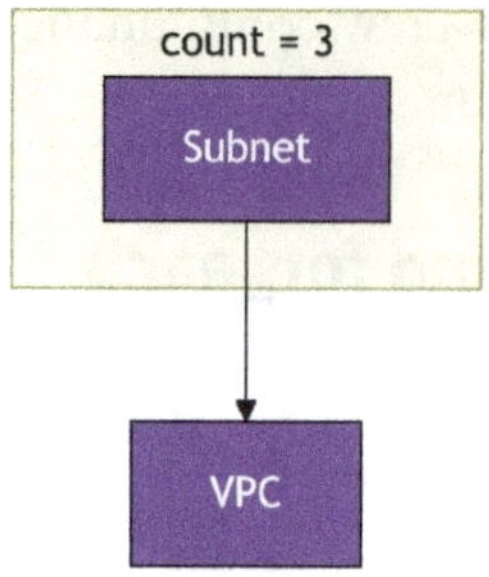

Figure 6.35. Using a fixed value for the count meta-argument

Here we create three subnets for the VPC. We can refer to the current *iteration* of the loop by **`count.index`**.

Most often we do not want to use a fixed number for the **`count`** meta-argument. Instead, we can use an expression (sample code available at GitHub.com[16]):

Figure 6.36. Using an expression for the count meta-argument

```
resource "aws_vpc" "this" {
  cidr_block = "10.0.0.0/16"
}

data "aws_availability_zones" "available" {
  state = "available"
}

resource "aws_subnet" "all" {
  # create one subnet for each availability zone in the region
  count = length(data.aws_availability_zones.available.names)

  vpc_id            = aws_vpc.this.id
  availability_zone = data.aws_availability_zones.available.names[count.index]
  cidr_block        = cidrsubnet(aws_vpc.this.cidr_block, 8, count.index)
}
```

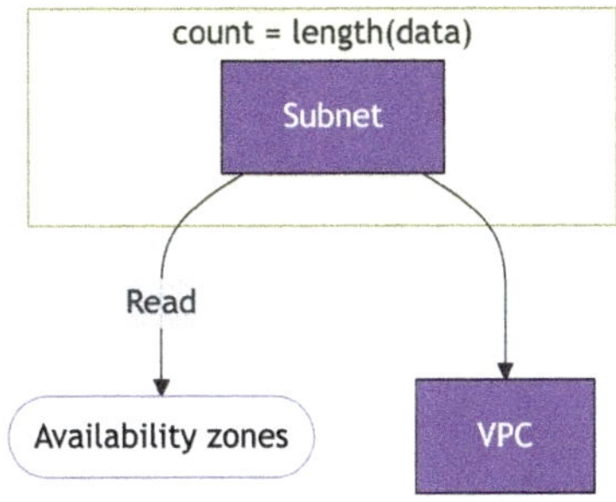

Figure 6.37. Using a dynamic value for the count meta-argument

In this example, we use the **`aws_availability_zones`** data source to query the AWS provider for all availability zones in the region. Then, we create one subnet for each of the availability zones by using the **`length()`** expression in the **`count`** meta argument. This Terraform configuration will work as expected no matter which AWS region we are targeting.

The **`for_each`** meta-argument creates one resource for each element in a **map** or **set of strings**. It has to be a map or set because both of these complex types can't have duplicate elements. This is a requirement since Terraform would complain if you tried to create two resources of the same type with identical resource names.

The **`for_each`** meta-argument in action looks like this (sample code available at GitHub.com[17]):

Figure 6.38. Using the for_each meta-argument with a map

```
locals {
  subnets = {
    "eu-west-1a" = {
      name = "subnet-a"
      cidr = "10.0.0.0/24"
    }
    "eu-west-1b" = {
      name = "subnet-b"
      cidr = "10.0.1.0/24"
    }
    "eu-west-1c" = {
      name = "subnet-c"
      cidr = "10.0.2.0/24"
    }
  }
}

resource "aws_vpc" "this" {
  cidr_block = "10.0.0.0/16"
```

```
}

resource "aws_subnet" "all" {
  for_each          = local.subnets
  vpc_id            = aws_vpc.this.id
  availability_zone = each.key
  cidr_block        = each.value.cidr

  tags = {
    Name = each.value.name
  }
}
```

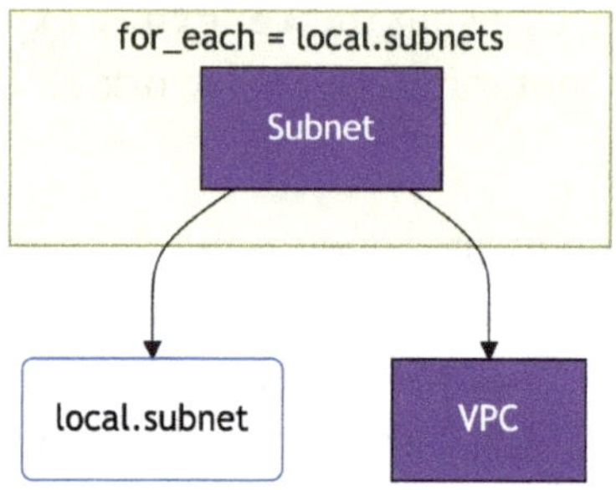

Figure 6.39. Using the for_each meta-argument with a local map value

Here we have again used local values. Read the box below for more details on the use of local values.

When we use a map in the **`for_each`** meta-argument we can reference the current element key by **`each.key`**, and the current element value by **`each.value`**. This means that for the first "iteration" of the **`for_each`** loop the **`each`** variable will be:

Figure 6.40. The value of the each variable in the first iteration

```
each = {
  key   = "eu-west-1a"
  value = {
    name = "subnet-a"
    cidr = "10.0.0.0/24"
  }
}
```

The basics of local values

Locals are values you can create and reference in other parts of your Terraform configuration as **`local.<name>`**.

Local values are great to modify some data from one form to another. You can create a "pipeline" of transformations, and verify that each step does what you expect.

You can include any number of **`locals`** blocks in your Terraform configuration. A best practice is to define the local value close to where you use it.

A concrete example of a local value pipeline

In a Terraform file, add a **`locals`** block with your transformation steps:

```
locals {
  step1 = file("inputdata.txt")
  step2 = split("\n", local.step1)
  step3 = [for value in local.step2 : upper(value)]
}
```

Next, add outputs for each step. You could use separate **`output`** blocks, or use a single **`output`** block:

```
output "steps" {
  value = {
    step1 = local.step1
    step2 = local.step2
    step3 = local.step3
  }
}
```

Imagine we have the following data in **`inputdata.txt`**:

```
data1
data2
data3
```

Apply the Terraform configuration (run **terraform apply -auto-approve**).

The output for step 1 is simply how Terraform has read the raw file:

```
step1 = <<EOT
data1
data2
data3
EOT
```

The output of step 2 shows that the raw file content has been split up by row and turned into a list:

```
step2 = tolist([
  "data1",
  "data2",
  "data3",
])
```

Finally, the output from step 3 has turned each string to uppercase format:

```
step3 = [
  "DATA1",
  "DATA2",
  "DATA3",
]
```

An example of using the **for_each** meta-argument with a set of strings (sample code available at GitHub.com[18]):

Figure 6.41. Using the for_each meta-argument with a set of strings

```
resource "aws_vpc" "all" {
  for_each = toset(["10.0.0.0/16", "192.168.0.0/16"])

  cidr_block = each.key
}
```

There is no way to create a literal set in Terraform, so the best we can do is to use the **toset()** function and pass in a list of strings.

When you use a set of strings in the **for_each** meta-argument both **each.key** and **each.value** will refer to the same value. So in the first "iteration" of the example above, the **each** variable will be:

Figure 6.42. The value of the each variable during the first iteration

```
each = {
  key =   "10.0.0.0/16"
  value = "10.0.0.0/16"
}
```

Once you have created a number of resources with either **count** or **for_each** it is relevant to know how to reference them.

To reference resources created using the **count** meta-argument you use the syntax:

- **aws_subnet.all[0]** for the first resource,
- **aws_subnet.all[1]**, for the second resource,
- and so on.

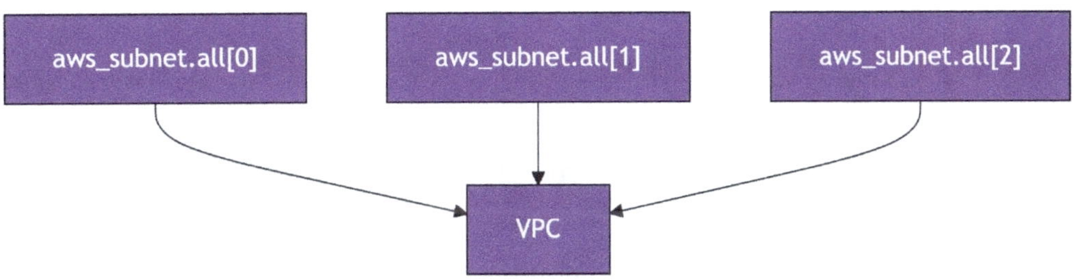

Figure 6.43. Resources created using the count meta-argument

You can only reference the resources using an index number, and it could get difficult to tell resources apart.

A concise way to reference all resources created using **count** is a **splat expression**. For instance, to get a list of subnet IDs you write **aws_subnet.all[*].id**.

To reference resources created using the **for_each** meta-argument you use the syntax:

- **aws_subnet.all["eu-west-1a"]** for the element with key **eu-west-1a**,
- **aws_subnet.all["eu-west-1b"]** for the element with key **eu-west-1b**,
- and so on.

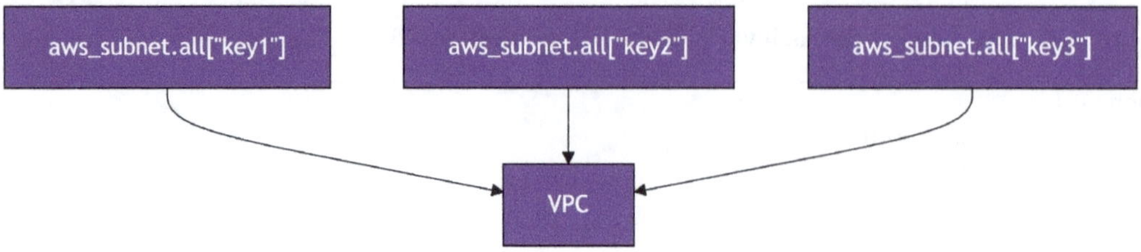

Figure 6.44. Resources created using the for_each meta-argument

The accessor is the key value used to create the resource. The key value will either be elements from a list (set) or keys from a map. You can easily tell resources apart, and you could also move or replace resources in your state more easily.

A simple example of moving a resource in your state:

Figure 6.45. Moving a resource created with the for_each meta-argument in your state

```
moved {
  from = aws_subnet.all["eu-west-1a"]
  to   = aws_subnet.some["eu-west-1a"]
}
```

We will see the **`moved`** block in action in Chapter 8 when we refactor Terraform configurations into modules.

When you decide on whether to use **`count`** or **`for_each`**, think about what input data you have and how you would like to reference the resources. If the identity of each individual resource is important, you should use **`for_each`**. If the identity of a resource is not of importance, all resources are basically identical and can be substituted with each other, then use **`count`**.

Another reason for using **`for_each`** over **`count`** is if you have **`aws_subnet.all[0]`**, **`aws_subnet.all[1]`**, **`aws_subnet.all[2]`** and attempt to remove or move element **`1`** then Terraform will delete elements **`1`** and **`2`** and recreate element **`2`** as element **`1`**. With **`for_each`** this is not an issue.

6.4.2: The dynamic Block

Some resources support multiple nested blocks of the same kind.

An example of this is the **`aws_security_group`** resource. It supports any number of nested **`ingress`** or **`egress`** blocks.

These nested blocks are used to define security group rules as part of the security group resource itself. Remember that you can create security group rules using separate resources (e.g. using **aws_vpc_security_group_egress_rule**). In fact, this is recommended.

An example of this resource (sample code available at GitHub.com[19]):

Figure 6.46. An AWS security group resource with nested ingress rules

```
resource "aws_vpc" "this" {
  cidr_block = "10.0.0.0/16"
}

resource "aws_security_group" "web" {
  vpc_id = aws_vpc.this.id

  ingress {
    from_port = 80
    to_port   = 80
    protocol  = "tcp"
  }

  ingress {
    from_port = 443
    to_port   = 443
    protocol  = "tcp"
  }
}
```

This example includes two nested **ingress** blocks. Imagine you have a large number of **ingress** blocks you want to define, this could get tedious quickly.

A simpler way of doing it is to use the **dynamic** block. An example of this (sample code available at GitHub.com[20]):

Figure 6.47. Using a dynamic block with a list to configure nested rules for a security group

```
locals {
  ports = [80, 443]
}

resource "aws_vpc" "this" {
  cidr_block = "10.0.0.0/16"
}

resource "aws_security_group" "web" {
  vpc_id = aws_vpc.this.id
```

```
  dynamic "ingress" {
    for_each = local.ports

    content {
      from_port = ingress.value
      to_port   = ingress.value
      protocol  = "tcp"
    }
  }
}
```

The **dynamic** block has one label representing the name of the block you want to repeat, in this case it is the **ingress** block. You control how many blocks will be generated using the **for_each** meta argument inside of the **dynamic** block. Finally, in a nested **content** block you create the content of the blocks, using the **ingress** reference to refer to each value from the **for_each** argument.

You can have nested **dynamic** blocks, but that is uncommon.

> A best practice is to avoid using **dynamic** blocks at all, if you can. A Terraform configuration with many **dynamic** blocks can quickly get complicated and difficult to read and understand.

An alternative to using a list in the **for_each** argument of the **dynamic** block is to use a map (sample code available at GitHub.com[21]):

Figure 6.48. Using a dynamic block with a map to configure rules for a security group

```
locals {
  ports = {
    http = {
      port     = 80
      protocol = "tcp"
    }
    https = {
      port     = 443
      protocol = "tcp"
    }
  }
}

resource "aws_vpc" "this" {
  cidr_block = "10.0.0.0/16"
}
```

```
resource "aws_security_group" "web" {
  vpc_id = aws_vpc.this.id

  dynamic "ingress" {
    for_each = local.ports

    content {
      from_port = ingress.value.port
      to_port   = ingress.value.port
      protocol  = ingress.value.protocol
    }
  }
}
```

6.4.3: The depends_on Meta-Argument

Resources often depend on each other. Terraform is usually very good at figuring out how resources depend on each other, and is able to create resources in the correct order. If there was no sense of dependency between resources it would be difficult to use Terraform successfully. The beauty of declarative infrastructure as code is that–if we follow certain rules–Terraform is able to handle the creation of resources for us, and we do not need to worry about how Terraform gets there.

For instance, when we create an **aws_vpc** resource and then add one or more **aws_subnet** resources that reference the **aws_vpc** resource, we create a dependency between each subnet resource and the VPC resource itself. This is how Terraform is able to know which resource to create in what order.

We can talk about two types of dependencies: **implicit** and **explicit** dependencies.

An example of an **implicit** dependency is when we reference attributes from one resource in the configuration of another resource:

Figure 6.49. An implicit dependency between two resources

```
resource "aws_vpc" "this" {
  cidr_block = "10.0.0.0/16"
}

resource "aws_security_group" "web" {
  vpc_id = aws_vpc.this.id # implicit dependency
}
```

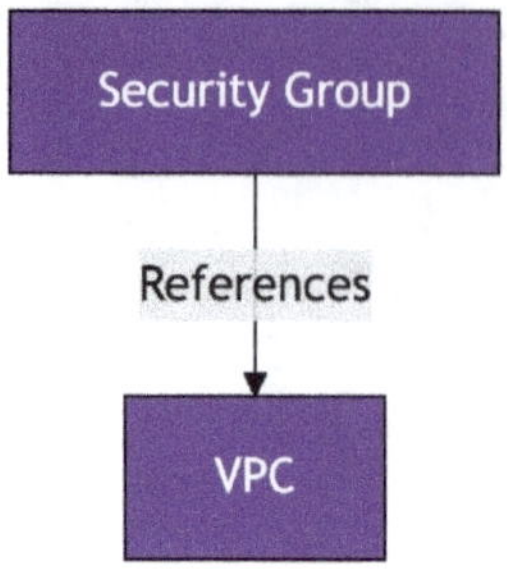

Figure 6.50. Implicit dependency between two resources

Here the **aws_security_group** resource references the **id** of the **aws_vpc** resource.

In general, there will be long chains of dependencies between your resources and data sources.

An **explicit** dependency is when we use the **depends_on** meta argument. This meta argument takes a list of resource addresses that we explicitly tell Terraform to treat as dependencies for this resource. This is useful if there is a hidden dependency that Terraform would not know about.

An example of how this looks (sample code available at GitHub.com[22]):

Figure 6.51. An example of an explicit dependency using the depends_on meta-argument

```
resource "time_sleep" "wait" {
  create_duration = "1m"
}

resource "aws_vpc" "this" {
  cidr_block = "10.0.0.0/16"

  depends_on = [
    time_sleep.wait, # explicit dependency
  ]
}
```

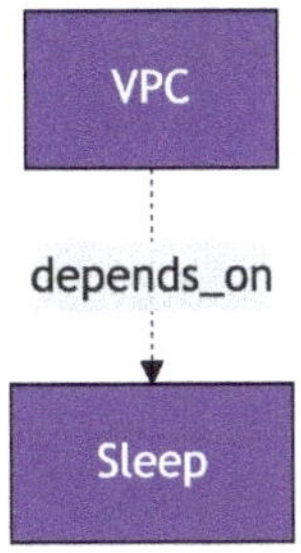

Figure 6.52. An explicit dependency between two resources using the depends_on meta-argument

In the example above, we use the **time provider** to add a sleep of one minute. We create an **`aws_vpc`** resource that specifies a **`depends_on`** argument with a reference to the **`time_sleep`** resource.

When we apply this configuration we get the following result:

Figure 6.53. Applying a Terraform configuration with an explicit dependency

```
$ terraform apply -auto-approve

Terraform used the selected providers to generate the following execution plan.
Resource actions are indicated with the following symbols:
  + create

Terraform will perform the following actions:

  # aws_vpc.this will be created
  + resource "aws_vpc" "this" {
      # details omitted
    }

  # time_sleep.wait will be created
  + resource "time_sleep" "wait" {
      # details omitted
    }

Plan: 2 to add, 0 to change, 0 to destroy.
time_sleep.wait: Creating...
time_sleep.wait: Still creating... [10s elapsed]
time_sleep.wait: Still creating... [20s elapsed]
time_sleep.wait: Still creating... [30s elapsed]
time_sleep.wait: Still creating... [40s elapsed]
time_sleep.wait: Still creating... [50s elapsed]
time_sleep.wait: Creation complete after 1m0s
aws_vpc.this: Creating...
aws_vpc.this: Creation complete after 2s [id=vpc-0cdbab81f00eaffd2]
```

```
Apply complete! Resources: 2 added, 0 changed, 0 destroyed.
```

We see that the **time_sleep.wait** resource is created first, and the creation takes one minute. Directly after it is complete the **aws_vpc** resource is created.

Apart from the meta-arguments we went through in this section there is one more of particular interest: the **provider** meta-argument. It is used to control which provider to use for a particular resource or data source. It is useful when you have configured multiple instances of the same provider. However, we leave the discussion of the **provider** meta-argument for Chapter 9 when we discuss providers at length.

6.5: Configure Input Variables and Outputs, Including Complex Types

Variables are **inputs** to your Terraform configuration. When you run plan and apply operations for your Terraform configuration you must provide values to the variables.

A variable can have a **default value**. If it has a default value, and no other value is provided during **terraform plan** and **terraform apply**, then the default value is used. When you design modules you should provide sensible default values for most variables, if possible.

Variables have **types**. There are a three **primitive types** in Terraform:

- The **string** type: e.g. **"my string"**.
- The **number** type: can be either a whole number (**1**, **999**, or **-40**) or decimal point number (**3.14** or **0.3**).
- The **bool** type: can be either **true** or **false**.

You can create input variables using any of these primitive types like so:

Figure 6.54. Creating variables with primitive types

```
variable "my_string" {
  type = string
}

variable "my_number" {
  type = number
}

variable "my_bool" {
  type = bool
}
```

Notice how the types (**string**, **number**, and **bool**) are keywords in the HCL language. However, they can only be used in this particular context, as the **type** for variables.

Then there are a few **complex types** or **collection types**:

- The **list** type: a collection of zero to many values of the same type (e.g. a list of strings **["one", "two", "three"]**).
- The **set** type: similar to a list, but it is a collection of unique values with no particular order.
- The **map** or **object** types: these are two types of key-value pair types (e.g. **{ Name = "Jane Doe", Age = 35 }**). Keys must always be strings. Values of a map must be of the same type, while this is not the case for objects.
- The **tuple** type: similar to a list but can contain values of different types (e.g. **["one", 2, "three", 4]**)

You can create variables using these complex types:

Figure 6.55. Creating variables with collection types

```
variable "my_list" {
  type = list(string)
}

variable "my_map" {
  type = map(string)
}

variable "my_object" {
  type = object({
    a = string
    b = number
  })
}
```

Each complex type can consist of nested complex types. As a general rule of thumb, do not make your variables more complicated than they need to be. In my experience the most common variable types are **string**, **number**, **bool**, **list(string)**, and **object({ ... })**. You should be familiar with how to define each variant of a variable and how to provide values for them.

Speaking of providing values to variables. In Chapter 5 we saw how to provide values inline in the **terraform plan** and **terraform apply** commands. We also saw that we can use **variable files**. For the exam I recommend that you use variable files to provide complex values to your Terraform configurations instead of having to provide the value inline.

As an example, if we have the following (fairly simple) variable:

Figure 6.56. An example of an object variable

```
variable "complex" {
  type = object({
    name = string
    details = object({
      age    = number
      height = number
    })
  })
}
```

Providing a value inline for **terraform plan** looks like this:

Figure 6.57. Providing values for collection types inline to the Terraform CLI

```
$ terraform plan -var='complex={name="jane",details={age=35,height=180}}'
...
```

While providing the value in a **terraform.tfvars** file looks like this:

Figure 6.58. Providing values to variables in a variable file

```
complex = {
  name = "jane"
  details = {
    age    = 35
    height = 180
  }
}
```

Using a variable file is easier, and it allows for quick updates of variables if needed instead of having to edit CLI commands.

The file named **terraform.tfvars** (or **terraform.tfvars.json**) is automatically picked up during **terraform plan** and **terraform apply**, and the same goes for files named ***.auto.tfvars** (or ***.auto.tfvars.json**).

A **variable** block takes a number of optional arguments. Here is a full example of a **variable** block:

Figure 6.59. A full example of a variable block

```
variable "my_variable" {
  type        = string
  description = "This is my variable"
  sensitive   = false
  nullable    = false
  default     = "My default value"
}
```

An overview of the arguments:

- The **type** argument represents the type of the variable (**string**, **number**, etc).
- Use the **description** argument to provide a clear description of what the variable represents. For the exam this is not important, but when designing modules for your production environment it is.
- To tell Terraform that the variable represents a sensitive value (secret, key, certificate, etc) specify **sensitive = true**. The default value is **false**. What this means is that Terraform will avoid printing this value in clear text to the terminal or in any other output, except for the state file.
- To allow a variable to be null, specify **nullable = true**.
- If possible, provide default values for your variables. You can do this in the **default** argument.

When it comes to configuring **outputs** from your Terraform configuration you use the **output** block. Outputs from your Terraform configurations or **modules** are used to pass values into other Terraform configurations or modules.

An **output** block looks like this:

Figure 6.60. An example of an output block

```
output "my_output" {
  description = "My VPC ID"
  value       = aws_vpc.this.id
}
```

The output block requires the `value` argument. This is what the output consists of. You do not need to specify a type of the output, this is taken care of automatically by Terraform. You can provide an optional `description` argument, as well as a `sensitive` argument to tell Terraform not to print the value of the output in logs.

An `output` block also supports the `depends_on` meta-argument. This meta-argument allows you to tell Terraform not to calculate the value of the output before the resources listed in the `depends_on` argument are created.

Earlier in this chapter we also saw that the `output` block supports adding a nested `lifecycle` block with a nested `precondition` block.

Once you have applied a configuration that has outputs defined, you can use the Terraform CLI to get the values of these outputs:

Figure 6.61. Reading output values using the Terraform CLI

```
$ terraform output -raw my_name
mattias
```

The `-raw` flag is useful to get a value without quotes around it.

Use the `terraform output` command to verify that an output has the format that you expect. You could also open up the Terraform state file (if you have direct access to it) to see what output values you have.

6.6: Analyze Best Practices For Managing Sensitive Data, Such as Using Vault for Secrets Management

First of all, I can assure you that you are not expected to set up a Vault cluster during the exam to be able to keep your secrets safe.

This sub-objective uses the wording: "*Analyze ...*". Essentially what this means is that parts of what is covered here will most likely appear as multiple-choice questions, not as part of a lab.

There are some best-practices to be aware of when it comes to secrets.

Let's first go through secrets in the context of Terraform itself without the use of any external system.

You can declare a variable in Terraform as **sensitive**. What this means is that Terraform will avoid outputting the value as plain text in logs. You declare a variable as sensitive by setting the **`sensitive`** argument of the variable to **`true`**:

Figure 6.62. Declaring a sensitive variable

```
variable "password" {
  type      = string
  sensitive = true
}
```

Likewise, you can declare output values as sensitive:

Figure 6.63. Declaring a sensitive output value

```
output "password" {
  value     = aws_rds_instance.main.password
  sensitive = true
}
```

Does that solve the problem of secrets once and for all? Not really. You should be aware that the Terraform state file is available in plain text, including values that are declared as sensitive. This means that if someone gets ahold of your state file they will be able to read your secret values.

To see this in action, use the following simple Terraform configuration:

Figure 6.64. A simple Terraform configuration to demonstrate sensitive values in a state file

```
variable "password" {
  type      = string
  sensitive = true
}

output "password" {
  value     = var.password
  sensitive = true
}
```

Create a **`terraform.tfvars`** file and provide a value for the **`password`** variable:

Figure 6.65. Terraform variable file terraform.tfvars

```
password = "thisismypassword"
```

Apply the configuration:

Figure 6.66. Apply the sample Terraform configuration

```
$ terraform apply -auto-approve

Changes to Outputs:
  + password = (sensitive value)

You can apply this plan to save these new output values to the Terraform state,
without changing any real infrastructure.

Apply complete! Resources: 0 added, 0 changed, 0 destroyed.

Outputs:

password = <sensitive>
```

We see that the output is masked as **`<sensitive>`**. But if we inspect the state file **`terraform.tfstate`** we see the following:

Figure 6.67. A Terraform state file with sensitive values in plain text

```
{
  "version": 4,
  "terraform_version": "1.9.5",
  "serial": 1,
  "lineage": "5671ff24-1f78-fbd8-0d12-671312cb3536",
  "outputs": {
    "password": {
      "value": "thisismypassword",
      "type": "string",
      "sensitive": true
    }
  },
  "resources": [],
  "check_results": null
}
```

The sensitive password appears as plain text! So even though the password started out as a sensitive input value, and was output as a sensitive value, it still appears in plain text in the state file.

> This highlights an important best practice: keep your state file secure. A best practice is to use a remote state storage (see Chapter 7). When the state is stored remotely it will only be held in memory during Terraform execution, and it will not appear in plain text where Terraform is executing.

It does not stop there. If your resources have attributes that are considered sensitive, they are also available in the state file. An example of this is when we create an AWS IAM user with access keys using Terraform (sample code available at GitHub.com[23]):

Figure 6.68. Create an AWS IAM user with access keys

```
resource "aws_iam_user" "terraform" {
  name = "terraform"
}

resource "aws_iam_access_key" "terraform" {
  user = aws_iam_user.terraform.name
}
```

After applying this configuration with **`terraform apply`** we end up with the following state file (only the relevant parts are shown):

Figure 6.69. A state file with AWS access keys in plain text

```
{
  "resources": [
    {
      "type": "aws_iam_access_key",
      "name": "terraform",
      "instances": [
        {
          "attributes": {
            "id": "AKIAAE64MWFAH64QDZ41",
            "secret": "/8zX3KL9W5MaJ1VGbGi49J1Z2dk82H5aGOH6RQxa",
          }
        }
      ]
    }
  ]
}
```

We clearly see the access key ID and secret access key in plain text in the state file.

HashiCorp Vault is a full-fledged secrets management tool. Explaining all the things that Vault can do is beyond the scope of this book, but for the purpose of the exam you need to know that Terraform can read secrets stored in Vault. Vault can also be used to generate short-lived dynamic secrets.

To work with Vault in Terraform you must use the **Vault provider**:

Figure 6.70. Add the Vault provider to a Terraform configuration

```
terraform {
  required_providers {
    vault = {
      source = "hashicorp/vault"
      version = "4.4.0"
    }
  }
}

provider "vault" {
  # configuration arguments
}
```

The Vault provider must be configured with details of where the Vault cluster is and with credentials to authenticate to it. The details of this are beyond the scope of the exam.

With the Vault provider configured you can access secret values using data sources.

Vault has the concept of **secrets engines** to work with secrets of various types. A simple example is the **key-value secrets engine** which stores secrets as key-value pairs.

Use the **`vault_kv_secret_v2`** data source to access a secret from the key-value secrets engine:

Figure 6.71. Read a secret from HashiCorp Vault using a data source

```
data "vault_kv_secret_v2" "db" {
  mount = "kv"
  name  = "database/prod/reader"
}
```

You would now be able to reference attributes of this data source elsewhere in your configuration using **`data.vault_kv_secret_v2.db.data`**.

What happens if we apply this configuration? Assuming Vault has been configured and set up with the key-value secrets engine and a secret has been set at the path **database/prod/reader** then we end up with the following state file (again, only the relevant parts of the state file are shown):

Figure 6.72. A Terraform state file with secrets from Vault in plain text

```
{
  "resources": [
    {
      "mode": "data",
      "type": "vault_kv_secret_v2",
      "name": "db",
      "instances": [
        {
          "attributes": {
            "data": {
              "password": "s3cr3t",
              "username": "admin"
            },
            "data_json": "{\"password\":\"s3cr3t\",\"username\":\"admin\"}",
            "name": "database/prod/reader",
          }
        }
      ]
    }
  ],
}
```

The secret appears not only once, but twice! How come? We have used HashiCorp Vault for secrets, shouldn't we be in the clear?

Vault is not a silver bullet that automatically solves the issue of secrets management. You need to utilize more advanced features of Vault in order to achieve better secrets management with Terraform.

One such feature is the **vault_aws_access_credentials** data source. You can configure an AWS secrets engine in Vault that produces short-lived credentials. You can then use these credentials in Terraform to create other resources in AWS. The details of this are outside the scope of this book.

In Chapter 9 we will look more at securely providing credentials to the AWS provider, and in Chapter 10 we will see how we can authenticate the AWS provider from HCP Terraform using no explicit credentials at all.

6.7: Summary

This chapter has covered a lot of details of HCL and how to create dynamic configurations.

The key takeaways from this chapter are:

- We learned about custom conditions to create validation logic for variables, resources, and outputs. We also learned about the `check` block to create validations that are not directly tied to the lifecycle of a specific resource.
- You create resources with Terraform using the `resource` block in HCL.
- You can read data from existing infrastructure (i.e. infrastructure that is not part of your current Terraform configuration) using data sources, defined using the `data` block in HCL. Data sources are very powerful.
- HCL has a large number of built-in functions to help you perform various tasks. In this chapter we looked closer at functions interacting with the local filesystem, as well as functions for working with IP addresses.
- We learned about meta-arguments. The `count` and `for_each` meta-arguments allow us to create multiple resources of the same type in a simpler way. The `depends_on` meta-argument allows us to explicitly define resource dependencies where they are not apparent to Terraform. The `dynamic` block allows us to create multiple nested blocks in a simpler way.
- We looked at how to provide input to our Terraform configuration using the `variable` block in HCL, as well as how to get outputs from our configurations using the `output` block.
- As much as possible, avoid storing sensitive values (secrets, keys, certificates, etc) in the state file. Sensitive values are stored in plaintext in the state file, and if this file would get lost you should consider all the sensitive values to be leaked.

Notes

1. https://github.com/mattias-fjellstrom/terraform-professional-book-sample-code/tree/main/aws/chapter06/figure6.01

2. https://github.com/mattias-fjellstrom/terraform-professional-book-sample-code/tree/main/aws/chapter06/figure6.03

3. https://github.com/mattias-fjellstrom/terraform-professional-book-sample-code/tree/main/aws/chapter06/figure6.05

4. https://github.com/mattias-fjellstrom/terraform-professional-book-sample-code/tree/main/aws/chapter06/figure6.06

5. https://github.com/mattias-fjellstrom/terraform-professional-book-sample-code/tree/main/aws/chapter06/figure6.08

6. https://github.com/mattias-fjellstrom/terraform-professional-book-sample-code/tree/main/aws/chapter06/figure6.14

7. https://registry.terraform.io/providers/hashicorp/aws/latest/docs/data-sources/vpc

8. See https://registry.terraform.io/providers/hashicorp/aws/latest/docs/resources/subnet

9. https://github.com/mattias-fjellstrom/terraform-professional-book-sample-code/tree/main/aws/chapter06/figure6.17

10. https://docs.aws.amazon.com/cli/latest/reference/ec2/describe-images.html

11. https://developer.hashicorp.com/terraform/language/functions

12. https://github.com/mattias-fjellstrom/terraform-professional-book-sample-code/tree/main/aws/chapter06/figure6.29

13. https://github.com/mattias-fjellstrom/terraform-professional-book-sample-code/tree/main/aws/chapter06/figure6.30

14. https://github.com/mattias-fjellstrom/terraform-professional-book-sample-code/tree/main/aws/chapter06/figure6.32

15. https://github.com/mattias-fjellstrom/terraform-professional-book-sample-code/tree/main/aws/chapter06/figure6.34

16. https://github.com/mattias-fjellstrom/terraform-professional-book-sample-code/tree/main/aws/chapter06/figure6.36

17. https://github.com/mattias-fjellstrom/terraform-professional-book-sample-code/tree/main/aws/chapter06/figure6.38

18. https://github.com/mattias-fjellstrom/terraform-professional-book-sample-code/tree/main/aws/chapter06/figure6.41

19. https://github.com/mattias-fjellstrom/terraform-professional-book-sample-code/tree/main/aws/chapter06/figure6.46

20. https://github.com/mattias-fjellstrom/terraform-professional-book-sample-code/tree/main/aws/chapter06/figure6.47

21. https://github.com/mattias-fjellstrom/terraform-professional-book-sample-code/tree/main/aws/chapter06/figure6.48

22. https://github.com/mattias-fjellstrom/terraform-professional-book-sample-code/tree/main/aws/chapter06/figure6.51

23. https://github.com/mattias-fjellstrom/terraform-professional-book-sample-code/tree/main/aws/chapter06/figure6.68

Chapter 7: Develop Collaborative Terraform Workflows

You would not be using Terraform to its full potential if you only use it in isolation on your local system. Terraform can, and should, be used collaboratively with others. However, developing collaborative Terraform workflows comes with a few challenges:

- One issue is **dependency management**. The Terraform binary, all provider binaries, and any external Terraform module you reference all come in different versions. To successfully collaborate on a Terraform configuration everyone must agree on which versions of these components to use.
- The most notable challenge you will face is the need to share the Terraform state file among all collaborators. Sharing the state file requires the use of a remote state backend, preferably one with a state file locking mechanism.
- Most likely, you will need to externalize the execution of your Terraform workflows to a remote CI/CD system or HCP Terraform to avoid running Terraform on individual developer laptops.
- If you and your organization manage many Terraform configurations there will eventually be a need to pass data between them. There are a few options for how you can achieve this.

The **develop collaborative Terraform workflows** exam objective covers the following sub-objectives:

- Manage the Terraform binary, providers, and modules using version constraints
- Configure remote state
- Use the Terraform workflow in automation
- Share data across configurations and workspaces

7.1: Manage the Terraform Binary, Providers, and Modules Using Version Constraints

We have already seen a few examples of how to specify required versions of the Terraform providers we use. An example of specifically requiring version **`5.61.0`** of the AWS provider looks like this:

Figure 7.1. Requiring a specific version of the AWS provider

```
terraform {
  required_providers {
    aws = {
      source  = "hashicorp/aws"
      version = "5.61.0"
    }
  }
}
```

We can also specify the required Terraform binary version, this is also done in the **`terraform`** block:

Figure 7.2. Add a requirement for the Terraform binary version

```
terraform {
  required_version = "~> 1.6.0"

  required_providers {
    aws = {
      source  = "hashicorp/aws"
      version = "5.61.0"
    }
  }
}
```

The Terraform Block

You can repeat the **`terraform`** block multiple times in a Terraform configuration. Terraform will merge the contents of all the blocks into one.

You could do this:

```
terraform {
  required_version = "~> 1.6.0"
}

terraform {
  required_providers {
    aws = {
      source  = "hashicorp/aws"
      version = "5.61.0"
    }
```

```
  }
}

terraform {
  backend "s3 {
    # backend configuration ...
  }
}
```

This behavior could be of interest if you programmatically create parts of your Terraform configuration (e.g. the use of specific provider versions), or if you want to split your Terraform configuration into logical pieces using different files (e.g. **terraform.tf**, **providers.tf**, and **backend.tf**).

Do we need to specify required versions for Terraform and our providers? It turns out we don't have to. You can omit the entire **terraform** block from your configuration, as Terraform will automatically discover the providers referenced in your configuration. This is good to remember if you encounter a Terraform configuration with no **terraform** block.

There are a few drawbacks with this approach:

- The AWS provider must still be configured with credentials and a specific AWS region name. These can be picked up from the default AWS CLI configuration, if it is set up on your system.
- You have no control over which version of the AWS provider will be installed. The latest available version (at the time **terraform init** is run) will be used. This can be concerning if your configuration has dependencies on a specific major version.
- The installed version of Terraform will be used, even if it is not compatible with the current configuration.
- Your Terraform configuration is harder to read and it is not clear what dependencies it has.

A best practice is to specify the required versions for both Terraform and for any provider that you use.

As for the Terraform binary and provider binaries, we can also specify required versions of the external **modules** (sample code available at GitHub.com[1]):

Figure 7.3. Requiring a specific version of an external module

```
module "vpc" {
  source  = "terraform-aws-modules/vpc/aws"
  version = "5.13.0"
}
```

You specify required versions for the Terraform binary, providers, and modules using **version constraints**. There are a few common version constraints you will see in practice:

- To specify an **exact** version, set the constraint equal to the version number (e.g. `version = "5.56.0"`, or less commonly this can be written as `version = "=5.56.0"`)
- To use a specific **major** and **minor** version, but use the latest available **patch number** use the `~>` constraint (e.g. `version = "~> 5.56.0"` allows for versions such as `5.56.1`, `5.56.2`, etc)
- To use a specific **major** version, but use the latest available **minor** and **patch number** again use the `~>` constraint but leave out the patch number (e.g. `version = "~> 5.56"` allows for versions such as `5.56.1`, `5.61.2`, etc)
- If your configuration requires a feature that is available from a specific version of a provider (and all following versions) you can use a version constraint such as `version = ">= 5.61.0"`.

Semantic Versioning

The Terraform binary and provider binaries, as well as modules, follow semantic versioning. The full details of this is beyond the scope of this book but the basics is that a version is specified using this format:

```
<major version>.<minor version>.<patch number>
```

A new version updates these numbers according to some rules:

- Backward incompatible changes increase the **major version**. This means that if you upgrade from version `4.x.x` to version `5.x.x` your configuration could stop working.

- Backward compatible changes and new features increase the **minor version**. Upgrading from version **4.5.x** to version **4.6.x** will give you access to new features, but your configuration should continue to work as before.
- Bug fixes and similar changes increase the **patch version**. Upgrading from version **4.5.1** to version **4.5.2** will not cause any issues for your configuration, but perhaps a bug you discovered in **4.5.1** has been fixed in **4.5.2**.

When you write your Terraform configuration, keep the following in mind:

A best practice is to lock the versions of your providers and modules to a fixed version. This allows you to be in control of when you upgrade these to newer versions. If you want to loosen these restrictions a bit, you can allow for the patch version of the provider and module to update (using the **~>** constraint) whenever a new patch number is available.

A best practice for the Terraform binary is to use the latest available version, but specify a constraint that requires at the minimum a given version (e.g. **>= 1.6.0**).

Upgrading a provider version is a common task. Start with the following Terraform configuration:

Figure 7.4. A sample Terraform configuration to illustrate how to upgrade a provider version

```
terraform {
  required_providers {
    aws = {
      source  = "hashicorp/aws"
      version = "5.61.0"
    }
  }
}
```

Initialize the Terraform configuration using **terraform init**:

Figure 7.5. Initialize the Terraform configuration

```
$ terraform init
Initializing the backend...
Initializing provider plugins...
- Finding hashicorp/aws versions matching "5.61.0"...
- Installing hashicorp/aws v5.61.0...
- Installed hashicorp/aws v5.61.0 (signed by HashiCorp)

Terraform has been successfully initialized!
```

Update the AWS provider version to **`5.62.0`**:

Figure 7.6. Set the version of the AWS provider to 5.62.0

```
terraform {
  required_providers {
    aws = {
      source  = "hashicorp/aws"
      version = "5.62.0" # new version
    }
  }
}
```

Blindly running **`terraform init`** again yields the following result:

Figure 7.7. Error when running terraform init with a new provider version constraint

```
$ terraform init
Initializing the backend...
Initializing provider plugins...
- Reusing previous version of hashicorp/aws from the dependency lock file

│ Error: Failed to query available provider packages
│
│ Could not retrieve the list of available versions for provider hashicorp/aws:
│ locked provider registry.terraform.io/hashicorp/aws 5.61.0 does not match
│ configured version constraint 5.62.0; must use terraform init -upgrade
│ to allow selection of new versions
```

To solve this, follow the suggestion in the error message and add the **`-upgrade`** flag to the command:

Figure 7.8. Add the upgrade flag to the terraform init command to upgrade a provider version

```
$ terraform init -upgrade
Initializing the backend...
Initializing provider plugins...
- Finding hashicorp/aws versions matching "5.62.0"...
- Installing hashicorp/aws v5.62.0...
- Installed hashicorp/aws v5.62.0 (signed by HashiCorp)

Terraform has been successfully initialized!
```

Upgrading a provider (especially when performing a major upgrade) can introduce issues in your configuration. This could mean resource arguments change the expected value types, or resources are deprecated and removed from the provider. If you are using an IDE with support for Terraform then you will most likely be notified about this while editing your Terraform configuration.

In Chapter 5 we glossed over the file called **`.terraform.lock.hcl`**. This is the **dependency lock file**. When you specify a given version constraint for your providers and run the **`terraform init`** command for the first time, then Terraform will pick the latest available version fulfilling the version constraint. Terraform records the chosen version in the dependency lock file.

The next time you run **`terraform init`** for this configuration Terraform will consult the dependency lock file to determine which version of your providers to use. This ensures that the same versions are used no matter where the **`terraform init`** command is run (e.g. on someone's laptop or in a CI system).

For the updated Terraform configuration above the lock file has the following content, the details of it is beyond the scope of this book and the exam:

Figure 7.9. The Terraform dependency lock file .terraform.lock.hcl

```
# This file is maintained automatically by "terraform init".
# Manual edits may be lost in future updates.

provider "registry.terraform.io/hashicorp/aws" {
  version     = "5.62.0"
  constraints = "5.62.0"
  hashes = [
    "h1:X3LAZdkVhb/77gTlhPwKYCA9oblBCSu866fZDDOojPY=",
    "zh:1f366cbcda72fb123015439a42ab19f96e10ce4edb404273f4e1b7e06da20b73",
    "... details omitted ...",
    "zh:ffb40a66b4d000a8ee4c54227eeb998f887ad867419c3af7d3981587788de074",
  ]
}
```

The dependency lock file should be committed to your version control system along with the Terraform configuration. This ensures that if someone else checks out the repository and runs **`terraform init`** then the same provider versions will be downloaded and used.

Why do you have to use a version constraint for the Terraform binary itself? This is useful if your configuration is using a feature that is only available from a given Terraform version. One example is the use of a **`check`** block, this block is available from Terraform version 1.5 (sample code available at GitHub.com[2]):

Figure 7.10. The use of a check block requires Terraform 1.5 or newer

```
terraform {
  required_version = ">= 1.5"
}

check "liveness" {
  data "http" "mattias_engineer" {
    url = "https://mattias.engineer"
  }

  assert {
    condition     = data.http.mattias_engineer.status_code == 200
    error_message = "My blog is not responding!"
  }
}
```

Version constraints for modules have the same benefits as for providers. If the module publisher follows semantic versioning, you know that upgrading major versions could mean you need to make a lot of changes to your Terraform configuration to accommodate the breaking changes in the module.

> A best practice is to always read the release notes of the providers and modules that your Terraform configuration is referencing so that you have an idea if a specific version upgrade will have an impact for you.
>
> Test the upgrade in a controlled environment before you push the change out into production.

7.2: Configure Remote State

Terraform keeps track of all the resources it manages and all of their attributes in the **state file**. The state file is stored in a **state backend**. The name of the state file is usually `terraform.tfstate`, but this is not a requirement. The state file contains JSON content, and is stored in plain text.

Unless otherwise told, Terraform uses the **local state backend**. The local state backend stores the Terraform state file in the directory where your Terraform configuration is. This is fine during experimentation and early prototyping, but it does not fit well into a collaborative environment.

To work with Terraform collaboratively you should configure a **remote state backend** (or remote state storage). Of special interest for the exam is the **AWS S3** remote state backend. This is the only native option for state storage on AWS.

AWS S3

AWS S3 (the name refers to the following three words starting with an S: Simple Storage Service) is a storage service for blobs (or binary large objects). Think of it as a data dump for most types of unstructured data.

The primary storage resource in S3 is a **bucket**. Bucket names must be **globally unique**, so it is unlikely that your bucket will have a nice name such as `terraform-state-storage`.

Blobs are stored in a flat structure within a bucket, with no directories or other type of file hierarchy. However, S3 has a virtual directory structure built up by using filenames with one or more `/`-characters. So it is common to store a file under a name such as `state/prod/terraform.tfstate`.

You can configure Terraform to use another state backend than the local backend using the `backend` block nested inside the `terraform` block. An example of using the AWS S3 backend:

Figure 7.11. Configuring an AWS S3 backend for a Terraform configuration

```
terraform {
  # other configuration omitted ...

  backend "s3" {
    bucket = "terraform-state-storage"
    key    = "state/prod/terraform.tfstate"
    region = "eu-west-1"
  }
}
```

The **`backend`** block has one label representing the name of the state backend. For AWS S3 the name is simply **`s3`**. The arguments of this block vary depending on the type of backend. For the AWS S3 backend the important arguments are:

- The **`bucket`** argument specifies the AWS S3 bucket name.
- The **`key`** argument specifies the filename of the state file, this can include virtual directories (e.g. **`state/prod/terraform.tfstate`**). Using virtual directories allows you to store multiple state files in the same bucket in a logical order.
- The **`region`** argument is the AWS region name used for this backend.

Terraform must be configured with credentials that allow it to read and write to the S3 bucket. You can use the same credentials that you use to configure the AWS provider, or you can use a different set of credentials. See Chapter 9 for details on different options on how to configure the AWS provider (and thus the S3 backend) with credentials.

A best practice for state storage in AWS S3 is to create specific AWS credentials for each Terraform configuration that allows it to read and write its specific state file. All Terraform configurations should not have access to all Terraform state files.

To take it one step further you should have different credentials for the state backend as for the AWS provider itself.

Also, you should ideally be configuring IAM roles with read/write permissions for the Terraform state. These roles should be assumed when required.

Configuring state storage on AWS using a single S3 bucket is a valid solution. However, there is one important feature missing from this setup: **state file locking**.

State file locking is an important feature used to prevent multiple people or processes from using the state file concurrently. Writing to a state file from multiple sources at the same time is a recipe for disaster and will lead to a broken and inconsistent state file.

Some backends (such as the Azure backend) support state file locking natively. This is not true for the AWS S3 backend. However, we can add a state file locking mechanism to the backend using a **DynamoDB table**[3].

> ### Amazon DynamoDB
>
> Amazon DynamoDB is a NoSQL database service. Data is stored in a **table**.
>
> For the purpose of the state locking mechanism, think of this as a key-value store that maps from a given state file to a state (*locked* or *not locked*). The exact details of the contents in the DynamoDB table is beyond the scope of this book and the exam.
>
> When you run a Terraform operation that will update the state file, Terraform locks the file by updating the corresponding state in the DynamoDB table. If another Terraform process tries to update the state file at the same time, it will discover that the state file is locked and report an error message about this.

During the exam there might be a need to set up remote state storage on AWS, or to configure Terraform to use an existing state storage that has been created for you. Certainly in real-life you might end up having to use AWS S3 for state storage. So this is an important concept to master.

> ### What Came First, the State or the State Storage?
>
> A common problem when setting up remote state storage (outside of HCP Terraform or a similar SaaS product) is:
>
> > *Where should you store the state file for the Terraform configuration creating the remote state storage resources?*

There are a few solutions to this problem. Taking AWS S3 as an example:

1. You could create the required resources using the AWS CLI.
2. You could create the required resources using another infrastructure-as-code tool (e.g. AWS CloudFormation).
3. You could create the resources using Terraform and the local backend, then migrate the state to use the AWS S3 state storage. State inception anyone?

The first two options mean we leave the resources outside of Terraform, and let AWS keep track of the state.

In the demonstration that follows we will see what the third option looks like.

Setting up an S3 state storage from scratch starts with creating a new Terraform file named **main.tf** with the following contents:

Figure 7.12. A new main.tf file

```
terraform {
  required_providers {
    aws = {
      source  = "hashicorp/aws"
      version = "5.63.0"
    }
  }
}

variable "aws_region" {
  type    = string
  default = "eu-west-1"
}

provider "aws" {
  region = var.aws_region
}
```

The final configuration will contain an AWS S3 bucket, a DynamoDB table, and an output with the value of a **backend** block template.

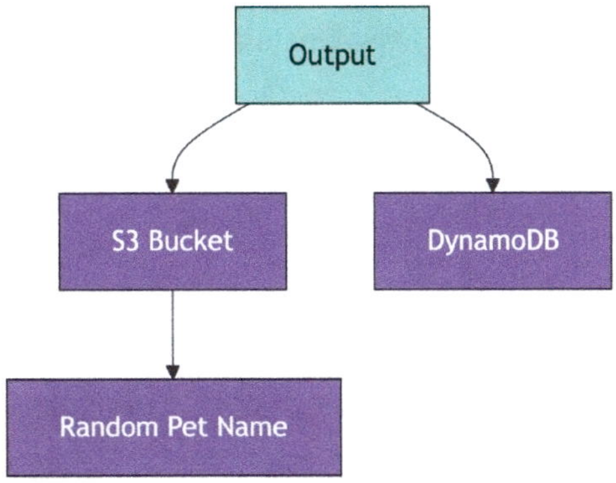

Figure 7.13. Relationship between the resources and outputs in the Terraform configuration for the AWS remote state storage solution

Add the S3 bucket resource to the end of the **main.tf** file:

Figure 7.14. Add the AWS S3 bucket resource to main.tf

```
# other code is omitted ...
resource "aws_s3_bucket" "state_storage" {
  bucket = "terraform-state-storage"
}
```

Remember above when I mentioned that the S3 bucket name must be globally unique? Chances are that the **terraform-state-storage** bucket is already taken by somebody else. How can we get a unique name? One option is to use the **random** provider. Add it to the **terraform** block:

Figure 7.15. Add the random provider to the Terraform configuration

```
terraform {
  required_providers {
    # other providers omitted ...
    random = {
      source  = "hashicorp/random"
      version = "3.6.3"
    }
  }
}
```

This provider has a number of resources to generate random numbers, strings, and so on. Let's use the **random_pet** resource to generate a fun pet name for our bucket. Add this resource to the configuration in **main.tf**:

Figure 7.16. Add a random pet name resource to main.tf

```
# other code is omitted ...
resource "random_pet" "bucket" {
  prefix = "terraform"
  length = 2
}
```

The **length** argument indicates how many parts this name will consist of. Each part will be separated by a dash (-). Update the **aws_s3_bucket** resource to use this name:

Figure 7.17. Update the S3 bucket to use the random pet name

```
# other code is omitted ...
resource "aws_s3_bucket" "state_storage" {
  bucket = random_pet.bucket.id # get the resulting random name
}
```

Next, we add a DynamoDB table, because we are interested in using the state file locking mechanism. Add the following code to the **main.tf** file:

Figure 7.18. Add a DynamoDB table to main.tf

```
# other code is omitted ...
resource "aws_dynamodb_table" "state_locking" {
  name         = "terraform-state-locking"
  billing_mode = "PAY_PER_REQUEST"
  hash_key     = "LockID"

  attribute {
    name = "LockID"
    type = "S"
  }
}
```

The names of DynamoDB tables do not have to be globally unique, so here it is fine to use a name such as **terraform-state-locking**. An important detail to get right of the DynamoDB table is the **hash_key** argument. Terraform requires this key to be **LockID**.

Finally, let's add an output that constructs a boilerplate AWS S3 backend block that we can copy (sample code available at GitHub.com[4]):

Figure 7.19. Add an output to main.tf for the configuration of the S3 backend

```
# other code is omitted ...
output "backend" {
  value = <<-EOF
  backend "s3" {
    bucket         = "${aws_s3_bucket.state_storage.bucket}"
    key            = "<REPLACE ME>"
    region         = "${var.aws_region}"
    dynamodb_table = "${aws_dynamodb_table.state_locking.name}"
  }
  EOF
}
```

Run through **`terraform init`**, **`terraform plan`**, and **`terraform apply`** for this configuration. For simplicity I use **`terraform apply -auto-approve`**:

Figure 7.20. Apply the configuration to set up the remote state storage resources

```
$ terraform apply -auto-approve
# details are omitted ...

Outputs:

backend = <<EOT
backend "s3" {
  bucket         = "terraform-wise-tick"
  key            = "<REPLACE ME>"
  region         = "eu-west-1"
  dynamodb_table = "terraform-state-locking"
}

EOT
```

So far we have created the resources required for a working AWS S3 state backend. However, it is clear from the contents of our working directory that we currently have a state file in plain text locally:

Figure 7.21. Terraform configuration with a local state file

```
$ tree .
.
├── main.tf
└── terraform.tfstate
```

To onboard the state file for this Terraform configuration into the new remote state storage we add the **backend** block from the output of our Terraform configuration. If you lost the output from the previous apply you can use the **terraform output** command to get it back:

Figure 7.22. Get the backend output using the Terraform CLI

```
$ terraform output -raw backend
backend "s3" {
  bucket         = "terraform-wise-tick"
  key            = "<REPLACE ME>"
  region         = "eu-west-1"
  dynamodb_table = "terraform-state-locking"
}
```

Add this content to the **terraform** block, and edit the **key** argument to a suitable name of the state file (sample code available at GitHub.com[5]):

Figure 7.23. Reconfigure the terraform block to use the new S3 state backend

```
terraform {
  # other code is omitted ...

  backend "s3" {
    bucket         = "terraform-wise-tick"
    key            = "state/state-storage-setup/terraform.tfstate"
    region         = "eu-west-1"
    dynamodb_table = "terraform-state-locking"
  }
}
```

We are ready to perform a **state migration**. This is the process of moving the state file from one backend to another backend. Note that this should not be done by simply copying the file from one location to the next manually. Instead, use the **terraform init** command with the **-migrate-state** flag:

Figure 7.24. Migrate the state file to the new AWS S3 state backend

```
$ terraform init -migrate-state
Initializing the backend...
Do you want to copy existing state to the new backend?
  Pre-existing state was found while migrating the previous "local" backend to the
  newly configured "s3" backend. No existing state was found in the newly
  configured "s3" backend. Do you want to copy this state to the new "s3"
  backend? Enter "yes" to copy and "no" to start with an empty state.

  Enter a value: yes

Successfully configured the backend "s3"! Terraform will automatically
use this backend unless the backend configuration changes.
Initializing provider plugins...
- Reusing previous version of hashicorp/random from the dependency lock file
- Reusing previous version of hashicorp/aws from the dependency lock file
- Using previously-installed hashicorp/aws v5.63.0
- Using previously-installed hashicorp/random v3.6.3

Terraform has been successfully initialized!
```

There we have it, we have successfully migrated the state file and we have a Terraform configuration that sets up the storage backend where it stores its own state file.

To use the AWS backend for other Terraform configurations, we must remember one important detail. We do not want to overwrite any other state file that we are already storing in the backend, so we must make sure to use a distinct **`key`** in the **`backend`** block for each Terraform configuration.

The state backend we created is expected to be long lived. After all, most of your other Terraform state files will live in this bucket. But you might still wonder what happens if you run **`terraform destroy`** for this Terraform configuration? After all, it will delete the very bucket where the state file is located. For the sake of science, let's see what happens:

Figure 7.25. Destroy the Terraform configuration for the state backend

```
$ terraform destroy
random_pet.bucket: Refreshing state... [id=terraform-wise-tick]
aws_dynamodb_table.state_locking: Refreshing state... [id=terraform-state-locking]
aws_s3_bucket.state_storage: Refreshing state... [id=terraform-wise-tick]

Terraform used the selected providers to generate the following execution plan.
Resource actions are indicated with the following symbols:
  - destroy

Terraform will perform the following actions:

  # aws_dynamodb_table.state_locking will be destroyed
  - resource "aws_dynamodb_table" "state_locking" {
      # attributes ...
    }

  # aws_s3_bucket.state_storage will be destroyed
  - resource "aws_s3_bucket" "state_storage" {
      # attributes ...
    }

  # random_pet.bucket will be destroyed
  - resource "random_pet" "bucket" {
      # attributes ...
    }

Plan: 0 to add, 0 to change, 3 to destroy.

Do you really want to destroy all resources?
  Terraform will destroy all your managed infrastructure, as shown above.
  There is no undo. Only 'yes' will be accepted to confirm.

  Enter a value: yes

aws_dynamodb_table.state_locking: Destroying... [id=terraform-state-locking]
aws_s3_bucket.state_storage: Destroying... [id=terraform-wise-tick]
aws_dynamodb_table.state_locking: Destruction complete after 4s

| Error: deleting S3 Bucket (terraform-wise-tick): operation error S3: ...
| ... error BucketNotEmpty: The bucket you tried to delete is not empty
|
| Error: Error releasing the state lock ...
```

A bunch of errors occur. The primary error is that S3 will not allow you to delete a bucket that has at least one object inside of it. To circumvent this we could have first updated the S3 bucket resource to the following:

Figure 7.26. Add the force_destroy argument to allow deleting a non-empty bucket

```
# other code is omitted ...
resource "aws_s3_bucket" "state_storage" {
  bucket        = random_pet.bucket.id
  force_destroy = true # add this
}
```

However, at this point it is easier to manually delete the S3 bucket and DynamoDB table. It is not ideal but it was a scientific experiment after all[6]. Remember that this will not be a regular occurrence, because the state storage bucket will most likely be the resource with the longest lifetime of all your resources.

You can configure details of the state backend using the **`-backend-config`** flag of the **`terraform init`** command. Any value provided in the **`terraform init`** command will be merged with the details of the **`backend`** block in the Terraform configuration.

As an example, start with the following partially configured **`backend`** block:

Figure 7.27. A partially configured backend block

```
terraform {
  backend "s3" {
    bucket         = "terraform-wise-tick"
    region         = "eu-west-1"
    dynamodb_table = "terraform-state-locking"
  }
}
```

The **`key`** argument is missing from the **`backend`** block. Provide the key in the **`terraform init`** command instead:

Figure 7.28. Provide backend configuration in the terraform init command

```
$ terraform init -backend-config="key=state/example/terraform.tfstate"
...
```

You can provide additional configuration values by specifying the **`-backend-config`** flag multiple times.

7.3: Use the Terraform Workflow in Automation

Terraform comes in the form of a CLI you can install on your own computer. We briefly went through this in Chapter 3.

Of course you could also install and use Terraform from a continuous integration (CI) system as well. This allows you to automate much, or all, of the Terraform commands.

I want to take the opportunity here to introduce two additional Terraform CLI commands that were not covered in Chapter 5:

- **`terraform fmt`** formats your HCL code to follow the standard format. This is beneficial so that everyone follows the same style to avoid inconsistency in style. It might be tempting to put this command in your CI pipeline, but it would be much better to run it as a pre-commit hook. If you are strict about formatting you can include this command in your CI pipeline if you also add the **`-check`** flag. This flag will cause the pipeline to fail if the format is not following the canonical style.
- **`terraform validate`** performs validations of the syntax as well as making sure you are following provider schemas (e.g. not passing a number where a string is expected). This should be part of your normal workflow, and definitely part of your CI pipelines.

You will not be asked to set up a CI system for your Terraform configurations during the exam, so for the purpose of this book it does not make sense to cover a specific tool for this.

Instead we can simulate all the CI systems using a simple Bash script named **`ci.sh`**. This script can most likely be used directly, or customized to fit your favorite CI system. You could also use a similar script on your local system. An example of what **`ci.sh`** could look like:

Figure 7.29. A simple Bash script to run a number of Terraform CLI commands

```
#!/bin/bash
set -Eeuo pipefail

echo "Initializing Terraform"
terraform init -upgrade

echo "Validating syntax and provider schema"
terraform validate

echo "Creating a Terraform plan"
terraform plan -out="actions.tfplan"

echo "Creating a JSON representation of the plan"
terraform show -json actions.tfplan | jq > actions.json
```

This simple script runs through most of the commands we have seen so far. The output of the script is a Terraform plan in JSON format in the **`actions.json`** file. This file could be used for policy-as-code or other purposes.

The script does not run the **`terraform apply`** command. You can think of this script as a CI script that you can run multiple times during development of the Terraform configuration. It will format and validate your code as well as giving you an idea of what will happen when you eventually run **`terraform apply`**.

There is a lot of Bash magic you can add to this script, but in modern CI systems you will not need that type of magic so it is unnecessary to go through these details here.

The benefit of externalizing the execution of Terraform from your developer workstations to an external CI system is that you can control the number of concurrent executions, as well as restrict who can access the Terraform state from all your developers down to only the CI system.

> A best practice is to use an external CI system, or a SaaS product such as HCP Terraform, to run Terraform for you and your team. This allows you to control how Terraform is executed instead of relying on your developers to follow the desired steps.
>
> It also allows you to lock down access to the state file to the system running Terraform.

7.4: Share Data Across Configurations and Workspaces

Sometimes it makes sense to split a larger infrastructure into smaller separate Terraform configurations. However, this leads to issues of how to pass data between different configurations.

In Chapter 10 we will learn about sharing data between different workspaces in HCP Terraform. In this chapter we will see how we can share data between different configurations outside of HCP Terraform.

Start by creating a new Terraform configuration with the boilerplate pieces in place. This Terraform configuration will be referred to as the **producer configuration**. If you deleted the remote state backend from the previous section, recreate it first[7]. Add the backend block to this new configuration:

Figure 7.30. The producer Terraform configuration with remote state storage

```
terraform {
  required_providers {
    aws = {
      source  = "hashicorp/aws"
      version = "5.64.0"
    }
  }

  backend "s3" {
    bucket         = "terraform-absolute-humpback"
    key            = "state/sharing/network/terraform.tfstate"
    region         = "eu-west-1"
    dynamodb_table = "terraform-state-locking"
  }
}

variable "aws_region" {
  type    = string
  default = "eu-west-1"
}

provider "aws" {
  region = var.aws_region
}
```

Create a VPC resource in the producer configuration and output its VPC ID:

Figure 7.31. Add a VPC resource to the producer configuration and an output for its ID

```
# ... previous code is omitted
resource "aws_vpc" "this" {
  cidr_block = "10.0.0.0/16"

  tags = {
    Name = "vpc-${var.aws_region}"
  }
}

output "vpc_id" {
  value = aws_vpc.this.id
}
```

Run through the `terraform init`, `terraform plan`, and `terraform apply` commands to create the VPC in AWS.

Next, imagine we work for a different team creating a different Terraform configuration where we want to read the VPC resource ID from the output of this other configuration. There are three options we can consider:

1. Hardcode the value of the AWS VPC ID.
2. Use an `aws_vpc` data source to read the VPC resource ID.
3. Use the `terraform_remote_state` data source.

There is a fourth alternative when using HCP Terraform, more on that in Chapter 10.

The first alternative is self-explanatory. We have seen examples of how to use the second alternative earlier in the book.

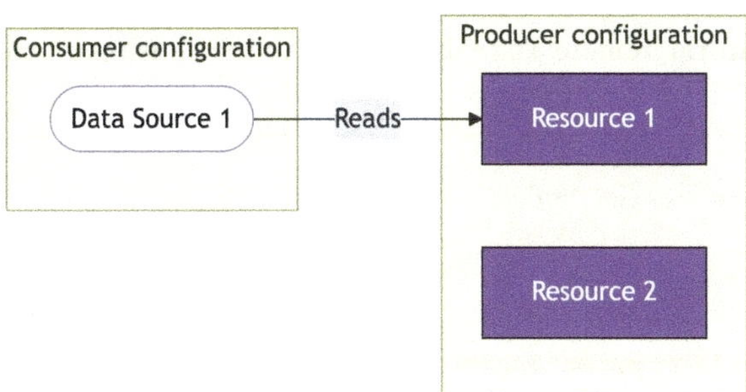

Figure 7.32. Sharing data between Terraform configurations using a resource and data source pair

Below we will consider the third option.

Create a new Terraform configuration for the team who want to use the VPC ID. This Terraform configuration will be referred to as the **consumer configuration**. Start with the boilerplate code:

Figure 7.33. The consumer Terraform configuration that will read data from the producer configuration

```
terraform {
  required_providers {
    aws = {
      source  = "hashicorp/aws"
      version = "5.64.0"
    }
  }

  backend "s3" {
    bucket         = "terraform-absolute-humpback"
    key            = "state/teams/team1/terraform.tfstate"
    region         = "eu-west-1"
    dynamodb_table = "terraform-state-locking"
  }
}

variable "aws_region" {
  type    = string
  default = "eu-west-1"
}

provider "aws" {
  region = var.aws_region
}
```

Next, add the **`terraform_remote_state`** data source to the consumer configuration:

Figure 7.34. Add a terraform_remote_state data source to the consumer configuration to read the output from the producer configuration

```
# ... previous code is omitted
data "terraform_remote_state" "vpc" {
  backend = "s3"
  config = {
    bucket         = "terraform-absolute-humpback"
    key            = "state/sharing/network/terraform.tfstate"
    region         = "eu-west-1"
    dynamodb_table = "terraform-state-locking"
  }
}
```

The configuration of the **terraform_remote_state** data source should match the **backend** block for the producer Terraform configuration exposing the output we want to read. You do not necessarily have to use the same credentials to access the storage.

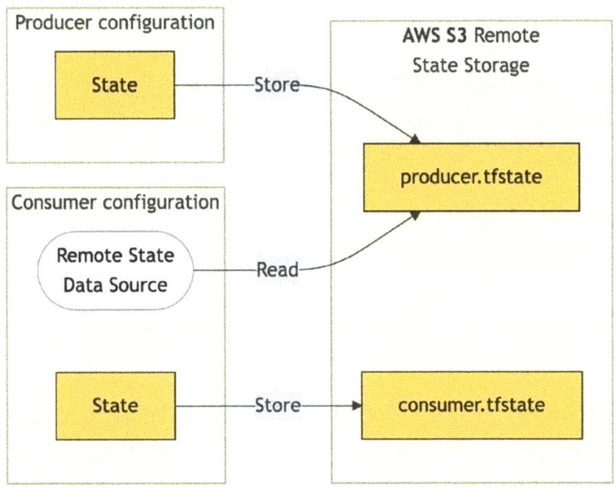

Figure 7.35. Sharing data between Terraform configurations using the remote state data source

> A best practice when sharing state between Terraform configurations is to provide read-only credentials to the system or team reading your state outputs.
>
> However, understand that in practice you allow read access to the complete state file. This could be more than you intend or want to share.

With the **terraform_remote_state** data source in place in the consumer configuration we can reference it and read output values that it exposes. In the consumer configuration, create a subnet in the VPC using the output for the VPC ID coming from the producer configuration:

Figure 7.36. Use data from the terraform_remote_state data source

```
# ... previous code omitted
resource "aws_subnet" "web" {
  vpc_id = data.terraform_remote_state.vpc.outputs.vpc_id
  cidr_block = "10.0.10.0/24"
}
```

Wait a minute! We only output the VPC ID, and nothing else about the VPC. Currently the **cidr_block** of the subnet is hardcoded, but what if it does not match with the CIDR block of the VPC?

Instead of just outputting the VPC ID you could output an object representing the VPC. Update the **output** in the producer configuration (sample code available at GitHub.com[8]):

Figure 7.37. Update the output in the producer configuration

```
output "vpc" {
  value = {
    id         = aws_vpc.this.id
    cidr_block = aws_vpc.this.cidr_block
  }
}
```

Now we can add additional details to the VPC output to accommodate future needs. Note that it is generally not a good idea to just dump the entire resource object as an output since it could contain sensitive values.

Apply the updates to the producer configuration containing the VPC to output the new value:

Figure 7.38. Apply the changes in the producer configuration to get the new output value

```
$ terraform apply -auto-approve

...

Apply complete! Resources: 0 added, 0 changed, 0 destroyed.

Outputs:

vpc = {
  "cidr_block" = "10.0.0.0/16"
  "id" = "vpc-01b03084b5311b186"
}
```

Now update the consumer configuration to use the **cidr_block** value from the VPC (sample code available at GitHub.com[9]):

Figure 7.39. Update the subnet resource in the consumer configuration

```
# ... previous code omitted
resource "aws_subnet" "web" {
  vpc_id = data.terraform_remote_state.vpc.outputs.vpc.id
  cidr_block = cidrsubnet(
    data.terraform_remote_state.vpc.outputs.vpc.cidr_block, 8, 10
  )
}
```

Why is the **`terraform_remote_state`** data source not the preferred method to share state? To be able to use this data source you need to have read access to the entire state file. Even if the Terraform configuration can only access the outputs.

If the state file you are reading is managed by a different team, they might not be keen to give you read access to the entire state just to read the VPC output value. This is why it is better to use a data source for the specific resource you want to read data from. In that case you only need read access to the specific cloud resource and nothing else.

In HCP Terraform there is a similar data source available to read data from another workspace. This is the **`tfe_outputs`** data source. There is an immediate benefit with this data source, it only reads outputs from a given workspace and nothing else. See Chapter 10 for additional details on how to use this data source in HCP Terraform.

7.5: Summary

In this chapter we have seen how we can start to collaborate around our Terraform configurations. Collaboration introduces a few challenges, mainly of making sure everyone is using the same versions of Terraform, providers, and modules, and making sure the state file is stored in a central location accessible by everyone.

Key takeaways from this chapter:

- Use **version constraints** when you specify what Terraform version your configuration requires, what providers you are using, and what modules you are referencing. This will make sure everyone is using compatible versions.
- Store the state file in a central location (a **Terraform backend** or **remote state storage**). In AWS you can build a Terraform backend using an S3 bucket and a DynamoDB table.

- Using Terraform in automation is as simple as installing the Terraform binary as a step in your pipelines and running Terraform CLI commands. A basic pipeline for Terraform can include **`init`**, **`validate`** and **`plan`** commands. Optional steps include checking the plan using policy-as-code and maybe even automatically running **`terraform apply`**.
- Passing data between Terraform configurations is best done using a data source. Create the resource in one configuration using a **`resource`** block, and read it in a different configuration using a **`data`** block.
- Use the **`terraform_remote_state`** data source to read outputs from other Terraform configurations.

Notes

1. https://github.com/mattias-fjellstrom/terraform-professional-book-sample-code/tree/main/aws/chapter07/figure7.03

2. https://github.com/mattias-fjellstrom/terraform-professional-book-sample-code/tree/main/aws/chapter07/figure7.10

3. Note that in newer versions of Terraform native state locking for AWS S3 is available and you no longer need to use a DynamoDB table.

4. https://github.com/mattias-fjellstrom/terraform-professional-book-sample-code/tree/main/aws/chapter07/figure7.19

5. https://github.com/mattias-fjellstrom/terraform-professional-book-sample-code/tree/main/aws/chapter07/figure7.23

6. It is possible to get out of this situation with Terraform, it almost always is. However, it is outside the scope of the exam so we will skip it.

7. Since I broke my remote state storage in the end of the previous section I have recreated it here.

8. https://github.com/mattias-fjellstrom/terraform-professional-book-sample-code/tree/main/aws/chapter07/figure7.37

9. https://github.com/mattias-fjellstrom/terraform-professional-book-sample-code/tree/main/aws/chapter07/figure7.39

Chapter 8: Create, Maintain, and Use Terraform Modules

Terraform **modules** are reusable pieces of Terraform configuration that encapsulates a logical piece of infrastructure.

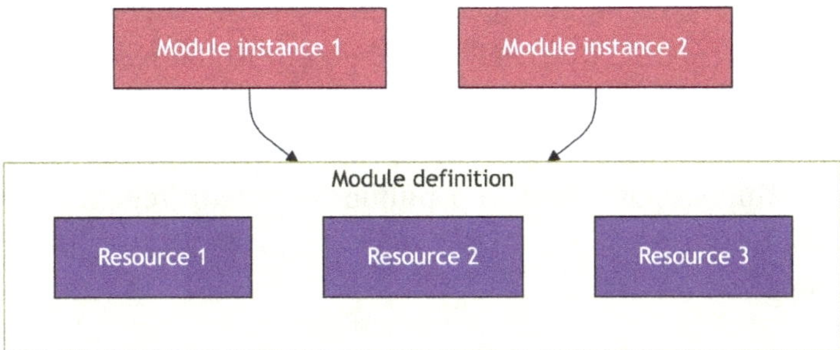

Figure 8.1. Terraform modules

The benefit of using modules is that you can package a working piece of infrastructure and make it available to others, or just create multiple copies of it in a convenient manner.

The design of great modules is a difficult task and it is beyond the scope of this book and the exam. However, there are key concepts and operations related to modules that are important to master for the exam.

The **create, maintain, and use Terraform modules** exam objective covers the following sub-objectives:

- Create a module
- Use a module in configuration
- Refactor a module and use module versioning
- Refactor an existing configuration into modules

8.1: Create a Module

Every Terraform configuration is a module.

The definition of a module is a set of Terraform configuration files in a given directory. The module where you execute Terraform CLI commands (**`terraform init`**, **`terraform plan`**, and **`terraform apply`**) is known as the **root module**. The root module is a special module. The root module is the only module that has a corresponding state file.

Every module, except for the root module, will be of one of the following two types:

1. **Local modules**: available in a local directory close to your root module. You reference a local module by specifying the path to the module. Local modules are generally stored together with the root module, and added to the same git repository. A local module does not support versioning.
2. **External modules**: published to a public or private registry, possibly to the official Terraform module registry. External modules in the Terraform module registry supports versioning.

How you create a new module depends a little bit on what type of module it is.

8.1.1: Creating a Local Module

Most of what has been covered about Terraform configurations in previous chapters still applies when creating a local or external module.

Creating a new module means creating a new directory containing a number of Terraform configuration files. There are some things that differ between a root module and any other module.

Let's go through an example of creating a module. For the sake of having an example to work with, imagine we want to create a number of security groups on AWS. All security groups look similar. They have ingress rules, and they have egress rules.

Figure 8.2. Examples of AWS security groups with ingress rules and egress rules

We could do this by either intelligently utilizing the **`count`** or **`for_each`** meta-arguments (see Chapter 6 for details on meta-arguments) or just repeating multiple **`resource`** blocks manually. However, extracting a module from similar infrastructure is a recipe that scales well when your infrastructure grows.

We start out with the following working directory:

Figure 8.3. Starting working directory

```
$ tree .
.
├── main.tf
└── modules

2 directories, 1 file
```

Initially, the **`modules`** directory is empty. The **`main.tf`** file contains the following boilerplate code:

Figure 8.4. Root module main.tf

```
terraform {
  required_providers {
    aws = {
      source  = "hashicorp/aws"
      version = "> 5.63.0"
    }
  }
}

variable "aws_region" {
  type    = string
  default = "eu-west-1"
}

provider "aws" {
  region = var.aws_region
}
```

Create a new sub-directory inside of the **modules** directory named **security-group** and create a **providers.tf** file inside of this directory:

Figure 8.5. Create the directory for the security group module

```
$ tree .

.
├── main.tf
└── modules
    └── security-group
        └── providers.tf

3 directories, 2 files
```

Add the following content to **providers.tf**:

Figure 8.6. modules/security-group/providers.tf

```
terraform {
  required_providers {
    aws = {
      source  = "hashicorp/aws"
      version = ">= 5.60"
    }
  }
}
```

Note that we do not add a **provider** block to configure the AWS provider inside of the module.

> A best practice is for your modules to inherit the provider configurations of the root module. This means you should not include **provider** blocks inside of the modules to configure anything related to the provider.
>
> However, you still specify required providers in the module and you specify version constraints for each provider.

Add a new file in the **security-group** directory named **variables.tf** with the following content:

Figure 8.7. modules/security-group/variables.tf

```
variable "vpc_id" {
  type = string
}

variable "tags" {
  type = map(string)
}

variable "rules" {
  type = list(object({
    name        = string
    direction   = string
    protocol    = string
    from_port   = number
    to_port     = number
    source      = optional(string)
    destination = optional(string)
  }))
}
```

This module takes three inputs:

- The VPC ID of the VPC where this security group will exist.
- A map of strings which will be applied as tags to the security group resource.
- A list of objects that represents the security group rules we want to add to the security group.

Add a new file in the **security-group** directory named **main.tf**. First add the security group resource:

Figure 8.8. modules/security-group/main.tf

```
resource "aws_security_group" "this" {
  vpc_id = var.vpc_id
  tags   = var.tags
}
```

We configure the security group with the input values for the VPC ID and the map of tags.

To create the security group rules we will use the **for_each** meta-argument. To do this successfully we must transform the input we receive in the **rules** variable. We create a map for ingress rules and a map for egress rules:

Figure 8.9. modules/security-group/main.tf

```
# ... previous code is omitted
locals {
  ingress_rules = {
    for rule in var.rules : rule.name => rule if rule.direction == "in"
  }
  egress_rules = {
    for rule in var.rules : rule.name => rule if rule.direction == "out"
  }
}
```

The **for** expressions goes through each rule, filters out the correct rules based on the value of the **direction** key and then creates a map where the rule name is the key and the full rule object is the value.

With this in place we can create the ingress and egress rules:

Figure 8.10. modules/security-group/main.tf

```
# ... previous code is omitted
resource "aws_vpc_security_group_ingress_rule" "all" {
  for_each = local.ingress_rules

  security_group_id = aws_security_group.this.id
  ip_protocol       = each.value.protocol
  from_port         = each.value.from_port
  to_port           = each.value.to_port
  cidr_ipv4         = each.value.source
}

resource "aws_vpc_security_group_egress_rule" "all" {
  for_each = local.egress_rules

  security_group_id = aws_security_group.this.id
  ip_protocol       = each.value.protocol
  from_port         = each.value.from_port
  to_port           = each.value.to_port
  cidr_ipv4         = each.value.destination
}
```

Add one last file in the **security-group** directory named **outputs.tf** with the following contents:

Figure 8.11. modules/security-group/outputs.tf

```
output "security_group" {
  value = {
    id = aws_security_group.this.id
  }
}
```

The local module is complete. The working directory now look like this:

Figure 8.12. Contents of the working directory

```
$ tree .

.
├── main.tf
└── modules
    └── security-group
        ├── main.tf
        ├── outputs.tf
        ├── providers.tf
        └── variables.tf

3 directories, 5 files
```

Back in our root module we would now like to use the security group module. How to use modules will be covered more in the next section of this chapter, but in essence we add a **module** block to the **main.tf** file in the root module (sample code available at GitHub.com[1]):

Figure 8.13. Root module main.tf

```
# ... previous code is omitted
resource "aws_vpc" "this" {
  cidr_block = "10.0.0.0/16"
}

module "web_security_group" {
  source = "./modules/security-group"

  vpc_id = aws_vpc.this.id
  tags = {
    Name = "web"
  }
  rules = [
    {
      name        = "HTTP"
```

```
      direction = "in"
      protocol  = "tcp"
      from_port = 80
      to_port   = 80
      source    = "0.0.0.0/0"
    },
    {
      name      = "HTTPS"
      direction = "in"
      protocol  = "tcp"
      from_port = 443
      to_port   = 443
      source    = "0.0.0.0/0"
    }
  ]
}
```

I also added a VPC resource to be able to pass in a valid VPC ID to the module.

We can verify that the module works by first running **`terraform init`**:

Figure 8.14. Initialize the Terraform configuration

```
$ terraform init
Initializing the backend...
Initializing modules...
- web_security_group in modules/security-group
Initializing provider plugins...
- Finding hashicorp/aws versions matching ">= 5.60.0, > 5.63.0"...
- Installing hashicorp/aws v5.67.0...
- Installed hashicorp/aws v5.67.0 (signed by HashiCorp)

Terraform has been successfully initialized!
```

Next we apply the configuration using **`terraform apply`**:

Figure 8.15. Apply the Terraform configuration

```
$ terraform apply -auto-approve

Terraform used the selected providers to generate the following execution plan.
Resource actions are indicated with the following symbols:
  + create

Terraform will perform the following actions:

# ... details omitted ...
```

```
Plan: 4 to add, 0 to change, 0 to destroy.

aws_vpc.this: Creating...
aws_vpc.this: Creation complete after 1s [id=vpc-04199f201e14bf1c2]
module.web_security_group.aws_security_group.this: Creating...
... details omitted ...

Apply complete! Resources: 4 added, 0 changed, 0 destroyed.
```

Everything seems to work!

8.1.2: Creating an External Module

There is one important difference between a local module and an external module. External modules should preferably be created in a separate git repository. This allows you to handle the software development life cycle of the module in isolation from the rest of your Terraform configuration and other modules.

When you make an update to an external module you should publish a new version following the semantic versioning rules (see Chapter 7 concerning details of semantic versioning and dependency management for external modules).

The canonical example of an external module in the AWS context is the **VPC module**. At the time of writing the latest available version of this module is **`5.13.0`**.

If you browse the documentation[2] for the VPC module you can see examples of how it is used.

As you can tell from the number of input variables to this module (230 of them) and the number of outputs (111 of them) AWS VPC is much more complex and capable than what we have seen so far in this book. However, there are **no required variables**.

> A best practice when designing a Terraform module is to provide sensible defaults to all input variables. This allows the module to fit the most common needs with little or no configuration. Following this practice makes your module user-friendly.
>
> Imagine having a module with 230 inputs and all of them are required? Chances are nobody will use your module.

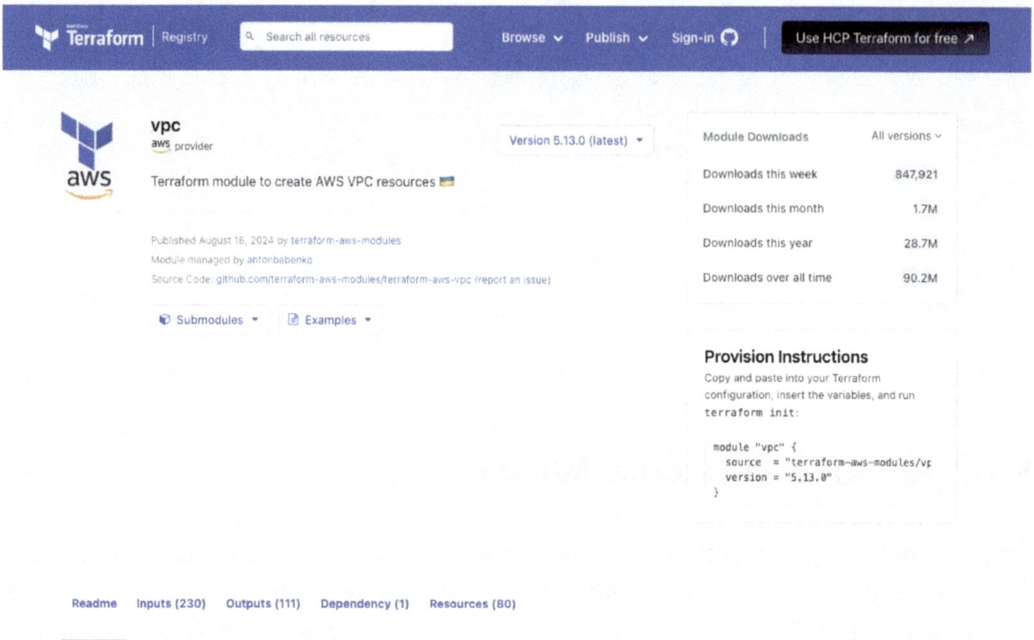

Figure 8.16. AWS VPC module documentation page on the official HashiCorp Terraform registry

Other than placing the source code for a module in a separate git repository there is no difference in how you design an external module compared to a local module. In practice this means what we did in the previous subsection is still valid for external modules, but the **`security-group`** directory should be made into a separate git repository.

There is a small difference between how you use a local and an external module in a Terraform configuration, more on that in the next section.

8.2: Use a Module In Configuration

Using a module in your Terraform configuration is straight-forward.

To create an *instance* of a module you use the **`module`** block:

Figure 8.17. A simple instance of a (local) module

```
module "networking" {
  source = "modules/networking"
}
```

The **module** block takes one label representing the **module name**.

You can reference your module from other parts of your configuration using the syntax **module.<name>**.

A module has one required argument: **source**. The **source** specifies where the module configuration is located. The source value can be a path on your local filesystem or a URL to a git repository or the official Terraform module registry.

The module block above references a local path at **modules/networking**. The contents of that directory is expected to contain one or more Terraform files.

Referencing an external module follows the same pattern. If the external module is located in the official Terraform module registry you can reference it like this:

Figure 8.18. Implicitly referencing an external module in the official Terraform module registry

```
module "network" {
  source = "terraform-aws-modules/vpc/aws"
}
```

The **source** argument for modules in the official Terraform module registry is simplified, the full URL can also be specified like this:

Figure 8.19. Explicitly referencing an external module in the official Terraform module registry

```
module "network" {
  source = "registry.terraform.io/terraform-aws-modules/vpc/aws"
}
```

In Chapter 7 we learned that we should specify a **version constraint** when we reference external modules. If we don't, then the latest available version when running **terraform init** will be used.

To specify a version constraint add the **version** argument:

Figure 8.20. Referencing an external module with a version constraint

```
module "network" {
  source  = "terraform-aws-modules/vpc/aws"
  version = "5.13.0"
}
```

If the local or external modules expects input variables you provide values for these directly in the **module** block:

Figure 8.21. Providing input values to module variables

```
module "network" {
  source  = "terraform-aws-modules/vpc/aws"
  version = "5.13.0"

  # input variables
  name = "vpc-${var.aws_region}"

  # ...
  # 229 other input values you could configure
  # ...
}
```

What happens when we run **terraform init** if our Terraform configuration includes references to external modules? If we start out with the following simplified Terraform configuration we can see what happens (sample code available at GitHub.com[3]):

Figure 8.22. A Terraform configuration referencing an external module

```
terraform {
  required_providers {
    aws = {
      source  = "hashicorp/aws"
      version = "5.67.0"
    }
  }
}

provider "aws" {
  region = "eu-west-1"
}

module "network" {
  source  = "terraform-aws-modules/vpc/aws"
  version = "5.13.0"
}
```

Save the contents to a file named **main.tf** and run **terraform init**:

Figure 8.23. Initializing the Terraform configuration with references to external modules

```
$ terraform init
Initializing the backend...
Initializing modules...
Downloading registry.terraform.io/terraform-aws-modules/vpc/aws 5.13.0 for networ\
k...
- network in .terraform/modules/network
Initializing provider plugins...
- Finding hashicorp/aws versions matching ">= 5.46.0, 5.67.0"...
- Installing hashicorp/aws v5.67.0...
- Installed hashicorp/aws v5.67.0 (signed by HashiCorp)

Terraform has been successfully initialized!
```

We see that Terraform downloads the external module from the Terraform module registry. This is a new behavior that we did not observe when we ran **`terraform init`** in Chapter 5. We did not use any modules in that chapter, so it makes sense.

Next we see an interesting behavior in the provider download step:

Figure 8.24. Multiple version constraints in use at the same time

```
Finding hashicorp/aws versions matching ">= 5.46.0, 5.67.0"...
```

The VPC module has one version constraint for the AWS provider and our configuration has another (**`version = ">= 5.46.0"`** and **`version = "5.67.0"`**, respectively). Terraform takes both version constraints into account.

For the sake of science, what would have happened if our Terraform configuration specified a version constraint that is not compatible with the version constraint specified in the module? Updating our configuration to require version **`5.45.0`** specifically gives the following result:

Figure 8.25. Initializing a Terraform configuration with incompatible version constraints for a provider

```
$ terraform init -upgrade
Initializing the backend...
Upgrading modules...
Downloading registry.terraform.io/terraform-aws-modules/vpc/aws 5.13.0
for network...
- network in .terraform/modules/network
Initializing provider plugins...
- Finding hashicorp/aws versions matching "5.45.0, >= 5.46.0"...
```

```
│ Error: Failed to query available provider packages
│
│ Could not retrieve the list of available versions for provider hashicorp/aws:
│ no available releases match the given constraints 5.45.0, >= 5.46.0
```

You are informed that there is no version that can fulfill both version constraints.

How would you handle a situation like this? You have two options:

1. Upgrade your Terraform configuration so that it is compatible with a newer version of the AWS provider.
2. Downgrade the required version of the VPC module to a version that is compatible with your version of the AWS provider.

We have seen how to configure a module and how to provide inputs to it. We also know that modules can have outputs. You can reference these output values in other parts of your configuration with the reference **`module.<name>.<output>`**.

As an example, imagine we have a simplified VPC module with the following **`output`** block:

Figure 8.26. A module output

```
output "vpc" {
  value = {
    id         = aws_vpc.this.id
    cidr_block = aws_vpc.this.cidr_block
  }
}
```

We can use this module and access its outputs like this (sample code available at GitHub.com[4]):

Figure 8.27. Using an output from a module

```
module "network" {
  source = "./modules/network"
}

resource "aws_subnet" "web" {
  vpc_id     = module.network.vpc.id
  cidr_block = cidrsubnet(
    module.network.vpc.cidr_block, 8, 10
  )
}
```

Similarly, we can pass data between two different modules (sample code available at GitHub.com[5]):

Figure 8.28. Passing data between modules

```
module "module_a" {
  source = "./modules/a"
}

module "module_b" {
  source = "./modules/b"

  name = module.module_a.name
}
```

Just like for resources and data sources, this creates a dependency between the two modules:

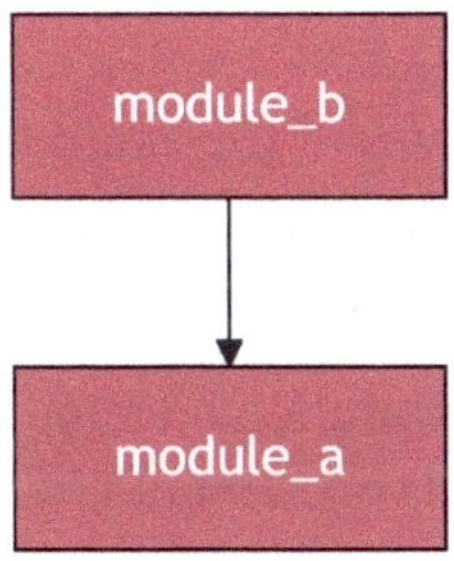

Figure 8.29. Module dependency, module_b depends on module_a

Just be careful to not create a dependency loop like this:

Figure 8.30. Circular dependency between two modules

```
module "module_a" {
  source = "./modules/a"

  name = module.module_b.name
}

module "module_b" {
  source = "./modules/b"

  name = module.module_a.name
}
```

In this situation Terraform can't proceed because there is a circular dependency between the two modules.

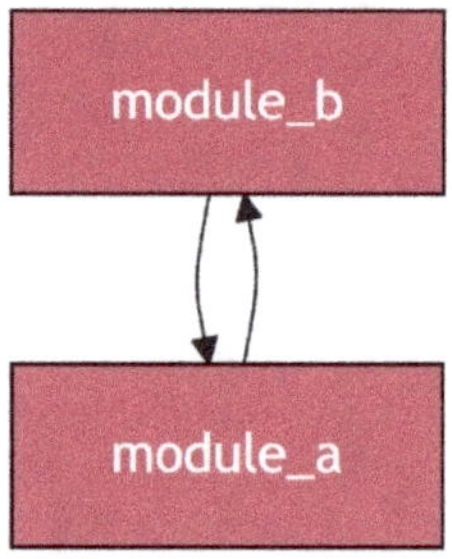

Figure 8.31. Circular dependency between modules

8.3: Refactor a Module and Use Module Versioning

This is the first of two sub-objectives of the exam that concerns refactoring. In this section we will see how to refactor parts of a module, and in the next we will see how to refactor parts of a root module into separate modules.

When you publish changes to a module, you should make sure to follow semantic versioning (see Chapter 7 for details on semantic versioning). Ideally all the updates you make will be backwards compatible, this simplifies the life of your module consumers. However, this is not always possible of course.

Breaking changes include:

- Removal of an input variable.
- Removal of an output value.
- Introducing a new major version of a provider in order to use new features of the provider.

Performing these types of updates is fairly self-explanatory, and we do not need to see examples of these.

Sometimes we want to introduce internal changes to a module that are not necessarily visible to the module consumer. Changes of this type include changing the resource names or data source names. In practice this means moving a resource from one location to another in the state.

Let's look at one example of how to do this. We will reuse the security group module from the previous section where we discussed creating local modules.

In the **main.tf** file of the module we had the following definition for ingress rules:

Figure 8.32. Ingress rule resource in modules/security-group/main.tf

```
resource "aws_vpc_security_group_ingress_rule" "all" {
  for_each = local.ingress_rules

  security_group_id = aws_security_group.this.id
  ip_protocol       = each.value.protocol
  from_port         = each.value.from_port
  to_port           = each.value.to_port
  cidr_ipv4         = each.value.source
}
```

What if we change the resource name from **all** to **web**:

Figure 8.33. Updating the name of the ingress rule resource in modules/security-group/main.tf

```
resource "aws_vpc_security_group_ingress_rule" "web" {
  for_each = local.ingress_rules

  security_group_id = aws_security_group.this.id
  ip_protocol       = each.value.protocol
  from_port         = each.value.from_port
  to_port           = each.value.to_port
  cidr_ipv4         = each.value.source
}
```

If we blindly apply the configuration we would see the following plan output:

Figure 8.34. Planning changes after renaming a resource

```
$ terraform plan

...
Plan: 2 to add, 0 to change, 2 to destroy.
```

This change is pretty harmless, but it will not always be safe to replace resources. To mitigate this we can include a **moved** block to tell Terraform that we are changing the name of this resource:

Figure 8.35. Adding a moved block to move a resource in modules/security-group/main.tf

```
moved {
  from = aws_vpc_security_group_ingress_rule.all
  to   = aws_vpc_security_group_ingress_rule.web
}
```

If we run the **terraform plan** command again things look better:

Figure 8.36. Planning changes with the moved block

```
$ terraform plan
aws_vpc.this: Refreshing state... [id=vpc-0825914329167d60d]
module.web_security_group.aws_security_group.this: Refreshing state...

Terraform will perform the following actions:

  # module.web_security_group.aws_vpc_..._ingress_rule.all["HTTP"]
  # has moved to module.web_security_group.aws_vpc_..._ingress_rule.web["HTTP"]
    resource "aws_vpc_security_group_ingress_rule" "web" {
        id                    = "sgr-01b6b12093f1d46f6"
        # (8 unchanged attributes hidden)
    }

  # module.web_security_group.aws_vpc_..._ingress_rule.all["HTTPS"]
  # has moved to module.web_security_group.aws_vpc_..._ingress_rule.web["HTTPS"]
    resource "aws_vpc_security_group_ingress_rule" "web" {
        id                    = "sgr-0462f0823a89df23c"
        # (8 unchanged attributes hidden)
    }

Plan: 0 to add, 0 to change, 0 to destroy.
```

This looks much better. Your module consumers will see the same changes when they run **terraform plan**, but since the change is harmless they can proceed with ease.

Another typical change you might make to your modules is to remove a resource that is no longer required. In general you would also like to delete the resource from AWS, so there is nothing to do but to remove the resource and any reference to it from the module configuration. Remember to warn the module consumers that this is an expected change.

> A new **removed** block was introduced in Terraform 1.7. This block allows you to remove a resource from the state without having Terraform remove the actual resource. However, since the exam only covers up to Terraform 1.6 this is not encountered during the exam.

8.4: Refactor an Existing Configuration Into Modules

When you work on a new Terraform configuration it starts out small and only contains some, if any, code duplication. As your code base grows, duplications tend to creep in. A good idea can be to break out duplicate parts into modules in order to simplify your configuration.

Refactoring a Terraform configuration with no existing state is a breeze: you just refactor it to what you want and then you are done. However, a Terraform configuration with an existing state file requires a careful approach. Apart from updating the configuration, you will also need to update the state file.

Examples of refactoring a configuration into modules can be very complex in real-life, involving hundreds of resources. On the exam you will not have to worry about migrating hundreds of resources, but there could be refactoring at a smaller scale.

Let's start with a root module and no other local or external modules. The structure of the working directory should look like this (the full sample code for this example is available at GitHub.com[6]):

Figure 8.37. Starting working directory

```
$ tree .
.
├── main.tf
├── providers.tf
├── terraform.tf
└── variables.tf

1 directory, 4 files
```

The **terraform.tf** file has the following content:

Figure 8.38. terraform.tf

```
terraform {
  required_version = ">= 1.6.0"
}
```

And the **providers.tf** file has the following content:

Figure 8.39. providers.tf

```
terraform {
  required_providers {
    aws = {
      source  = "hashicorp/aws"
      version = "~> 5.67.0"
    }
  }
}

provider "aws" {
  region = var.aws_region
}
```

In the **variables.tf** file we have two variables configured with default values:

Figure 8.40. variables.tf

```
variable "aws_region" {
  type    = string
  default = "eu-west-1"
}

variable "vpc_cidr_block" {
  type    = string
  default = "10.0.0.0/16"
}
```

Finally, in the **main.tf** file we have created a single VPC and two different security groups with corresponding rules and dependencies between them. The VPC resource looks like this:

Figure 8.41. main.tf

```
resource "aws_vpc" "this" {
  cidr_block = var.vpc_cidr_block
}
```

The first security group is that for a web server:

Figure 8.42. main.tf

```
# ... previous code is omitted
resource "aws_security_group" "web" {
  vpc_id = aws_vpc.this.id
}

resource "aws_vpc_security_group_ingress_rule" "http" {
  security_group_id = aws_security_group.web.id
  ip_protocol       = "tcp"
  from_port         = 80
  to_port           = 80
  cidr_ipv4         = "0.0.0.0/0"
}

resource "aws_vpc_security_group_ingress_rule" "https" {
  security_group_id = aws_security_group.web.id
  ip_protocol       = "tcp"
  from_port         = 443
  to_port           = 443
  cidr_ipv4         = "0.0.0.0/0"
}

resource "aws_vpc_security_group_egress_rule" "database" {
  security_group_id = aws_security_group.web.id
  ip_protocol       = "tcp"
  from_port         = 5432
  to_port           = 5432
  cidr_ipv4         = var.vpc_cidr_block
}
```

The web server security group has three rules:

- It allows **ingress** traffic from the internet (`0.0.0.0/0`) on both port 80 and port 443.
- It allows **egress** traffic on port 5432 inside the VPC.

The second security group is that for a database:

Figure 8.43. main.tf

```
# ... previous code is omitted
resource "aws_security_group" "database" {
  vpc_id = aws_vpc.this.id
}

resource "aws_vpc_security_group_ingress_rule" "web" {
  security_group_id            = aws_security_group.database.id
  ip_protocol                  = "tcp"
  from_port                    = 5432
  to_port                      = 5432
  referenced_security_group_id = aws_security_group.web.id
}
```

This security group has a single rule:

- It allows **ingress** traffic on port 5432 from the web server security group.

An overview of the resources and their dependencies is shown in the following figure.

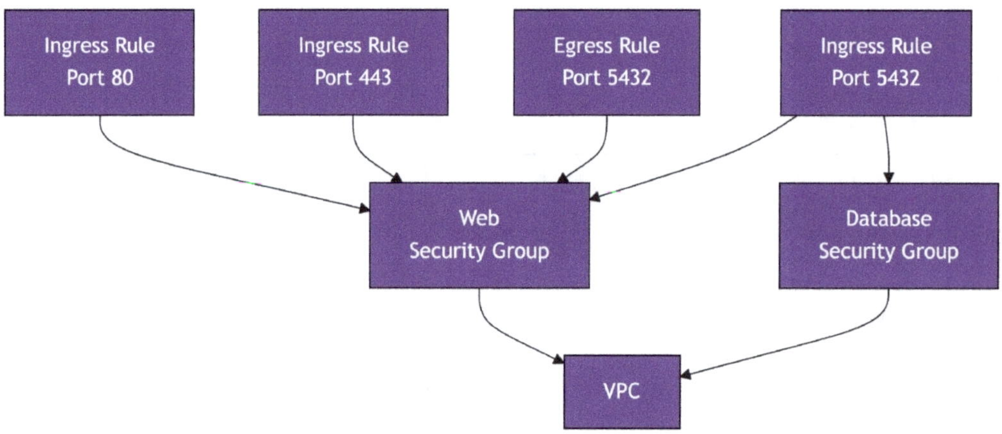

Figure 8.44. Resource dependencies before refactoring into modules

Before we move on, let's apply this Terraform configuration so that we have an existing state file:

Figure 8.45. Apply the initial Terraform configuration

```
$ terraform apply -auto-approve
...
Apply complete! Resources: 7 added, 0 changed, 0 destroyed.
```

We can verify that we have resources in our state using the **`terraform state list`** command:

Figure 8.46. View the current resources in our Terraform state

```
$ terraform state list
aws_security_group.database
aws_security_group.web
aws_vpc.this
aws_vpc_security_group_egress_rule.database
aws_vpc_security_group_ingress_rule.http
aws_vpc_security_group_ingress_rule.https
aws_vpc_security_group_ingress_rule.web
```

It is clear from the contents of **`main.tf`** that we have an opportunity to create a security group module and create each security group using an instance of the module instead.

The first step to achieve this is to create a new directory for our module:

Figure 8.47. Create a directory for the new module

```
$ mkdir -p modules/security-group
```

The working directory should now look like this:

Figure 8.48. The current view of the working directory

```
$ tree .
.
├── main.tf
├── modules
│   └── security-group
├── providers.tf
├── terraform.tf
├── terraform.tfstate
└── variables.tf

3 directories, 5 files
```

We will create a number of new files in the **security-group** directory.

The **providers.tf** file specifies one required provider:

Figure 8.49. modules/security-group/providers.tf

```
terraform {
  required_providers {
    aws = {
      source  = "hashicorp/aws"
      version = "~> 5.67.0"
    }
  }
}
```

The **variables.tf** file configures two variables:

Figure 8.50. modules/security-group/variables.tf

```
variable "vpc_id" {
  type = string
}

variable "rules" {
  type = list(object({
    name        = string
    direction   = string
    protocol    = string
    from_port   = number
    to_port     = number
    source      = optional(string)
    destination = optional(string)
  }))
}
```

The **outputs.tf** file has one output:

Figure 8.51. modules/security-group/outputs.tf

```
output "security_group" {
  value = {
    id = aws_security_group.this.id
  }
}
```

A **locals.tf** file that processes the values passed to the **rules** variable:

Figure 8.52. modules/security-group/locals.tf

```
locals {
  ingress_rules = {
    for rule in var.rules : rule.name => rule if rule.direction == "in"
  }
  egress_rules = {
    for rule in var.rules : rule.name => rule if rule.direction == "out"
  }
}
```

Finally, the **main.tf** file configures one security group with both ingress and egress rules:

Figure 8.53. modules/security-group/main.tf

```
resource "aws_security_group" "this" {
  vpc_id = var.vpc_id
}

resource "aws_vpc_security_group_ingress_rule" "all" {
  for_each = local.ingress_rules

  security_group_id = aws_security_group.this.id
  ip_protocol       = each.value.protocol
  from_port         = each.value.from_port
  to_port           = each.value.to_port
  cidr_ipv4 = can(
    regex("^[0-9./]+$", each.value.source)
  ) ? each.value.source : null
  referenced_security_group_id = can(
    regex("^sg-[a-z0-9]+$", each.value.source)
  ) ? each.value.source : null
}

resource "aws_vpc_security_group_egress_rule" "all" {
  for_each = local.egress_rules

  security_group_id = aws_security_group.this.id
  ip_protocol       = each.value.protocol
  from_port         = each.value.from_port
  to_port           = each.value.to_port
  cidr_ipv4 = can(
    regex("^[0-9./]+$", each.value.destination)
  ) ? each.value.destination : null
  referenced_security_group_id = can(
    regex("^sg-[a-z0-9]+$", each.value.destination)
  ) ? each.value.destination : null
}
```

A security group rule (either ingress or egress) can allow traffic based on the source or destination IP, as well as the source or destination security group. See the **cidr_ipv4** and **referenced_security_group_id** arguments:

```
resource "aws_vpc_security_group_ingress_rule" "all" {
  # arguments omitted ...
  cidr_ipv4 = can(
    regex("^[0-9./]+$", each.value.source)
  ) ? each.value.source : null
  referenced_security_group_id = can(
    regex("^sg-[a-z0-9]+$", each.value.source)
  ) ? each.value.source : null
}

resource "aws_vpc_security_group_egress_rule" "all" {
  # arguments omitted ...
  cidr_ipv4 = can(
    regex("^[0-9./]+$", each.value.destination)
  ) ? each.value.destination : null
  referenced_security_group_id = can(
    regex("^sg-[a-z0-9]+$", each.value.destination)
  ) ? each.value.destination : null
}
```

These expressions checks what type of value is provided (using the **regex** function), then uses the corresponding value for the correct argument. The other argument is set to **null**, effectively removing it from the Terraform configuration[7].

So far we have addressed one step: designing the new module. We have one important step left, migrating the root module to use the new module without destroying and recreating the resources in our state.

To address this we must use a few **moved** blocks in our root module.

We start by adding placeholders for our modules to **main.tf**:

Figure 8.54. Adding module blocks to main.tf

```
# ... previous code is omitted
module "web" {
  source = "./modules/security-group"
}

module "database" {
  source = "./modules/security-group"
}
```

Next we create the **moved** blocks for the security group resources:

Figure 8.55. Adding moved blocks for the security groups to main.tf

```
# ... previous code is omitted
moved {
  from = aws_security_group.web
  to   = module.web.aws_security_group.this
}

moved {
  from = aws_security_group.database
  to   = module.database.aws_security_group.this
}
```

Moving the security group rules will be more challenging. Let's start with the database security group rules because there is only one of them. We need to configure the corresponding **module** block at the same time to have an idea of what the resource address will be for the rule resource:

Figure 8.56. Configuring the database module block and moving the ingress rule

```
# ... other code is omitted
module "database" {
  source = "./modules/security-group"

  vpc_id = aws_vpc.this.id
  rules = [
    {
      name      = "web"
      direction = "in"
      protocol  = "tcp"
      from_port = 5432
      to_port   = 5432
      source    = module.web.security_group.id
    }
  ]
}

moved {
  from = aws_vpc_security_group_ingress_rule.web
  to   = module.database.aws_vpc_security_group_ingress_rule.all["web"]
}
```

You need to be intimately familiar with how the module is designed to be able to get the **moved** blocks correct. To figure out the correct resource addresses you just need to find where the resource is defined in the current state (look in your Terraform configuration or use **terraform state list**) and then find the corresponding resource address in the new module. In this case the destination (the **to** argument of the **moved** block) is found by following the trail:

Figure 8.57. Figuring out the destination address for the security group rule

```
-> module.database
-> aws_vpc_security_group_ingress_rule.all
(the for_each loop uses a map where the keys will be the resource indices
 and in this case the indices are the rule names)
-> ["web"]
```

Notice how I used the output of the **web** module to specify the source for the security group rule for the database security group.

Using the same approach we can fill in the details of the **web** module and add the corresponding **moved** blocks for all the rules:

Figure 8.58. Configuring the web module block and moving the ingress and egress rules

```
# ... other code omitted
module "web" {
  source = "./modules/security-group"

  vpc_id = aws_vpc.this.id
  rules = [
    {
      name      = "http"
      direction = "in"
      protocol  = "tcp"
      from_port = 80
      to_port   = 80
      source    = "0.0.0.0/0"
    },
    {
      name      = "https"
      direction = "in"
      protocol  = "tcp"
      from_port = 443
      to_port   = 443
      source    = "0.0.0.0/0"
    },
    {
      name        = "database"
      direction   = "out"
      protocol    = "tcp"
      from_port   = 5432
      to_port     = 5432
      destination = var.vpc_cidr_block
```

```
    }
  ]
}

moved {
  from = aws_vpc_security_group_ingress_rule.http
  to   = module.web.aws_vpc_security_group_ingress_rule.all["http"]
}

moved {
  from = aws_vpc_security_group_ingress_rule.https
  to   = module.web.aws_vpc_security_group_ingress_rule.all["https"]
}

moved {
  from = aws_vpc_security_group_egress_rule.database
  to   = module.web.aws_vpc_security_group_egress_rule.all["database"]
}
```

The last thing to remember to do is to remove (or comment out) the resources that have been moved in the root module. If you don't, Terraform will complain that the moved resources still exist in the configuration.

If you have followed along this far, your final Terraform configuration in **main.tf** should now look similar to this (sample code available at GitHub.com[8]):

Figure 8.59. Final main.tf in the root module

```
resource "aws_vpc" "this" {
  cidr_block = var.vpc_cidr_block
}

# DATABASE ---------------------------------
module "database" {
  source = "./modules/security-group"

  vpc_id = aws_vpc.this.id
  rules = [
    {
      name      = "web"
      direction = "in"
      protocol  = "tcp"
      from_port = 5432
      to_port   = 5432
      source    = module.web.security_group.id
    }
  ]
}
```

```
moved {
  from = aws_security_group.database
  to   = module.database.aws_security_group.this
}

moved {
  from = aws_vpc_security_group_ingress_rule.web
  to   = module.database.aws_vpc_security_group_ingress_rule.all["web"]
}

data "aws_security_group" "database" {
  id = module.database.security_group.id
}

# WEB ---------------------------------------
module "web" {
  source = "./modules/security-group"

  vpc_id = aws_vpc.this.id
  rules = [
    {
      name      = "http"
      direction = "in"
      protocol  = "tcp"
      from_port = 80
      to_port   = 80
      source    = "0.0.0.0/0"
    },
    {
      name      = "https"
      direction = "in"
      protocol  = "tcp"
      from_port = 443
      to_port   = 443
      source    = "0.0.0.0/0"
    },
    {
      name        = "database"
      direction   = "out"
      protocol    = "tcp"
      from_port   = 5432
      to_port     = 5432
      destination = data.aws_security_group.database.id
    }
  ]
}

moved {
  from = aws_security_group.web
```

```
  to   = module.web.aws_security_group.this
}

moved {
  from = aws_vpc_security_group_ingress_rule.http
  to   = module.web.aws_vpc_security_group_ingress_rule.all["http"]
}

moved {
  from = aws_vpc_security_group_ingress_rule.https
  to   = module.web.aws_vpc_security_group_ingress_rule.all["https"]
}

moved {
  from = aws_vpc_security_group_egress_rule.database
  to   = module.web.aws_vpc_security_group_egress_rule.all["database"]
}
```

A visual representation of how the modules and resources depend on each other is shown in the following figure.

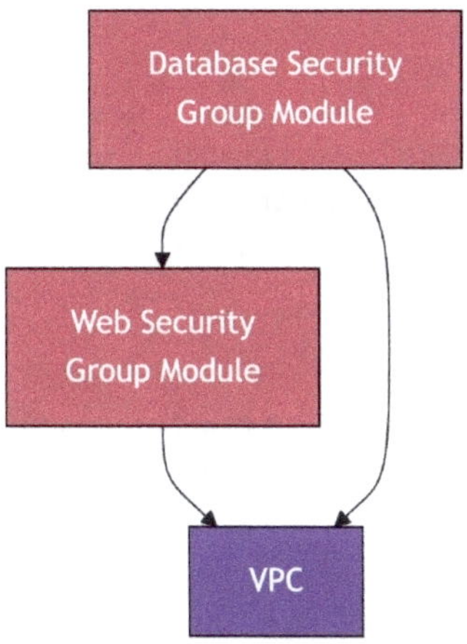

Figure 8.60. Module and resource dependencies after refactoring into modules

We can verify that everything is as we expect by running a **`terraform plan`**:

Figure 8.61. Planning after refactoring the Terraform configuration to modules

```
$ terraform plan
aws_vpc.this: Refreshing state... [id=vpc-0bec3272177d29e19]

...

Terraform will perform the following actions:

  # aws_security_group.database has moved to
  # module.database.aws_security_group.this
    resource "aws_security_group" "this" {
        # attributes
    }

  # aws_vpc_security_group_ingress_rule.web has moved to
  # module.database.aws_vpc_security_group_ingress_rule.all["web"]
    resource "aws_vpc_security_group_ingress_rule" "all" {
        # attributes
    }

  # aws_security_group.web has moved to
  # module.web.aws_security_group.this
    resource "aws_security_group" "this" {
        # attributes
    }

  # aws_vpc_security_group_egress_rule.database has moved to
  # module.web.aws_vpc_security_group_egress_rule.all["database"]
    resource "aws_vpc_security_group_egress_rule" "all" {
        # attributes
    }

  # aws_vpc_security_group_ingress_rule.http has moved to
  # module.web.aws_vpc_security_group_ingress_rule.all["http"]
    resource "aws_vpc_security_group_ingress_rule" "all" {
        # attributes
    }

  # aws_vpc_security_group_ingress_rule.https has moved to
  # module.web.aws_vpc_security_group_ingress_rule.all["https"]
    resource "aws_vpc_security_group_ingress_rule" "all" {
        # attributes
    }

Plan: 0 to add, 0 to change, 0 to destroy.
```

Nothing will be created, changed, or destroyed. This looks like a successful migration!

You should practice doing these types of operations, a lot. They will help you during the exam and they will help you in real life.

Performing migrations is a scary operation and many tend to avoid it altogether, but using the declarative approach with **`moved`** blocks makes the process close to foolproof.

8.5: Summary

In this chapter we looked at Terraform modules.

We saw how to build a Terraform module, how to use it in our Terraform configurations, and how to perform different types of refactoring operations related to modules.

Key takeaways from this chapter include:

- Designing a great module is an art. In this chapter we did not concentrate on module design philosophy but instead focused on the **how** of modules.
- Creating an instance of a module in your Terraform configuration is done using the **`module`** block.
- There are two types of modules: internal and external modules. Internal modules are co-located with your Terraform configuration, while external modules live in their own git repository and follow their own software development lifecycle.
- Performing migrations inside of an existing module is often fairly simple. The most common operation will include moving resources around in the state using **`moved`** blocks. Other module refactoring could include adding or removing variables and outputs. Whenever you do these types of changes, remember to follow semantic versioning to notify your module consumers of the types of changes you are introducing.
- Migrating resources from a root module to separate modules is fairly easy with the use of **`moved`** blocks. You just have to be comfortable in knowing how you find resource addresses and then use the **`terraform plan`** command a lot until you are certain everything looks good.
- Practice migrations as much as possible!

Modules is one of the more important topics in Terraform.

Notes

1. https://github.com/mattias-fjellstrom/terraform-professional-book-sample-code/tree/main/aws/chapter08/figure8.13

2. https://registry.terraform.io/modules/terraform-aws-modules/vpc/aws/latest

3. https://github.com/mattias-fjellstrom/terraform-professional-book-sample-code/tree/main/aws/chapter08/figure8.22

4. https://github.com/mattias-fjellstrom/terraform-professional-book-sample-code/tree/main/aws/chapter08/figure8.27

5. https://github.com/mattias-fjellstrom/terraform-professional-book-sample-code/tree/main/aws/chapter08/figure8.28

6. https://github.com/mattias-fjellstrom/terraform-professional-book-sample-code/tree/main/aws/chapter08/figure8.37

7. The **`can()`** function tests its input. If the input produce an error, **`can()`** returns **`false`**. If it does not produce an error it returns **`true`**.

8. https://github.com/mattias-fjellstrom/terraform-professional-book-sample-code/tree/main/aws/chapter08/figure8.59

Chapter 9: Configure and Use Terraform Providers

By itself, Terraform is not able to work with external APIs to create resources in your favorite cloud providers and beyond. The heavy lifting is performed by **Terraform providers**, or simply **providers**. Terraform orchestrates the work that these providers perform. A provider is the link between Terraform and an external system or API.

The **configure and use Terraform providers** exam objective covers the following sub-objectives:

- Understand Terraform's plugin-based architecture
- Configure providers, including aliasing, versioning, sourcing, and managing upgrades
- Manage provider authentication
- Troubleshoot provider errors

9.1: Understand Terraform's Plugin-Based Architecture

Terraform consists of **Terraform core** and **Terraform providers**.

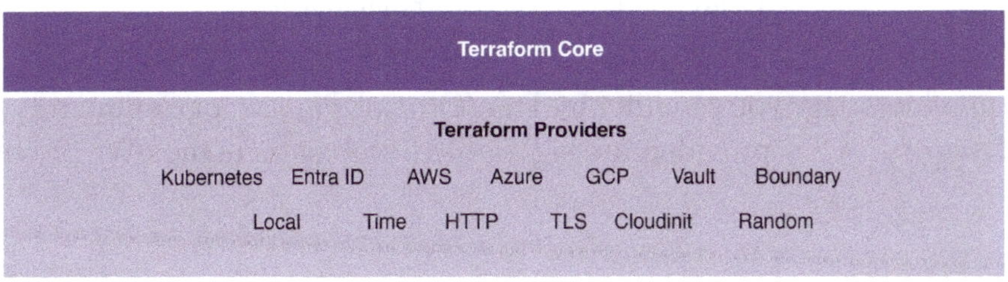

Figure 9.1. Terraform core and the Terraform provider ecosystem.

A provider comes in the form of a **separate binary** that you download as needed to allow Terraform to work with the external system represented by the provider. The provider works like a plugin to Terraform. Each provider exposes a number of resources and data sources.

Terraform core orchestrates the work of the providers. For the purpose of the certification exam it is not necessary to go deeper into the details of how Terraform works, but if you ever have the chance to work on a custom provider yourself, you will learn a lot about how Terraform works under the hood.

The separation of the core from the providers allows Terraform to interact with basically any system in a unified way, as long as someone has written a provider for it.

There are many providers available, some are managed by HashiCorp and its partners, and some are driven by third-party and open-source contributors.

To see the official list of available providers, go to the Terraform registry[1] and click on **Browse Providers** (see Figure 9.2).

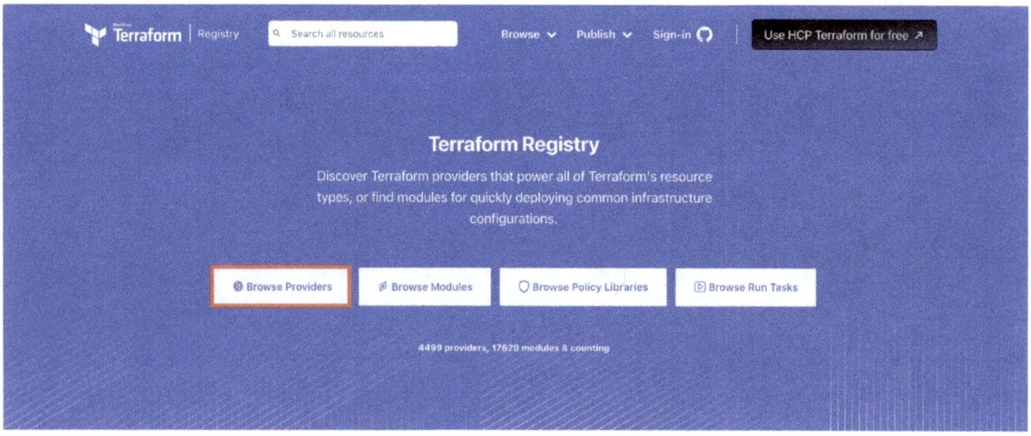

Figure 9.2. Terraform registry landing page

On the providers page you can filter by **Tier** (Official, Partner, or Community) as well as by **Category**. A few providers are highlighted, among them the AWS provider (see Figure 9.3)

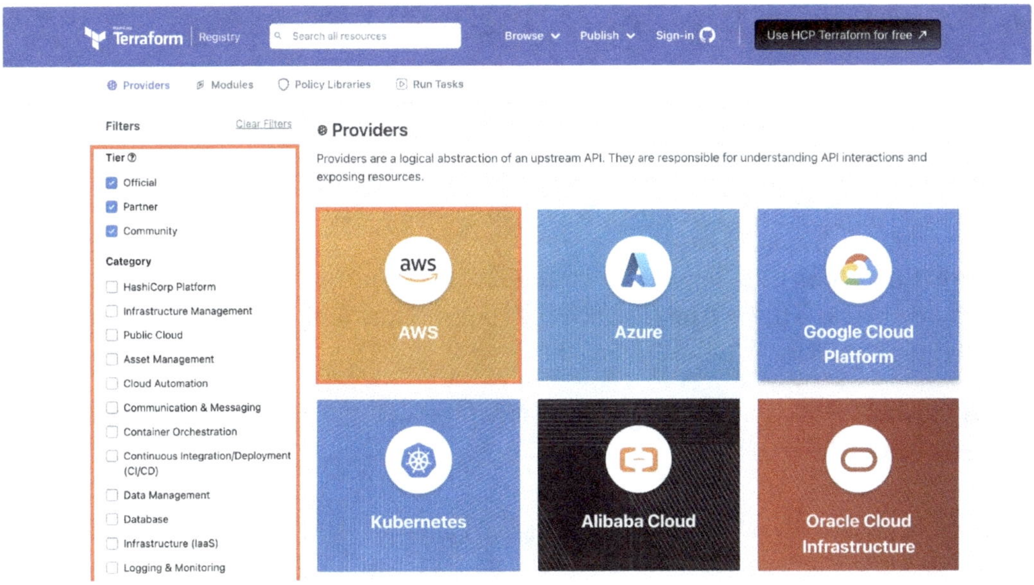

Figure 9.3. Filter by tier and category, or pick one of the highlighted providers (e.g. AWS)

There is a lot that goes into designing a good provider.

In general, a provider should be designed with a one-to-one mapping between a resource in Terraform and a resource in the underlying API. What constitutes a resource in the underlying API will vary depending on the provider. A Terraform resource can also represent something more abstract, like an association between a subnet and a route table.

Most AWS resources in Terraform represent a single resource in the AWS API, so a resource in Terraform (e.g. `aws_vpc`) corresponds to a single resource in AWS (e.g. an AWS VPC).

Instead of building providers that expose abstractions through its resource types, it is a better strategy to use Terraform modules to build these types of abstractions. Use simple providers, build advanced modules.

This also means that a single provider should only work with one underlying API. If you want to build something that is cross-cloud or cross-API, you should use multiple providers and not build a master provider that can work with all your target APIs. Single-purpose providers are better suited for many different types of use-cases.

9.2: Configure Providers, Including Aliasing, Versioning, Sourcing, and Managing Upgrades

We have already seen many examples of how we configure providers in Terraform, but it is worth repeating a few details.

The providers that our Terraform configuration requires are defined within the **terraform** block. This is true for both the root module and any internal or external modules that we use.

A **terraform** block with a single required provider looks like this (sample code available at GitHub.com[2]):

Figure 9.4. A Terraform configuration with a single required provider

```
terraform {
  required_providers {
    aws = {
      source  = "hashicorp/aws"
      version = "~> 5.63.0"
    }
  }
}
```

It is not uncommon for a Terraform configuration to require more than a single provider. You add all the providers that your Terraform configuration uses in the same **required_providers** block. An example of requiring multiple providers looks like this (sample code available at GitHub.com[3]):

Figure 9.5. A Terraform configuration with multiple required providers

```
terraform {
  required_providers {
    aws = {
      source  = "hashicorp/aws"
      version = "~> 5.67.0"
    }

    cloudinit = {
      source = "hashicorp/cloudinit"
      version = "2.3.5"
    }

    http = {
      source = "hashicorp/http"
```

```
      version = "3.4.5"
    }
  }
}
```

A best practice is to specify the required providers sorted by name. This is not a requirement, and it will not make any technical difference in your Terraform configuration. However, it can be very helpful for readers of your Terraform configuration if there is order among your providers.

In Chapter 7 we learned about **version constraints** for provider binaries. Managing the version of your provider can turn into a challenge when your Terraform footprint increases. However, it is still a good idea to be as explicit as possible when you select provider versions. You should test your infrastructure with the selected provider version, and test for every provider upgrade you perform.

We saw examples of how to upgrade a provider. You perform this operation by updating the version constraint of the provider:

Figure 9.6. Change the version of a provider

```
terraform {
  required_providers {
    aws = {
      source  = "hashicorp/aws"
      # version = "~> 5.61.0" # replace this
      version = "~> 5.63.0"   # with this
    }
  }
}
```

Next you run **`terraform init -upgrade`** to trigger Terraform to reevaluate the version constraint, download a new provider binary, and update the dependency lock file **`.terraform.lock.hcl`** to match the newly selected provider version.

The **`source`** argument is the URL to where the provider is published. If the provider is published to the official Terraform registry you do not need to specify the full URL, it is enough to specify the namespace (e.g. **`hashicorp`**) and the provider name (e.g. **`aws`**). The following two **`terraform`** blocks configure the same required version of the AWS provider:

Figure 9.7. Implicit and explicit provider source configuration

```
terraform {
  required_providers {
    aws = {
      source  = "hashicorp/aws"
      version = "5.63.0"
    }
  }
}

terraform {
  required_providers {
    aws = {
      source  = "registry.terraform.io/hashicorp/aws"
      version = "5.63.0"
    }
  }
}
```

For the exam it is enough to use providers available in the official Terraform registry, so we do not need to discuss how to handle a situation where the provider binary comes from somewhere else.

Once we have specified the required provider versions we should also configure our providers. Configuring a provider often entails authenticating the provider by providing it with some form of credentials (see Manage Provider Authentication later in this chapter).

Remember that the configuration of a provider should only be done in the root module, and not in any internal or external modules that you use.

The AWS provider is configured in the **provider** block:

Figure 9.8. A provider block for the AWS provider

```
provider "aws" {
  # configuration
}
```

Each provider has its own required and optional attributes. Some providers do not need to be explicitly configured, assuming you have configured it in some other way (e.g. environment variables or through AWS CLI in the case of the AWS provider). You should check the documentation for the providers you are using to understand the possible configuration arguments that are available.

There is one special argument which all providers support: the **alias** argument.

Provider aliases are used when configuring multiple instances of the same provider. Why would you want to do that?

In the case of AWS there are two common reasons for using multiple provider instances:

1. You want to create resources in multiple different AWS regions (e.g. **eu-west-1** and **us-east-1**).
2. You want to create resources in multiple different AWS accounts.

For the first case, remember that the **provider** block for the AWS provider takes a **region** argument:

Figure 9.9. Configuring the AWS provider for a specific AWS region

```
provider "aws" {
  region = "eu-west-1"
}
```

The **region** argument is a string, it does not accept a list of strings or anything else. To create resources in two different AWS regions in the same Terraform configuration we add an additional **provider** block for the AWS provider, and we add the **alias** argument to it:

Figure 9.10. Configuring two instances of the AWS provider, one with an explicit alias

```
provider "aws" {
  region = "eu-west-1"
}

provider "aws" {
  alias  = "us"
  region = "us-east-1"
}
```

There is no need to change anything in the **required_providers** block. There is still only a single provider binary in use, but it is configured in two different instances using different configuration values. You could also configure the providers to use different credentials.

The provider instance with no explicit **alias** is referred to as the **default provider instance**. Unless otherwise specified, this is the AWS provider instance that will be used. This means that if we add the following **resource** block to our configuration the default provider instance will be used:

Figure 9.11. A resource using the default provider instance

```
resource "aws_vpc" "eu" {
  cidr_block = "10.0.0.0/16"
}
```

To use a provider instance with an alias, add the **`provider`** meta-argument to the resource (see Chapter 6 for other meta-arguments):

Figure 9.12. A resource using an explicit provider alias

```
resource "aws_vpc" "us" {
  provider   = aws.us
  cidr_block = "192.168.0.0/16"
}
```

Putting everything together we have the following simple Terraform configuration that deploys resources to multiple AWS regions at the same time (sample code available at GitHub.com[4]):

Figure 9.13. A Terraform configuration creating resources in multiple AWS regions through the use of two AWS provider instances

```
terraform {
  required_providers {
    aws = {
      source  = "hashicorp/aws"
      version = "5.67.0"
    }
  }
}

provider "aws" {
  region = "eu-west-1"
}

provider "aws" {
  alias  = "us"
  region = "us-east-1"
}

resource "aws_vpc" "eu" {
  cidr_block = "10.0.0.0/16"
}

resource "aws_vpc" "us" {
  provider   = aws.us
  cidr_block = "192.168.0.0/16"
}
```

The other use-case mentioned above was *"You want to create resources in multiple different AWS accounts"*. This works the same way, you create two (or more) **provider** blocks, one for each account. However, there is no **account_id** argument that controls which AWS account is in use. Instead this is controlled using the credentials that you configure for the provider. More on credentials in Manage Provider Authentication later in this chapter.

It is possible that you will encounter modules that require more than one instance of the AWS provider (or a different provider for that matter). It is also possible that you design a module that uses two different AWS provider instances. So it is crucial that you know how this changes the module design, the changes are minor but we will go through them in the following discussion.

In this scenario we have the following local module stored in **modules/network**:

Figure 9.14. modules/network/main.tf

```
terraform {
  required_providers {
    aws = {
      source  = "hashicorp/aws"
      version = ">= 5.60.0"
    }
  }
}

resource "aws_vpc" "this" {
  cidr_block = "10.0.0.0/16"
}
```

Currently the module only has one instance of the AWS provider, the default provider instance.

Now we would like to add another provider instance that sets up a VPC resource in a different region. Remember that we do not add **provider** blocks in the module, so we must configure this in some other way.

It turns out that there is an optional argument in the provider definition in the **required_providers** block, called **configuration_aliases**:

Figure 9.15. Adding a configuration alias for the required provider in modules/network/main.tf

```
terraform {
  required_providers {
    aws = {
      source  = "hashicorp/aws"
      version = ">= 5.60.0"
      configuration_aliases = [
        aws.secondary
      ]
    }
  }
}

# the rest of the code is omitted ...
```

The **configuration_aliases** is a list where you configure aliases for the providers using the syntax **<provider>.<alias>**.

Then we can use the provider aliases like we did before. Add a new resource to the module:

Figure 9.16. Add a new VPC resource to modules/network/main.tf

```
# ... previous code is omitted
resource "aws_vpc" "that" {
  provider   = aws.secondary
  cidr_block = "192.168.0.0/16"
}
```

That was everything we needed to do in the module itself. What is left to do is to pass provider configurations into the module from the root module. We can do this in the **providers** meta-argument of the **module** block (sample code available at GitHub.com[5]):

Figure 9.17. Creating an instance of a module requiring two provider instances

```
# root module main.tf
terraform {
  required_providers {
    aws = {
      source  = "hashicorp/aws"
      version = "5.67.0"
    }
  }
}

provider "aws" {
  region = "eu-west-1"
}

provider "aws" {
  alias  = "us"
  region = "us-east-1"
}

module "network" {
  source = "./modules/network"
  providers = {
    aws.secondary = aws.us
  }
}
```

The **`providers`** meta-argument is a key-value map where the key represents the alias configured in the module, and the value represents the alias defined in the root module. The default provider from the root module is implicitly passed to the module, so there is no need to pass it explicitly.

Note that there is no limit to the number of provider aliases you can configure and pass around between your different modules.

9.3: Manage Provider Authentication

Most providers require some form of authentication[6]. How the authentication process works is built into the providers. However, you must provide some form of credentials so that the provider can perform its authentication. In general, provider credentials are provided as environment variables or through some form of credential file.

The AWS provider requires AWS credentials to be able to do anything at all in your AWS environment. Since the AWS provider is in focus for this exam we will concentrate on how to provide authentication credentials to this provider.

It turns out there are a few available methods to provide credentials to the AWS provider. In order of precedence, these methods are:

- Parameters in the provider configuration
- Environment variables
- Shared configuration and credentials files
- Container credentials
- Instance profile credentials and region

It could be beneficial to remember the order of these credentials options, because if you provide credentials through multiple methods at the same time it will be good to know which credentials will be used.

In the following subsections we will go through the first three methods in this list.

9.3.1: Parameters In the Provider Configuration

This is the most explicit method to configure the AWS provider with credentials. It involves setting the credentials explicitly in the **provider** block:

Figure 9.18. Configuring provider credentials directly in the provider block

```
provider "aws" {
  region     = "eu-west-1"
  access_key = "thisismyaccesskey"
  secret_key = "thisismysecretkey"
}
```

Instead of hardcoding the values in the provider you could pass them in as variables (sample code available at GitHub.com[7]):

Figure 9.19. Configuring provider credentials directly in the provider block but passing in the values as variables

```
variable "aws_region" {
  type = string
}

variable "aws_access_key_id" {
  type      = string
  sensitive = true
}

variable "aws_secret_access_key" {
  type      = string
  sensitive = true
}

provider "aws" {
  region     = var.aws_region
  access_key = var.aws_access_key_id
  secret_key = var.aws_secret_access_key
}
```

Then you can create a variables file named **`terraform.tfvars`** with the credentials:

Figure 9.20. Provider credentials in a Terraform variables file

```
aws_region            = "eu-west-1"
aws_access_key_id     = "thisismyaccesskey"
aws_secret_access_key = "thisismysecretkey"
```

Now you can run **`terraform init`**, **`terraform plan`**, and so on.

Note that it is **not** a best practice to provide credentials in this way, especially hardcoding them directly in the **`provider`** block. This is because there is a risk that you will accidentally commit the credentials to your source code repository.

However, during the exam this is the **fastest** way to provide credentials to the provider. Is it faster than environment variables? I would say yes. This is because when you set environment variables you generally do this using **`export AWS_ACCESS_KEY_ID=...`** commands in a given terminal window, and if you switch to a different window you do not have the environment variables available.

9.3.2: Environment Variables

In Chapter 3 we saw and used this option for providing credentials to the AWS provider. The environment variables must use these specific names:

- **AWS_ACCESS_KEY_ID** for the access key ID.
- **AWS_SECRET_ACCESS_KEY** for the corresponding secret key.

You could have these environment variables set in your Bash profile, or you can set them as needed in your current terminal session:

Figure 9.21. Setting environment variables for the AWS provider credentials

```
$ export AWS_ACCESS_KEY_ID=thisismyaccesskey
$ export AWS_SECRET_ACCESS_KEY=thisismysecretkey
```

The AWS provider will automatically pick these environment variables up for all Terraform CLI commands.

Note that this method does not support providing different credentials to different instances of the AWS provider.

9.3.3: Shared Configuration and Credentials Files

The AWS CLI uses configuration and credentials files to authenticate the AWS CLI. These files can also be used by Terraform.

Read the AWS documentation[8] for all the configuration options for these files. In the following demonstration we will see how to use these files, but we won't go into details about how you configure these files.

By default, the configuration and credentials files are located under the **~/.aws** directory (i.e. the **.aws** directory in your home directory):

Figure 9.22. The .aws directory content

```
$ tree .aws
.aws
├── config
└── credentials

1 directory, 2 files
```

The credentials are configured in the **credentials** file:

Figure 9.23. The AWS credentials file

```
[default]
aws_access_key_id=FIRSTACCESSKEY
aws_secret_access_key=FiRsTsEcReTkEy

[same-account-other-region]
aws_access_key_id=FIRSTACCESSKEY
aws_secret_access_key=FiRsTsEcReTkEy

[other-account]
aws_access_key_id=SECONDACCESSKEY
aws_secret_access_key=SeCoNdSeCrEtKeY
```

This file specifies two different sets of credentials. The section (or *profile*) named **`[default]`** will be used unless the AWS CLI and Terraform is told otherwise.

You can also configure the profiles in the **`config`** file:

Figure 9.24. The AWS config file

```
[default]
region=eu-west-1
output=json

[profile same-account-other-region]
region=us-east-1
output=json

[profile other-account]
region=eu-west-1
output=json
```

In your Terraform configuration you can use the profile names (e.g. **`default`** and **`same-account-other-region`**) from these configuration and credentials files:

Figure 9.25. Referencing the config and credentials files in a Terraform configuration

```
provider "aws" {
  shared_config_files      = ["/Users/mattias/.aws/config"]
  shared_credentials_files = ["/Users/mattias/.aws/credentials"]
  profile                  = "default"
}

provider "aws" {
  alias                    = "us"
  shared_config_files      = ["/Users/mattias/.aws/config"]
  shared_credentials_files = ["/Users/mattias/.aws/credentials"]
  profile                  = "same-account-other-region"
}
```

You could move the configuration and credentials files to somewhere else if you wish. I used the default ones available under my home directory **`/Users/mattias`**.

The important point to note is the connection between the profile in the configuration file, the corresponding credentials in the credentials file, and the **`profile`** argument of the AWS **`provider`** block.

I have skipped over a few details in this discussion. The credentials I have used above are **long-lived credentials**. It is possible to generate **short-lived credentials** (the details are outside the scope of the exam and this book), and along with these there is a third credential component included: **the session token**.

If you are provided with an access key, a secret access key, and a session token, then the only difference is that you need to also set the session token using the relevant method.

If you configure it directly in the **`provider`** block it looks like this:

Figure 9.26. Adding the session token argument to the provider block

```
provider "aws" {
  region     = "eu-west-1"
  access_key = "thisismyaccesskey"
  secret_key = "thisismysecretkey"
  token      = "thisismysessiontoken"
}
```

If you are using environment variables, you configure it in the **`AWS_SESSION_TOKEN`** variable like this:

Figure 9.27. Adding the session token as an environment variable

```
$ export AWS_SESSION_TOKEN=thisismysessiontoken
```

If you are using the credentials file method you set it like this:

Figure 9.28. Adding the session token in the AWS CLI credentials file

```
[default]
aws_access_key_id=thisismyaccesskey
aws_secret_access_key=thisismysecretkey
aws_session_token=thisismysessiontoken
```

No other changes are needed.

9.4: Troubleshoot Provider Errors

Troubleshooting provider errors is a broad topic and we will only scratch the surface of what types or errors can appear.

9.4.1: Logging

When performing any troubleshooting with Terraform a good idea is to change the log level from its default value. You can do this using the **TF_LOG** environment variable:

Figure 9.29. Configure the log level for the Terraform CLI

```
$ export TF_LOG=TRACE
```

The available log levels are **TRACE**, **DEBUG**, **INFO**, **WARN**, and **ERROR**. Note that setting it to **TRACE** or **DEBUG** will produce a lot of logs.

If you want to primarily concentrate on troubleshooting the provider, you can separate the log levels to skip a lot of logs from Terraform core:

Figure 9.30. Use separate log levels for the Terraform core and for the providers

```
$ export TF_LOG_CORE=ERROR
$ export TF_LOG_PROVIDER=TRACE
```

Also, if you want to store the log output in a file instead of in the standard out of the current terminal window you can set the **`TF_LOG_PATH`** environment variable:

Figure 9.31. Store the logs in a file instead of using the standard out

```
$ export TF_LOG_PATH=terraform.logs
```

9.4.2: Validating Using the CLI

The **`terraform validate`** command can find and report many mistakes and errors you have made in the resources and data sources of your configuration.

An example Terraform configuration that has an error which your editor will not find can look like this (sample code available at GitHub.com[9]):

Figure 9.32. A Terraform configuration with an error in the VPC CIDR block

```
terraform {
  required_providers {
    aws = {
      source = "hashicorp/aws"
    }
  }
}

provider "aws" {
  region = "eu-west-1"
}

resource "aws_vpc" "this" {
  cidr_block = "10.0.0.0/"
}
```

Running **`terraform validate`** for this configuration produces the following result:

Figure 9.33. Validating a Terraform configuration using the Terraform CLI

```
$ terraform validate

│ Error: expected cidr_block to contain a valid Value, got: 10.0.0.0/ with err:
│ invalid CIDR address: 10.0.0.0/
│
│   with aws_vpc.this,
│   on main.tf line 14, in resource "aws_vpc" "this":
│   14:     cidr_block = "10.0.0.0/"
```

The error messages are usually good at pinpointing what the error is. Imagine we update the configuration of the **aws_vpc** to this instead (sample code available at GitHub.com[10]):

Figure 9.34. Introducing a different error in the VPC CIDR block

```
resource "aws_vpc" "this" {
  cidr_block = "10.0.0.0/6"
}
```

If we rerun the validation command now we encounter two different errors:

Figure 9.35. Validating the new Terraform configuration using the Terraform CLI

```
$ terraform validate

│ Error: expected cidr_block to contain a valid network Value,
│ expected 8.0.0.0/6, got 10.0.0.0/6
│
│   with aws_vpc.this,
│   on main.tf line 14, in resource "aws_vpc" "this":
│   14:     cidr_block = "10.0.0.0/6"
│
│ Error: expected "cidr_block" to contain a network Value with
│ between 16 and 28 significant bits, got: 6
│
│   with aws_vpc.this,
│   on main.tf line 14, in resource "aws_vpc" "this":
│   14:     cidr_block = "10.0.0.0/6"
```

The first error comes from the fact that **10.0.0.0/6** is not a valid CIDR block to start with, and the second error means that the size of the VPC CIDR block must be between 16 and 28 (i.e. **10.0.0.0/16** to **10.0.0.0/28**).

As you can tell the **terraform validate** command can be very helpful.

Most errors caught by **terraform validate** are also caught by **terraform plan**. However, the **terraform validate** command will do this faster if time is of the essence (e.g. during the exam).

Other types of errors you might encounter include:

- Specifying a provider version in **required_providers** that does not exist. This will be caught by **terraform init**. See an example of this in Chapter 5.
- Invalid or no credentials are found. This will not be caught by either **terraform init** or **terraform validate**. However, it will be caught by **terraform plan**:

```
$ terraform plan
Planning failed. Terraform encountered an error while generating this plan.

│ Error: Retrieving AWS account details: validating provider credentials:
│ retrieving caller identity from STS: operation error STS:
│ GetCallerIdentity, https response error StatusCode: 403,
│ RequestID: <id>, api error InvalidClientTokenId: The security token
│ included in the request is invalid.
│
│   with provider["registry.terraform.io/hashicorp/aws"],
│   on main.tf line 9, in provider "aws":
│    9: provider "aws" {
```

- You are using a data source that does not exist. This might mean that you have configured your data source incorrectly, or that the provider is configured to look in the wrong region or the wrong AWS account.
- You try to create a resource that already exists. This is not as common for the AWS provider as for other providers. Many resource types in AWS have no name property that must be unique within your account or within AWS as a whole. However, one such resource is an S3 bucket. If you try to create an S3 bucket with a name that is already taken you will not discover this before you run **terraform apply**, but the error message will be clear (**BucketAlreadyExists**):

```
$ terraform apply -auto-approve
aws_s3_bucket.test: Creating...
...
| Error: creating S3 Bucket (test): operation error S3:
| CreateBucket, https response error StatusCode: 409,
| RequestID: <id>, HostID: <id>, BucketAlreadyExists:
|
|   with aws_s3_bucket.test,
|   on main.tf line 17, in resource "aws_s3_bucket" "test":
|   17: resource "aws_s3_bucket" "test" {
```

I hope this section has shown you that many errors are in fact easy to resolve due to the information presented in the error messages. Exactly what types of errors you will encounter is difficult to foresee, but this section has given you a few ideas of what it could be.

9.5: Summary

In this chapter we covered many details around providers, and the AWS provider in particular.

Key takeaways from this chapter include:

- Providers are the bridge between Terraform and external APIs and systems. Terraform orchestrates the creation of resources through the providers. A provider is a plugin to Terraform.
- You can create multiple instances of the same provider in the same Terraform configuration. To do this, you need to use provider aliases. In the case of the AWS provider you could configure multiple providers to target different AWS regions or different AWS accounts.
- You can use multiple provider instances in your modules as well. You need to specify a) what provider aliases are expected and b) where you configure what providers are required for the module. You configure the actual providers in the root module and pass them in to the module.
- You can provide authentication details to the AWS provider in a number of ways. The quickest way during the exam is to configure the credentials directly in the **`provider`** block. However, this is a bad idea in general. A relatively quick way and much more safe is to use environment variables. We also saw how to use the AWS CLI configuration and credentials files.
- Troubleshooting providers is something we all will require to do every now and then. During the exam there will not be a specific "troubleshoot this provider"

exercise, but troubleshooting will come up naturally when you write your configurations. A few common issues were discussed in this chapter, among them credential issues, missing data sources, conflicting resources and invalid resource configurations.

Notes

1. https://registry.terraform.io/
2. https://github.com/mattias-fjellstrom/terraform-professional-book-sample-code/tree/main/aws/chapter09/figure9.04
3. https://github.com/mattias-fjellstrom/terraform-professional-book-sample-code/tree/main/aws/chapter09/figure9.05
4. https://github.com/mattias-fjellstrom/terraform-professional-book-sample-code/tree/main/aws/chapter09/figure9.13
5. https://github.com/mattias-fjellstrom/terraform-professional-book-sample-code/tree/main/aws/chapter09/figure9.17
6. Simpler providers such as the local provider or the HTTP provider do not require any authentication.
7. https://github.com/mattias-fjellstrom/terraform-professional-book-sample-code/tree/main/aws/chapter09/figure9.19
8. https://docs.aws.amazon.com/cli/v1/userguide/cli-configure-files.html
9. https://github.com/mattias-fjellstrom/terraform-professional-book-sample-code/tree/main/aws/chapter09/figure9.32
10. https://github.com/mattias-fjellstrom/terraform-professional-book-sample-code/tree/main/aws/chapter09/figure9.34

Chapter 10: Collaborate on Infrastructure as Code Using HCP Terraform

The **HashiCorp Cloud Platform** (HCP) provides Software-as-a-Service (SaaS) versions of HashiCorp tools, including Terraform. The SaaS version of Terraform was known as **Terraform Cloud** up until April 2024 when it was rebranded as **HCP Terraform**.

HCP Terraform simplifies working with Terraform among teams in an organization. It provides a private Terraform registry, integrated testing, and policy evaluation, among other things. Some of these things will be covered in this chapter.

The **collaborate on infrastructure as code using HCP Terraform** exam objective covers the following sub-objectives:

- Analyze the HCP Terraform run workflow
- Understand HCP Terraform workspaces and their configuration options, including access management
- Manage provider credentials in HCP Terraform
- Analyze policy as code and governance features

This exam objective is only covered in **multiple-choice questions**. This means that you will not encounter the HCP Terraform portal during the exam.

You still need to be aware of the important features that HCP Terraform provides and how they work, and the benefits these bring to collaboration in your organization.

Before we dive into this exam objective it is useful to understand the resource hierarchy in HCP Terraform.

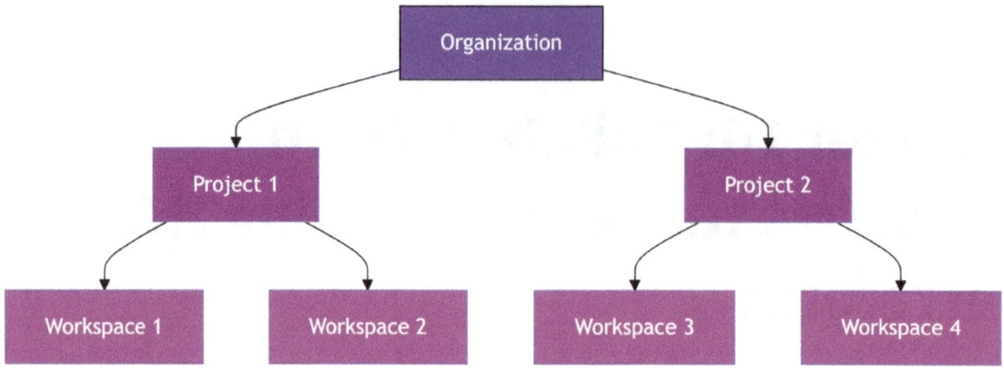

Figure 10.1. HCP Terraform resource hierarchy: organization, projects, workspaces

- At the top there is an **organization**.
- Each organization can contain any number of **projects**.
- Each project can contain any number of **workspaces**.
- Each workspace represents one Terraform configuration with a set of variable values and provider credentials.

You can apply permissions at each scope in order to allow different teams and users to perform their job and see the workspaces that they need.

Note that workspaces can be moved between projects. Projects or workspaces can't be moved between organizations.

10.1: Analyze the HCP Terraform Run Workflow

The run workflow in HCP Terraform can be thought of as a **state machine**. A run can be in one of many different states. Some states are more important to be aware of than others.

Before we go through the different phases of a run workflow, it is worth first thinking about what can **trigger** a workflow run.

You can trigger a run **manually**. This allows you to perform customization to the run, e.g. it allows you to replace resources. In the workspace page in HCP Terraform you can trigger a run manually by clicking on **+ New run** (see Figure 10.2).

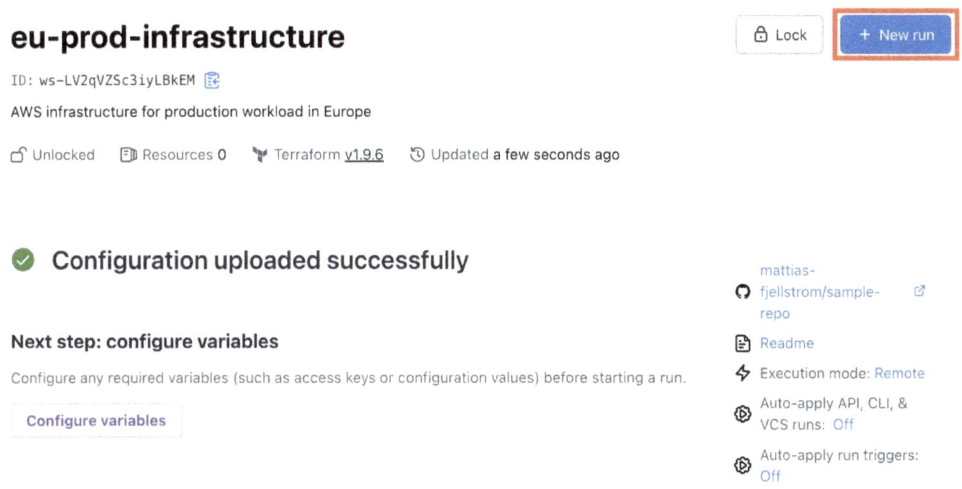

Figure 10.2. Manually trigger a workspace run

Apart from manually triggering a run from the UI, you could also trigger runs manually via the API or via the Terraform CLI. This depends a little bit on how your HCP Terraform workspace is configured. More on that in the next section.

If you have configured a VCS connection for your workspace (more on workspace configuration in the next section) there are additional trigger options. If you commit directly to the main branch of the repository (or the branch that the workspace is configured for) a new run is automatically triggered (see Figure 10.3).

If you open a pull-request targeting your **`main`** branch (or whichever branch you configured for your HCP Terraform workspace) in your VCS system there will be a simplified run triggered, simplified in the sense that it will only run a **`terraform plan`** operation, and also *cost estimation* and the *policy-as-code* phase (see Figure 10.4).

There are additional options for triggers for a VCS connected repository, for instance you could only trigger runs when git tags are created or only when files under a specific directory are changed.

One last trigger option to know about is a **run trigger**. This is when a successful run in one workspace automatically triggers a run in a different workspace.

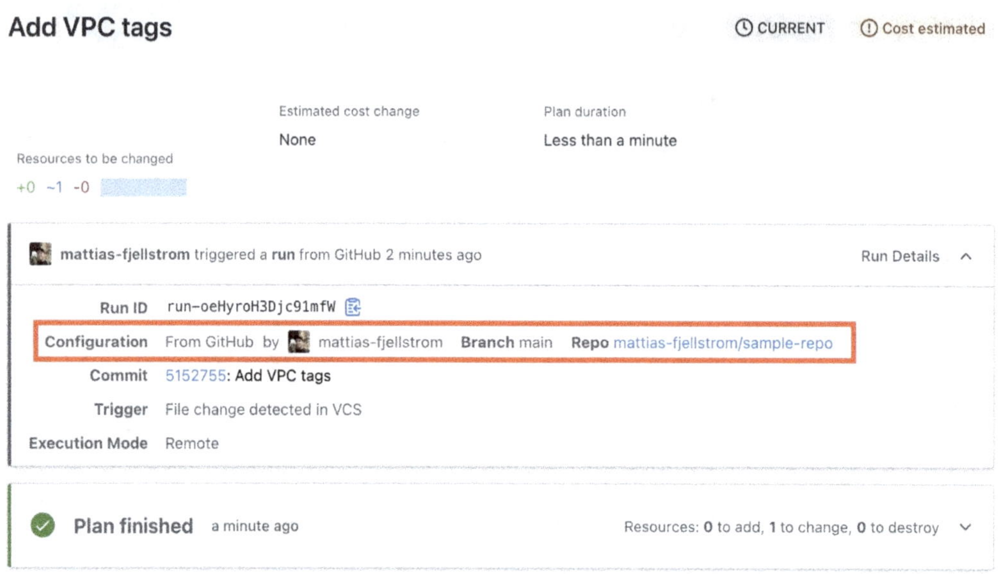

Figure 10.3. A run triggered by a commit to the `main` branch

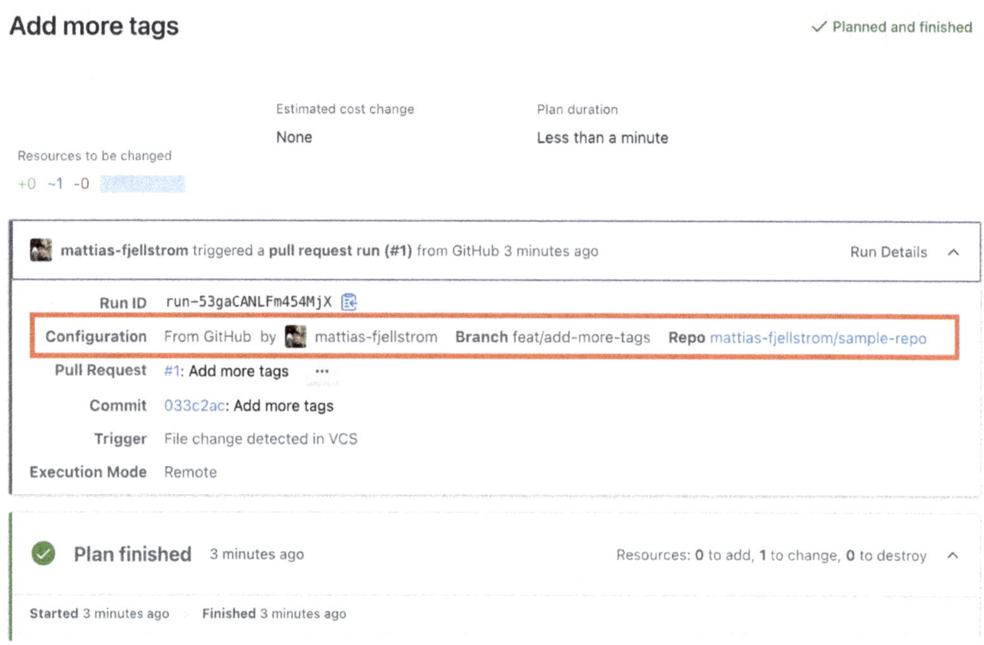

Figure 10.4. A speculative run (plan only) triggered by opening a pull-request targeting the `main` branch

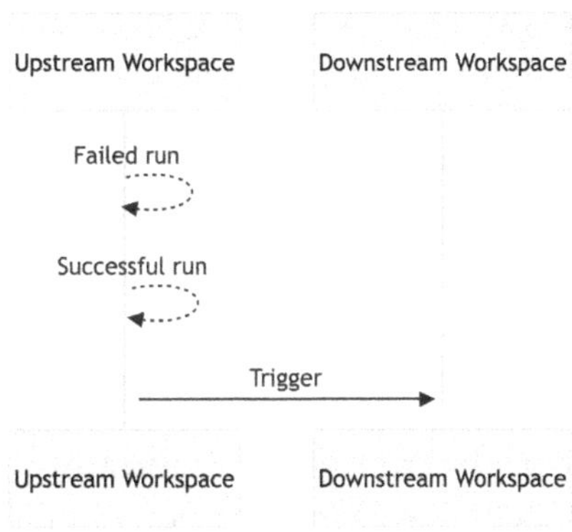

Figure 10.5. An upstream workspace triggering a downstream workspace using a run trigger

Run triggers allow you to configure dependencies between workspaces. For instance, if an upstream workspace outputs a value that is used in a downstream workspace, then you would want to run the downstream workspace whenever the output in the upstream workspace has changed.

Once a workspace run has been triggered, HCP Terraform follows the steps that you would run when using the Terraform CLI locally. However, there are some additional steps included.

First of all, HCP Terraform runs **`terraform init`** like you would have to do for any Terraform configuration, no matter where you are running Terraform. The **`terraform init`** command downloads the providers that your configuration requires, any modules you are referencing, and initializes the state storage. Speaking of state storage, HCP Terraform can be used for state storage and provides version control of your state.

Next, HCP Terraform runs a **`terraform plan`**. After the plan phase there is a major difference to the usual Terraform workflow you might be used to work with.

HCP Terraform runs a **cost-estimation phase** where it tries to estimate the cost of the changes you are about to apply. This is not available for all providers, but the AWS provider is probably the provider with the best support for this feature. Running a cost estimation is a good sanity check so that you have not made changes that will introduce exceptional charges that you were not aware of.

After the cost-estimation phase, HCP Terraform applies a **policy as code phase**. In this phase any policies that are configured for this workspace will be run. These policies can look at data from the cost estimation phase, your current state file, your Terraform configuration, and the planned changes output from the plan phase.

Policies can be configured directly in HCP Terraform, or kept in a remote git repository. More on policies later in this chapter.

Finally, if all goes well Terraform will move to the **`terraform apply`** phase. You can allow HCP Terraform to automatically run the apply phase if the plan phase did not encounter any errors, this can be convenient for development environments. For production environments you should leave the default behavior of asking for an approval before the apply phase starts.

That is the overall workflow of a run in HCP Terraform. An example of what a successful run looks like in HCP Terraform is shown in Figure 10.6.

Apart from the phases described above, there are a number of extension points in the workflow where you can apply additional checks and custom behavior. These are called **run tasks**. The details of how these work is beyond the scope of the exam and the book. See the following box for a short description of run tasks.

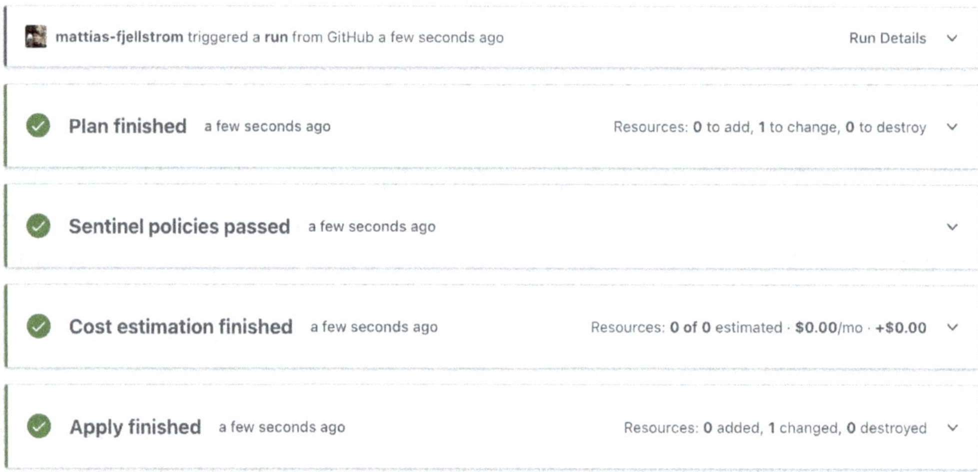

Figure 10.6. A successful run in a HCP Terraform workspace

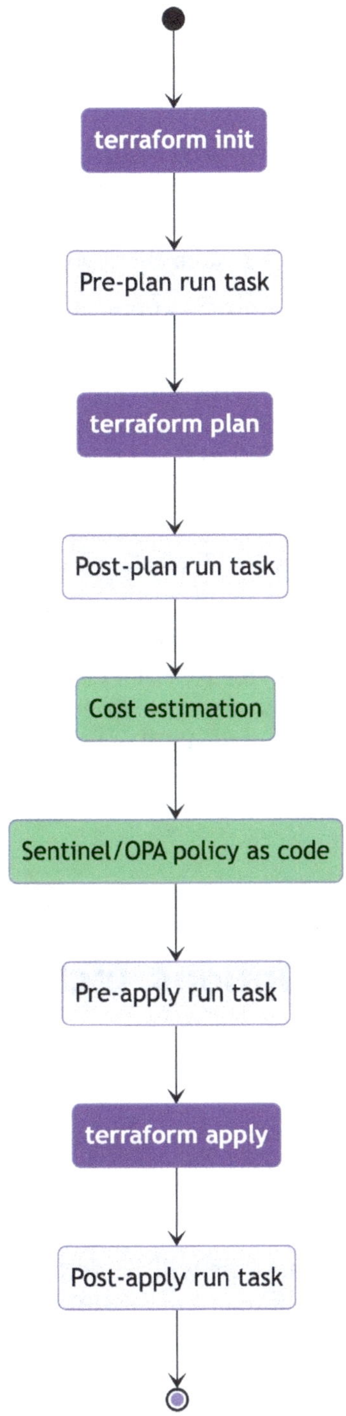

Figure 10.7. An HCP Terraform workspace run overview

Run Tasks

A run task is an integration with an external system. There are run tasks available from HashiCorp partners for various tasks. Common tasks include running static analysis of your Terraform configuration, state, or plan output. You can also build your own run tasks if you have a custom check you want to perform.

Run tasks can be applied at four distinct phases in the overall Terraform run:

- Pre-plan: right before HCP Terraform runs **`terraform plan`**.
- Post-plan: right after HCP Terraform has run **`terraform plan`**.
- Pre-apply: right before HCP Terraform runs **`terraform apply`**.
- Post-apply: right after HCP Terraform has run **`terraform apply`**.

Run tasks come with two different enforcement levels:

- An **advisory** run task will not stop a run from completing, but it will print a visible warning message in the HCP run UI.
- A **mandatory** run task will stop a run from completing along with printing a visible warning message in the HCP run UI.

10.2: Understand HCP Terraform Workspaces and Their Configuration Options, Including Access Management

A **workspace** in HCP Terraform is an instance of a Terraform configuration configured according to your needs.

When you create a new workspace in HCP Terraform you must decide on which project to place the workspace in. This will be determined by your organization's workspace structure. Most likely you will have different projects for different teams or departments. Place the workspace accordingly.

Remember that a project can have policies (see the discussion of policies later in this chapter) that are applied to all the workspaces that it contains. It could also have permissions and variable sets that will be inherited to the workspace.

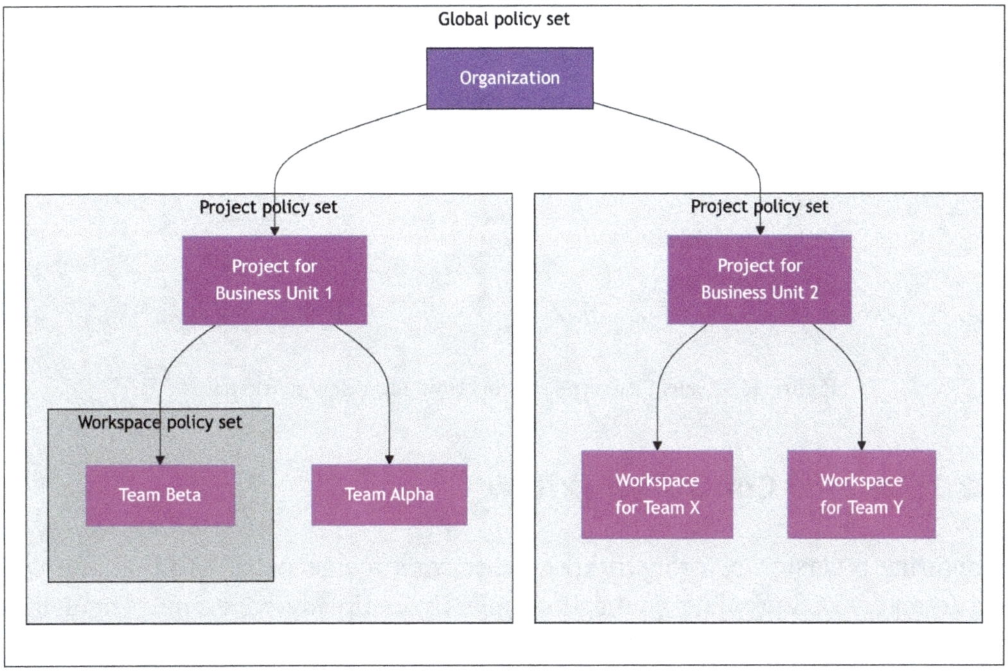

Figure 10.8. Organizing workspaces into projects and apply policy sets at different scopes

Next you need to decide on the type of workflow this workspace will use (see Figure 10.9):

- A **version control workflow** (commonly referred to as a VCS workflow) connects a git repository to the workspace.
- A **CLI-driven workflow** uses HCP Terraform as the engine for your Terraform runs, but you still use the Terraform CLI from your local system or CI system to trigger runs.
- An **API-driven workflow** allows you to build custom integrations with any tool that can send HTTP requests to the Terraform API. This is an advanced type of workflow and will not be covered in this book or during the exam.

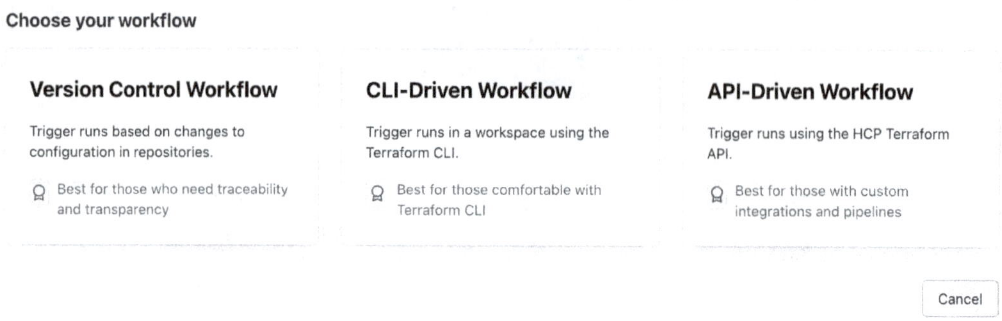

Figure 10.9. Select the type of workflow for a new workspace

10.2.1: Version Control Workflow

Configuring a version control workflow requires a few steps. First of all you will need to add a VCS provider connection unless you already have one. The details are outside the scope of this book and vary according to what VCS provider you are using. You can see the available options in Figure 10.10.

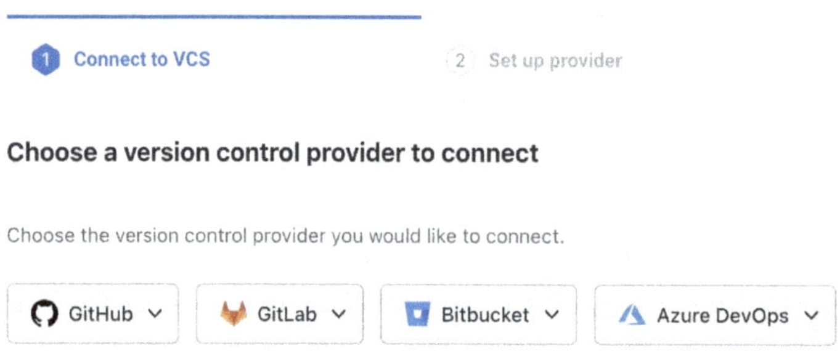

Figure 10.10. Add a new VCS provider to HCP Terraform

Once you have added a VCS provider you can create a new workspace using the version control workflow. You select the VCS provider that you want to use and select the repository from this provider that the workspace should be connected to.

There are a number of options you can specify for a version control workflow, a few are highlighted below.

You can configure your workspace to **auto-apply** your changes if the output from `terraform plan` is successful and any policies you have connected to the workspace passes.

You can configure your VCS system to trigger runs in this workspace in a few different ways. If you always want to trigger runs no matter what is changed in the repository then configure this accordingly (see Figure 10.11).

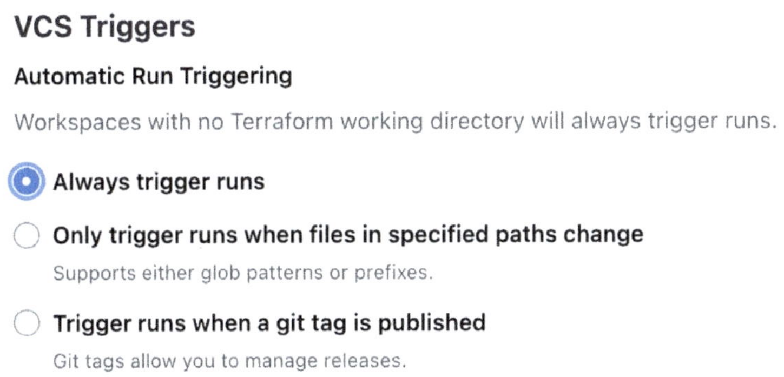

Figure 10.11. Trigger on all changes in the repository

You could also restrict trigger runs for when code in a certain directory (or directories) is changed (see Figure 10.12).

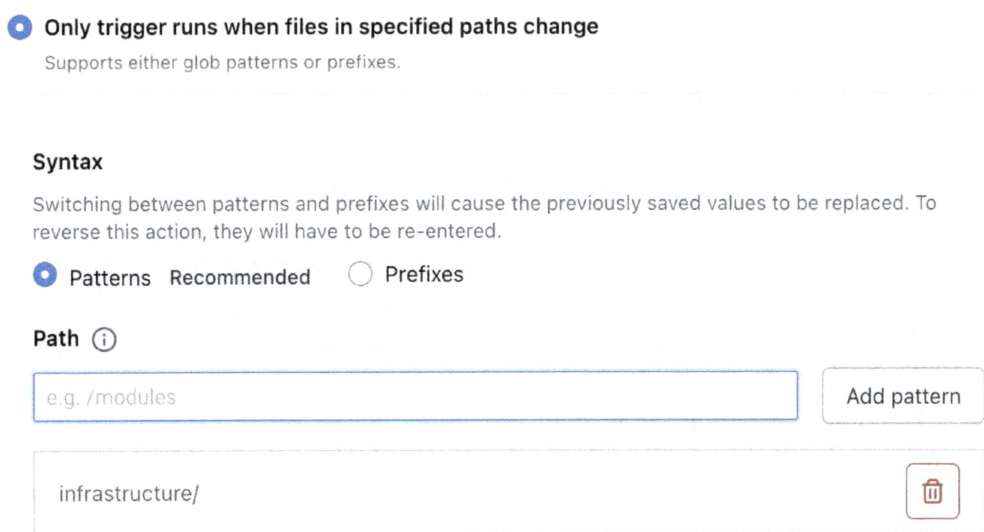

Figure 10.12. Trigger for changes following a pattern

Finally, you could restrict trigger runs for when git tags following a name convention are pushed (see Figure 10.13).

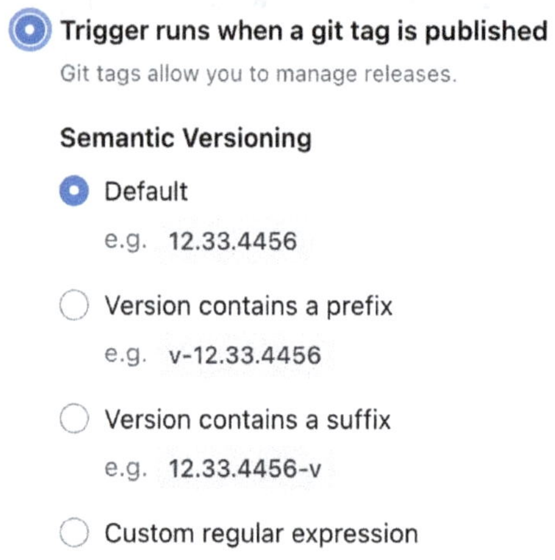

Figure 10.13. Trigger when certain tags are pushed

You can also configure the workspace to be triggered when a pull-request is opened. This will only trigger a **speculative plan**, this type of run does not include the apply phase.

Once your workspace is created, there are other settings made available to you. A few of them are covered in the following subsections.

10.2.1.1: Execution Mode

A Terraform workspace supports three types of execution modes:

- The **remote** execution mode is the default and it means that everything occurs on HCP Terraform's infrastructure.
- In the **local** execution mode you run plan and apply on your own infrastructure, and HCP Terraform is only used for state storage.
- In the **agent** execution mode, plan and apply happen on Terraform agents that you set up yourself. This allows you to deploy infrastructure to regulated environments that HCP Terraform does not have direct network access to. The agents polls HCP Terraform for jobs, and no inbound network traffic is required to the agents.

10.2.1.2: Remote State Sharing

You can allow other workspaces to use outputs from your state. This allows the other workspaces to configure **terraform_remote_state** data sources that read your state (see Chapter 7 for more on sharing state through this data source).

Note that HCP Terraform has a similar option for sharing state: the **HCP Terraform provider** for Terraform has a data source called **tfe_outputs** (the **tfe** prefix comes from *Terraform Enterprise*):

Figure 10.14. Sharing state using the tfe_outputs data source

```
data "tfe_outputs" "prod" {
  workspace = "prod-workspace"
}
```

To use the HCP Terraform provider you must configure it with HCP Terraform credentials.

10.2.1.3: Health Assessments

You can set up continuous health assessments for the resources of your infrastructure. Health assessments include **drift detection** and **continuous validation**.

Drift detection was discussed in Chapter 5. It will discover if something in your infrastructure managed by Terraform has changed through some other means. Most commonly this means that someone has manually updated resources managed by Terraform.

Continuous validation is a daily evaluation of every **check** block that your Terraform configuration contains. This allows you to be notified whenever the result of a **check** block evaluates to **false**. An example is to set up a health check for a website created through Terraform (see Chapter 6 for more on the **check** block).

10.2.1.4: Notifications

You can set up notifications for important events taking place in your workspace (see Figure 10.15).

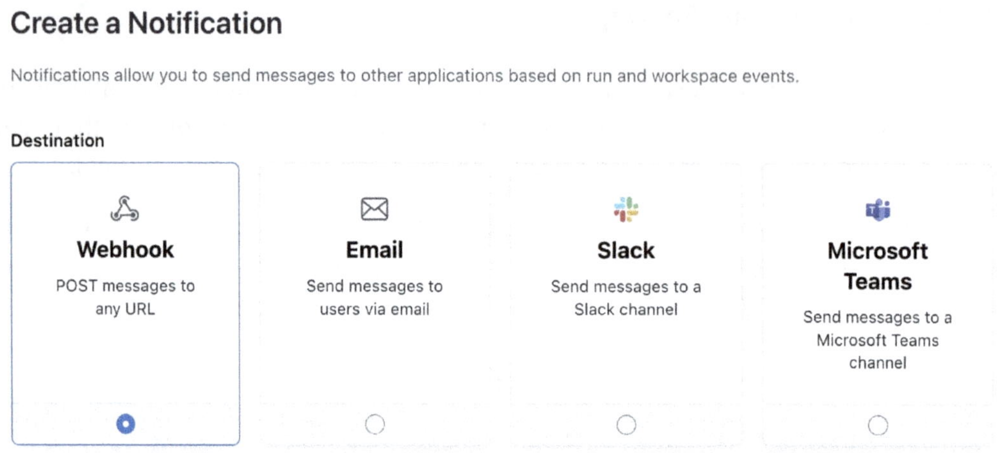

Figure 10.15. Set up a new notification for workspace events

These events include health assessment results, auto-destroy reminders, any state change in a run, and more.

10.2.1.5: Run Tasks

You can create and connect run tasks to various stages of a workflow run (see Figure 10.16).

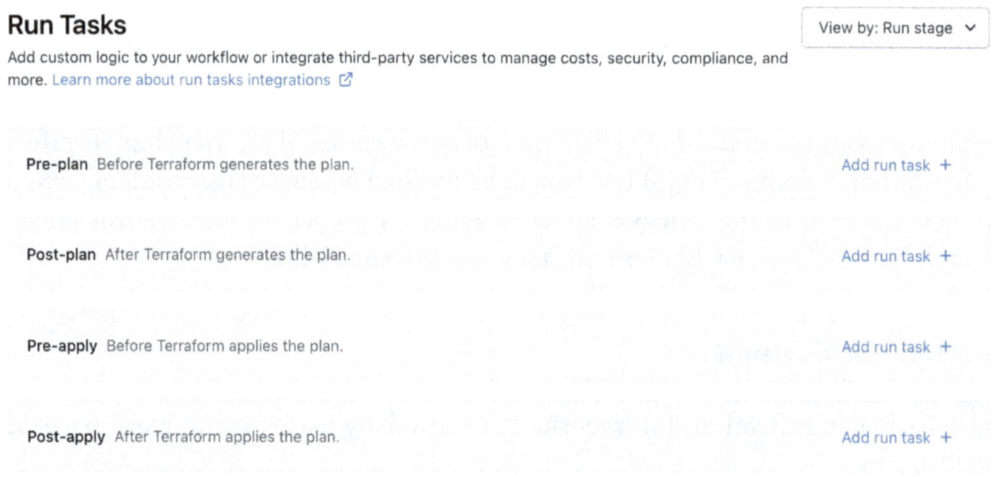

Figure 10.16. Create a run task for a workspace

See the box about run tasks earlier in this chapter for some details on what run tasks are.

10.2.2: CLI-Driven Workflow

Configuring a HCP Terraform workspace using the CLI-driven workflow is easy. Provide a name, an optional description, and what project the workspace should be a part of (see Figure 10.17).

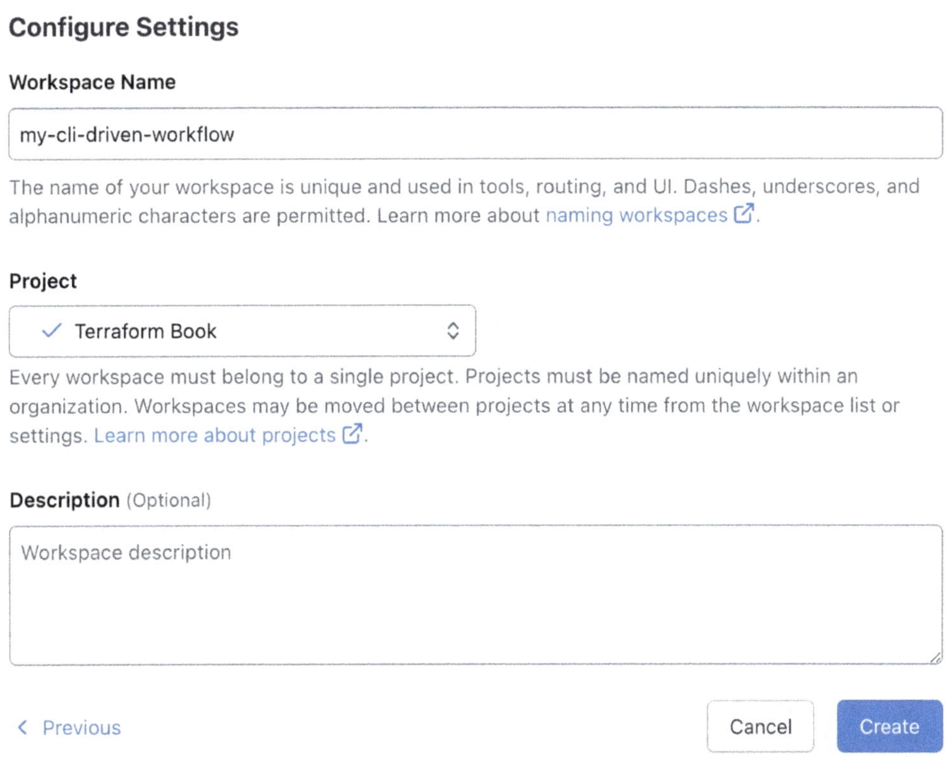

Figure 10.17. Configure a CLI-driven workflow

You are informed that you should add a new code block to your Terraform configuration for it to use this new workspace:

Figure 10.18. Configuring your Terraform configuration to use HCP Terraform

```
terraform {
  cloud {
    organization = "your-organization-name"

    workspaces {
      name = "my-cli-driven-workflow"
    }
  }
}
```

If you go down this route, you do not have to use a specific Terraform backend configured in a **backend** block inside of the **terraform** block (see Chapter 7 for details about the **backend** block). Instead, HCP Terraform will be used as the state backend.

When you have configured your Terraform code with the **cloud** block shown above, you can continue using the Terraform CLI as previously, with the exception that Terraform workflows will take place in HCP Terraform.

However, output from HCP Terraform will be streamed back to your terminal so it appears as if you are running Terraform locally. The state file is kept secure in HCP Terraform, and you can use state file versioning as well as other features of HCP Terraform (e.g. policy as code as discussed later in this chapter).

In HCP Terraform you have **users** and **teams**. You should add users to teams, and provide teams with the access that they need.

You can assign permissions for teams at any scope; organization, project, or workspace. How you structure this is a matter of the needs of your organization, but one common way is to give a team their own project, and let them be administrators of all workspaces in this project.

A better way of managing users and teams is to set up single sign-on (SSO) with your identity provider (see Figure 10.19).

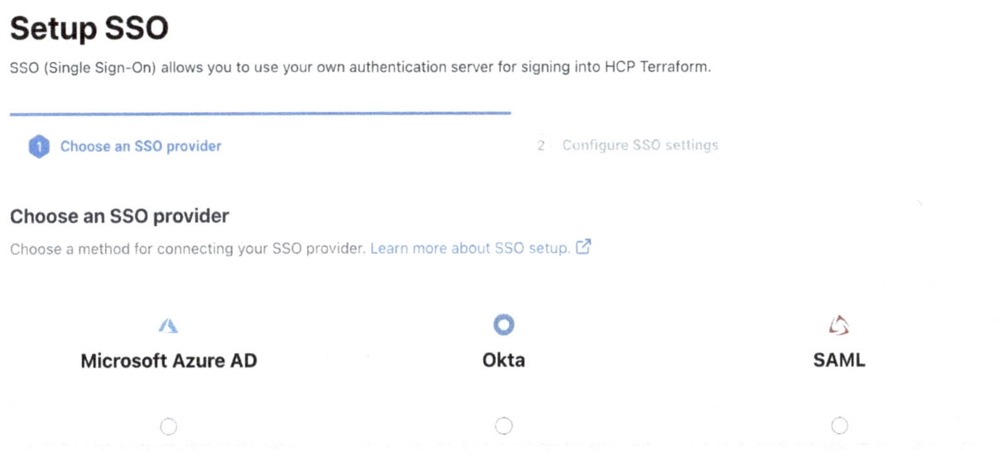

Figure 10.19. Set up single sign-on for your HCP Terraform organization

When you assign permissions on a workspace to a team you can select one of a few predefined permission groups, or create a custom permission group. The predefined permission groups at the workspace scope are:

- **Read**
- **Plan**
- **Write**
- **Admin**

The full details of what permissions each permission group grants is beyond the scope of this book and the exam.

In a similar fashion you can assign permissions for a team on a project. The predefined permission groups at the project scope are:

- **Read**
- **Write**
- **Maintain**
- **Admin**

Each user can create one or more **API tokens**. The API token can be used to programmatically access the HCP Terraform API as the user. Similarly, a team can create **one** (and only one) API token. This token can be useful to add to automation systems that should run as the team.

There are two additional types of tokens:

- An **organization token** can be used to manage teams and workspaces. However, it can't run Terraform workflows for a given workspace.
- An **audit token** is used to provide read-only access for the audit trails API. This token can be provided to auditors that request access to this information.

If you are a user using a user token, or part of a team using a team token, the token can be used in API-calls similar to the following example:

Figure 10.20. Using the HCP Terraform API with a user or team token

```
#!/bin/bash
TOKEN="user or team token"
curl \
  --header "Authorization: Bearer $TOKEN" \
  --header "Content-Type: application/vnd.api+json" \
  --request POST \
  --data @payload.json \
  https://app.terraform.io/api/v2/runs
```

10.3: Manage Provider Credentials In HCP Terraform

There are two primary ways of managing provider credentials in HCP Terraform:

- Static credentials through environment variables
- Dynamic credentials

10.3.1: Static Credentials

The most straightforward way of managing provider credentials in HCP Terraform is to provide them as environment variables. This is similar to what we saw in Chapter 9 when configuring credentials for the AWS provider locally.

Variables in HCP Terraform, **both Terraform variables** and **environment variables**, come in the form of variable sets and workspace variables.

A **variable set** is a collection of variables that you can apply to one or more HCP Terraform workspaces.

A variable set allows you to apply cloud credentials and other variables at scale to multiple workspaces. You can group workspaces into projects and allow all workspaces in a given project to have access to common credentials. You can even apply some variable sets globally for all workspaces.

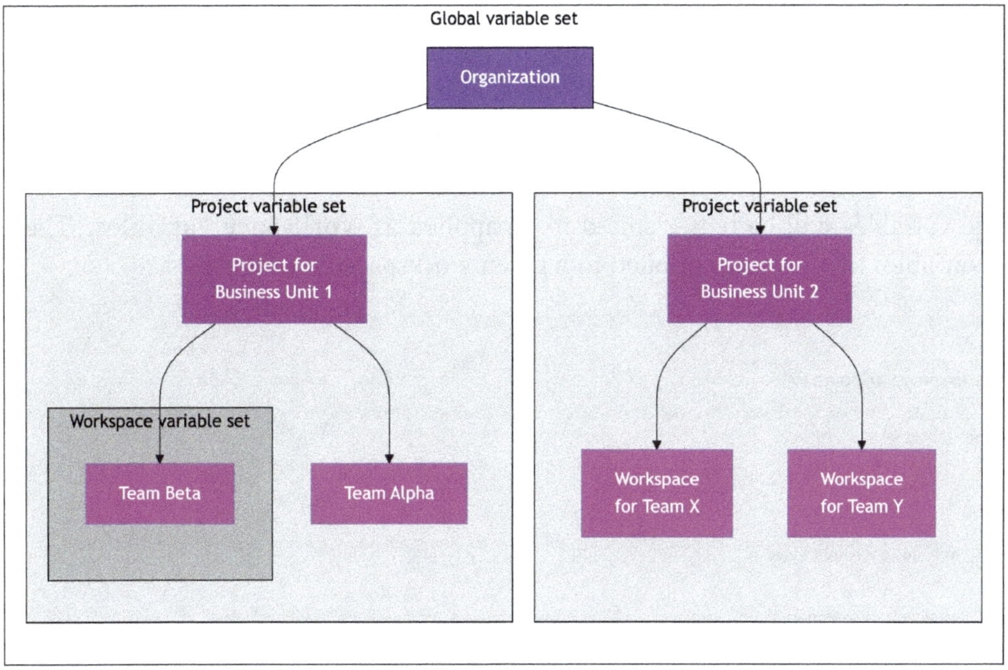

Figure 10.21. Apply variable sets at different scopes

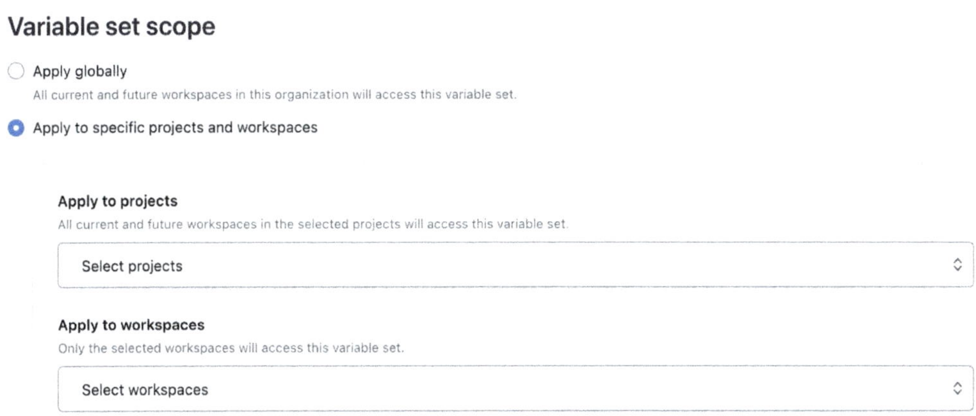

Figure 10.22. Configuring a variable set scope

As we learned in Chapter 9, you can provide AWS credentials in environment variables named **`AWS_ACCESS_KEY_ID`** and **`AWS_SECRET_ACCESS_KEY`**. Terraform will automatically pick these up and use them to authenticate the AWS provider. This is the most convenient way to provide AWS credentials to your workspaces.

Apart from the actual credentials you also have to configure the provider to use a specific AWS region. Either do this in the **`provider`** block of your Terraform configuration together with a regular Terraform variable or a hardcoded value, or add the **`AWS_REGION`** environment variable together with the credentials environment variables.

Some variables will be better suited to be applied as **workspace variables**. These are variables that are only applied to a given workspace (see Figure 10.23).

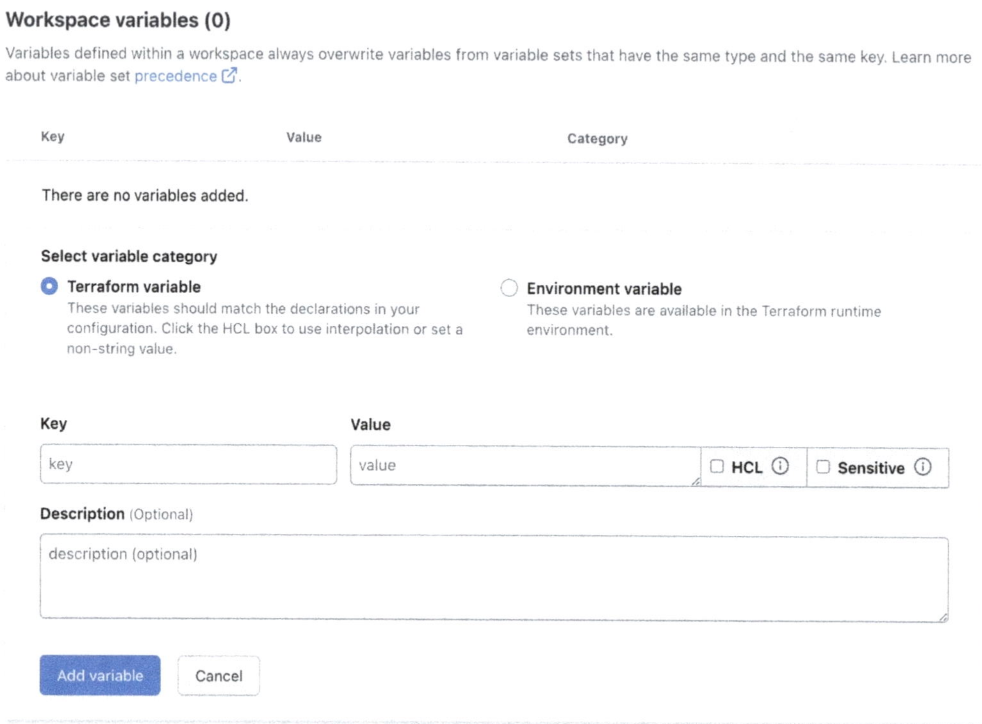

Figure 10.23. Configuring workspace variables for a given workspace

10.3.2: Dynamic Credentials

A better and more secure way to provide credentials for your providers is through **dynamic credentials**. Dynamic credentials involves setting up a trust relationship between your HCP Terraform workspace and your provider.

Once this trust relationship is set up, HCP Terraform can generate and send a token (called a workload identity token) to the provider, and the provider verifies that this token comes from HCP Terraform. If the identity can be verified, the provider returns temporary credentials that HCP Terraform can use in the subsequent run. The returned credentials are short-lived, meaning that the risk and impact of credentials being leaked is minimized.

A simplified overview of the interaction between HCP Terraform and AWS during dynamic credentials generation is shown in the following figure.

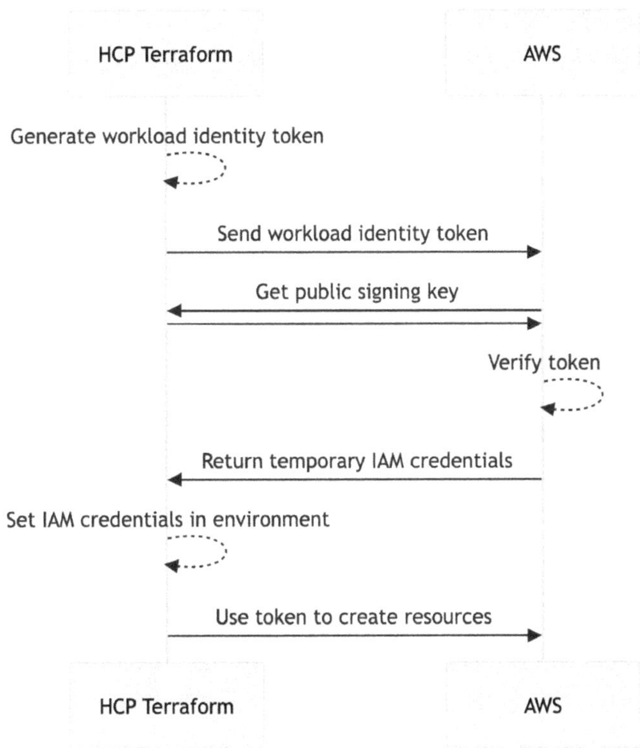

Figure 10.24. Workload identity token generation and exchange for temporary AWS IAM credentials

You do not need to set up dynamic credentials for the AWS provider during the exam, but it is important to be aware of the steps that are required. A high-level description follows.

You must configure both AWS and HCP Terraform to set up the trust relationship.

- On AWS, first create an **OIDC Identity Provider** resource. The OIDC identity provider must be configured with **`https://app.terraform.io`** as the provider URL and **`aws.workload_identity`** as the audience.

- Next, create a new **AWS IAM role** that has a trust relationship with the OIDC identity provider you created in the previous step. The IAM role should also have any IAM policies with permissions allowing it to perform its job (i.e. attach an S3 policy to work with S3, and so on). Exactly what permissions are needed is determined by what your Terraform configuration is trying to do.
- On HCP Terraform, configure the workspace you wish to use the dynamic credentials in with the following environment variables:
  - Set **`TFC_AWS_PROVIDER_AUTH`** to **`true`**.
  - Set **`TFC_AWS_RUN_ROLE_ARN`** to the IAM role ARN (Amazon Resource Name) of the role you created previously.

You must configure the provider with what AWS region you want to use. You can set this in the **`AWS_REGION`** environment variable.

If you remember one thing from this section let it be this:

> A best practice is to set up dynamic credentials to provide just-in-time access for HCP Terraform during plan and apply. No more long-lived credentials that are copied between configurations and laptops!
>
> If this feature is supported for your target provider (e.g. AWS) then you should use it.

For production scenarios, you should build Terraform modules that set up new HCP Terraform workspaces and automatically set up dynamic credentials for your cloud providers.

10.4: Analyze Policy as Code and Governance Features

Policy as code is the codification of **rules** around your Terraform infrastructure.

Remember in Chapter 6 where we introduced **custom conditions** for validating part of our infrastructure using features of HCL? Policy as code has some overlap with what you can do with custom conditions, but it is external to the HCL code and it scales much better when you want to apply the same rules for all of your Terraform configurations and modules.

A best practice is to use policy as code for rules that should target many (or all) of your Terraform configurations. These types of rules should not be part of individual module variable validations or other types of custom conditions.

In HCP Terraform you can apply policy as code using **HashiCorp Sentinel** or the **Open Policy Agent** (OPA) (see Figure 10.25).

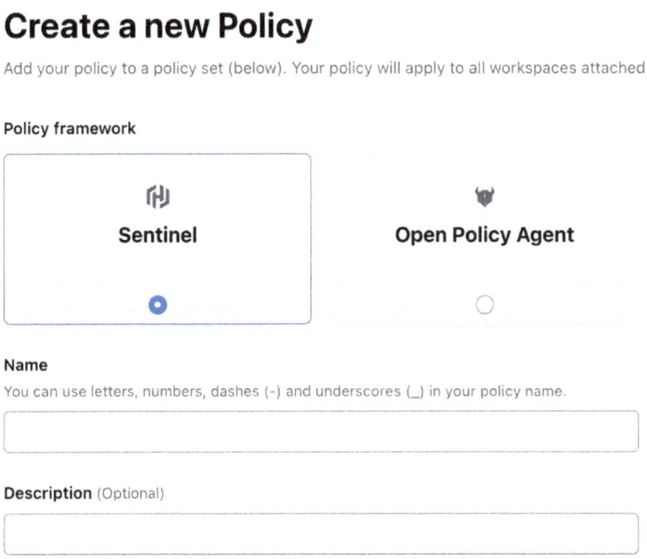

Figure 10.25. Create a new policy in HCP Terraform

For the exam you do not need to write policies, but you should be aware of what features are available in HCP Terraform for policy as code.

In HCP Terraform you can create one or more **policies**, and you can group policies into **policy sets**.

Policy sets allow you to group related policies (e.g. AWS policies, Azure policies, etc) and apply them at scale globally, or to certain projects or workspaces (see Figure 10.26).

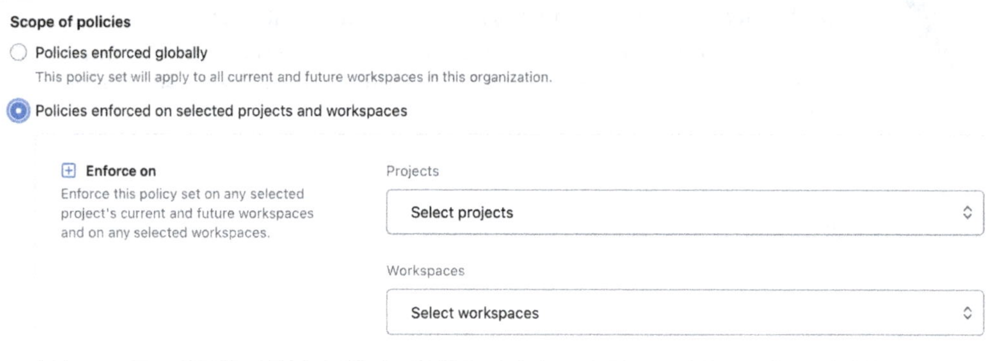

Figure 10.26. Select an appropriate scope for the new policy set

The full details of how to work with HashiCorp Sentinel or OPA is outside the scope of this book.

There are two ways of working with policies in HCP Terraform:

1. Define individual policies and policy sets directly in HCP Terraform.
2. Add policies to a git repository and connect it to your HCP Terraform organization as a policy set.

It is clear that the second option is a much more scalable way of adding policies.

A policy has one of three **enforcement modes**:

- An **advisory** policy will inform users if their Terraform configuration violates a policy, but the violation will not stop the Terraform run from completing.
- A **soft mandatory** policy will halt Terraform from continuing if a policy is violated, but you can specify exceptions for a given workspace if required.
- A **hard mandatory** policy will halt Terraform from continuing and there is no possibility of bypassing this policy through exceptions.

An example of an advisory policy evaluation that fails looks like in Figure 10.27.

Similarly, a failing soft-mandatory policy looks like in Figure 10.28 (notice the option to override and continue the run):

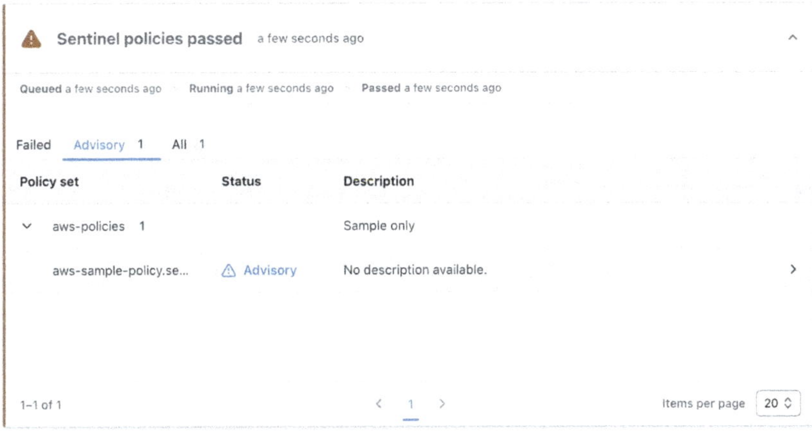

Figure 10.27. A failing advisory policy

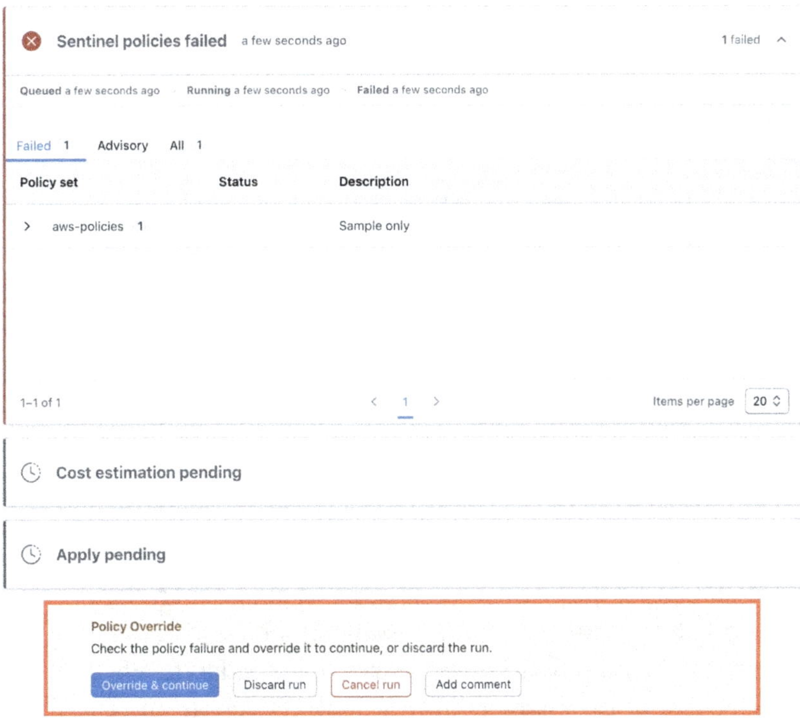

Figure 10.28. A failing soft-mandatory policy

What data are your policies taking decisions based on? You can write policies that take the following into account:

- Your Terraform configuration (your `*.tf` files including any external modules)

- Your Terraform state file
- Your `terraform plan` output
- Cost estimation data

Using these data sources allow you to write policies that restrict unwanted changes based on resource attributes, cost increases, current state attributes, and more.

A few best practices when working with policies are:

- Start out small with a few basic policies applied at a single scope.
- Increase the policy as code footprint in phases.
- Include testing of your policies to verify that they behave as expected.
- When introducing new policies for your teams, set them to be advisory to avoid disruptions. Give your teams a deadline to fix any advisory policy violations before you switch mode to either soft or hard mandatory.
- Use policy sets connected to a VCS repositories.

10.5: Summary

In this chapter we looked at features of HCP Terraform that enhance the developer experience of using Terraform and how it fosters collaborative workflows.

Key points from this chapter include:

- You can organize workspaces in HCP Terraform into projects. Both projects and workspaces can be used as a scope for applying policies and access permissions.
- The HCP Terraform run consists of a few additional steps than what we are used to from running Terraform locally. Notable differences are the cost estimation phase, the policy as code phase, and the various run task integration points.
- A run task is an integration with an external system that is called either before or after a plan operation, or before or after an apply operation.
- You can provide provider credentials using either static or dynamic credentials. Static credentials use environment variables, similar to what we have been doing in the rest of the chapters of this book. Dynamic credentials come from setting up a trust relationship between HCP Terraform and the provider (e.g. AWS). Dynamic credentials are single-use and short-lived, greatly enhancing security and simplifying credential management.
- You can introduce policy as code into HCP Terraform using either HashiCorp Sentinel policies or OPA policies. Policies are grouped into policy sets that you can apply to a workspace, a project, or globally.

Chapter 11: Final words

You have reached the end of this study guide.

If you have gone through each chapter and understand the concepts that have been presented, then you are well prepared for the exam. However, a book can only get you so far.

What I encourage you to do now is to:

> practice, practice, practice!

I wish to end this book by describing a fun anecdote around my experience of the exam.

My laptop has a small screen. This is convenient when you need to travel, or just carry your laptop around. It is not ideal for taking the Terraform Authoring and Operations Professional exam, or any other exam for that matter! I thought to myself that I better use an external monitor, so I connected my fairly large monitor. This monitor has a built-in webcam.

During the exam check-in the proctor asked me to move the camera around the room, and also show my entire desk area.

I explained that my webcam is built into the monitor and that I would have trouble performing what I was asked to do.

I did not want to risk anything by opening up my laptop screen (I assumed the system would immediately see that I was using two monitors, which is not allowed). So I ended up tilting, spinning, and moving my screen around.

This was quite a challenge!

So my last suggestion before you head into the exam is: **do not use an external monitor with a built-in webcam**.

Good luck with the exam! I am rooting for you!

If you found this book useful, please reach out on LinkedIn (scan the QR code below) to let me know!

Even if you didn't find the book that useful, reach out anyway! I appreciate all constructive feedback.

Since this book is published via Leanpub I can make changes to it and publish an updated version quickly.

Figure 11.1. QR code for my LinkedIn page–reach out!

www.ingramcontent.com/pod-product-compliance
Lightning Source LLC
LaVergne TN
LVHW060032210926
848481LV00013B/3845
* 9 7 8 1 8 0 7 7 8 4 7 5 1 *